CORPORATE HELL: A MEMOIR

Randy Zinn

SOR Press
GAITHERSBURG, MARYLAND

Randy Zinn/SOR Press
Gaithersburg, Maryland
www.randy-zinn.com

Publisher's Note: Any names, characters, or places have been changed to protect anonymity. Any resemblance to actual people, living or dead, or to businesses, companies, events, institutions, or locales is coincidental.

Corporate Hell: A Memoir / Randy Zinn. -- 1st ed.
ISBN 978-1-9536432-1-6 (paperback)
ISBN 978-1-9536432-2-3 (hardcover)

Contents

ACKNOWLEDGEMENTS

Special Thanks to Logan Russel
and Daniela Zorrilla

Cover design by JD&J Design

Preface

Thank you for opening my memoir! I have a few notes before we get started.

This book covers the first decade of my career as a software developer in the Washington, D.C. area, where I worked for companies that usually had a contract with a government agency. This included the Army, Navy, Marines, Internal Revenue Service (IRS), Transportation Security Administration (TSA), Department of Energy (DOE), and Environmental Protection Agency (EPA). Given the seriousness of some of the work, the shenanigans of the corporate world in which I worked were usually surprising. You may find equal doses of humor and disbelief in these pages.

I have kept a diary since 1990. This has allowed me to recount these events in unusual detail. I often write especially memorable conversations, but it is the nature of a memoir to recreate dialogue. There are no composite characters, and I have altered all names for privacy, with one exception: the names of government agencies. I also changed the identifies of companies for which I worked, but if any I invented matches a real company, that is a definitive sign that it is not that employer.

There is some overlap between this memoir and another called *The Wine-Dark Sea (A Silence Not So Golden, #3)*, which immediately precedes this one chronologically. Having read that book is unnecessary; in fact, this one is being published first. That book details a tendonitis injury and how it destroyed my life. My world was still in ruins when the events of this memoir began, so there is mention of my reinvention toward the beginning. My first corporate job is the one that set that rebirth in motion because I needed several things the job gave me: money, a new career, a new life, and a way to let my injured arms rest and recover. *The Wine-Dark Sea* covers the personal side of my transformation and alludes to the first job here, while this book covers the professional side and alludes to the personal; both books cover the time period with an attempt at minimal redundancy.

My given birth name was David, everyone calling me Dave. This only shows up in this story at the beginning because I changed it before long.

Free Book

A free eBook is available to newsletter subscribers.

CHAPTER ONE

The Threat

Gary said, "Ted's really upset with you." He shuffled into the cramped, windowless office we'd shared for a week. Removing his black leather bag from one shoulder, he tossed it on a table and put down his coffee. Then he unwound a grey scarf from his neck and doffed the wool raincoat, dumping them on an upholstered chair that had seen better days, the fabric torn, the arm rests scuffed, and the seat wobbling slightly when someone sat on it"

Being early in my career in the year 2000, I had not set foot in many government agencies yet, but the Department of Energy (DOE) headquarters was depressing everywhere I had gone. The Forrestal Building was decrepit, brutish, and ugly inside and out, its planned use to accommodate military personnel the likely reason our "office" seemed like a converted dorm room that once had bunk beds. The cabinets and furniture looked decades old in style, material, and wear, as if they hadn't been updated since the building's construction in the 1960s. White ceiling tiles, many stained with brown water marks, hung above us. Black marks from shoes streaked the light linoleum floor all over. Even the computers were ancient, the CRT monitors small.

Identifying smells had never been my strong suit, but the place reminded me of menthol.

Then again, maybe it was Gary. I had seen him pop a breath mint in his mouth once or twice, but he preferred Tic Tacs. He stood nearly as tall as my 6'3" and cut a distinguished figure, receding black, curly hair streaked with grey, shoulders a little hunched and his head always jutting forward. His voice was kind and calm. Nothing seemed to faze him, and I had always found him disarmingly pleasant. I regretted not working directly for him anymore. Not usually, anyway.

But he had announced his retirement and asked for my help to close out his project at the DOE. I really hadn't had a choice but would have said yes anyway because he was my first mentor in the corporate world, and my former boss. And I liked and respected him. I normally worked at our employer's headquarters in Northern Virginia (No-VA), but I was now working in Washington, D.C. for weeks.

Since I worked for someone else now, Gary's boss, Ted, had needed to request my services from my current boss, who had obliged. And so there I was, doing both Gary and Ted a favor. And that was why Gary's announcement that Ted was upset with me came as a surprise.

"You need to call him now," added Gary, settling into a creaking chair.

"What's he upset about?" I turned away from trying to fix some of Gary's coding mistakes on a desktop computer. The room was so narrow that if I needed to leave, he would have to stand to let me by.

"Just call him," Gary said. "Do it on speaker. I think I need to listen in."

I arched an eyebrow. I needed a witness? That sobered me. I had no idea what this could be about. Both of them had been almost like father figures at work to me, starting thirteen months earlier when I first entered the corporate world at age 27. I trusted them. And so I dialed Ted's number on speakerphone assuming the best despite the warning signs.

"Ted Gavin," said a voice on the other end.

"Hi, Ted. It's Randy. I—"

"Oh, *is it* now?" he interrupted sarcastically.

I did a double-take, assuming I'd misheard the big attitude. "Yeah, Gary told—"

"You have a lot of nerve, you know that?"

I hesitated, having never been spoken to like that at a job, and certainly not by Ted. "What are you talking about?"

"Don't play dumb with me. I know you're quitting and giving one week's notice."

I froze. How could Ted know I was leaving? I hadn't given notice, not to mention one week instead of the customary two. Gary's face wore an unreadable frown so that I couldn't tell if any of this was a surprise to him so far. What had Ted told him?

"Why do you think—"

Ted snapped, "Your recruiter friend Tina left me a message that you're starting somewhere in a week."

My eyes widened. Tina, a recruiter from another company, had just found me a job, but I hadn't received a written offer yet, just the verbal one, so I wouldn't give notice. I was waiting for the offer letter, which was now several days late. "She wasn't supposed to call you until I—"

"Well she *did*," Ted snapped. "You have to ask my permission to use me as a reference."

"Yeah, I know. I'm trying to expl—"

"You're being selfish," he interrupted.

I scowled, resenting that. That was not my nature, which should have been apparent to him by now, especially given the current favor I was doing him helping Gary.

His conclusion jumping didn't warrant the accusation, and it bothered me that someone I looked up to found it so easy to believe so little of me. I started getting an attitude of my own. "Yeah? How so?"

"Because you owe me, both personally and professionally."

I frowned harder, if that was possible. I didn't owe him shit. Personally, he hadn't done a thing for me and I hadn't asked him to, though he had supported me at work when I legally changed my name, promising to make everyone honor it, not that anyone had failed to. Professionally, he had given me my first corporate programming job, taking a chance on me despite my inexperience, but I had repaid him by doing excellent work for six months on a contract-to-hire basis—enough so that he had wanted to hire me but couldn't because the contract he managed couldn't afford me anymore. The result was that he lobbied to get another group at SysCorp to interview me. I had done the rest, securing the job as an employee. But that new group, my current one, didn't really need me and the job sucked. They had also lowballed me with Ted's help. I was not obligated to remain and hadn't worked for Ted in six months, so me leaving was really none of his business.

I asked, "You expect me to stay just because you helped me get this job?"

"Yes!"

"Then you're not being realistic."

"Yeah, well I *got* you this job and I can *take it away from you*!"

Startled, I glanced at Gary in time to see his expression change from shock to disapproval.

"Listen, Ted—"

"You know *nothing* about professional etiquette."

I stiffened. "Considering how you're talking to me, you're not much better." I saw Gary's eyes widen before he poorly suppressed a smile.

Ted growled, "You do *not* have my permission to use me as a reference. Ever!"

No longer wanting him to be, I replied, "I'm not asking you to be."

"Sure as hell sounded like the recruiter thinks you were."

"She's made a mistake. I—"

"No, that was *you!*"

"Ted, I can't explain anything if you don't let me finish a—"

"I don't want to hear any explanations from you!"

I snapped, "Then *why* are we having this conversation?"

Ted snarled, "Listen Goddamnit. I have this recruiter's name and phone number, so why don't you think about *that?*"

I pulled back from the speakerphone in shock at his threat to destroy my new job while making it clear this one was now destroyed. The line went dead. My worried eyes sought Gary, who looked as stunned as I felt, shaking his head, his mouth moving, but no words coming out.

"Jesus," he finally muttered. "I don't know what the hell's gotten into him."

I wasn't sure what to say about that but asked, "Can he really call the recruiter and say nasty stuff about me?"

Gary frowned. "No. It's illegal, and he'd just make SysCorp look bad. Don't worry about that. Did you really give one week's notice?"

"No. I have given no notice at all. I haven't gotten the job offer in writing." Quitting without the written offer wasn't wise. While I was new to the corporate world, this one I knew.

He nodded. "I didn't realize you were leaving, too."

I shrugged. "The job stinks. Working for you was great, but this group has no use for me. The work is garbage."

He smirked in approval. "I could've told you that. I'm not surprised you're going. Why does Ted think you've given notice?"

I sighed, pissed at Tina. "The recruiter told me she couldn't send me on the job interview without references on file, so I gave her Ted's name on the condition that she not call him until I got a job offer in writing. Then I would ask Ted's permission and if he said yes, tell her it was okay to call. She apparently didn't wait after all."

Gary rolled his eyes good-naturedly. "Never trust a recruiter. I'll go see Ted, talk some sense into him. It's really not appropriate, the way he was just acting." While Ted was his boss, Gary seemed older, and they acted like equals. I thought he had a good chance of getting Ted to be reasonable, but using Ted as a reference was certainly out. An apology from him would need to be good or I wouldn't even want to talk to him. I wondered if something else was going on in Ted's life for him to turn on me like that. I was still shocked.

But it greatly relieved me to hear Gary's take on this. I said emphatically, "Thank you."

He waved it off. "When's the job supposed to start?"

"What's today? Wednesday? I was supposed to get the offer Monday and didn't, so the date was going to be two weeks from then. With the letter late, I've been intending to get it, then call them and ask to move the date back so I can give two-week's notice."

He seemed to accept that, unlike Ted, who wouldn't even listen. This was a misunderstanding, one that hardly warranted his behavior. Having looked up to Ted made this worse, our mutual respect turning into mutual contempt, though I held mine in check pending the result of Gary's talk with him. I've always been forgiving, but Ted had me rattled. And I felt suddenly grateful for Gary, more so than ever. I hoped for the best and to still leave my first corporate job on good terms.

But Ted had other ideas.

The next day, an exasperated Gary told me to forget about Ted. They had gotten into a big argument when Gary learned what Ted had been doing back at HQ since that phone call. Ted was a Program Manager in one division and reported to its Vice President, John. I worked in another division that reported to John. Going down the hierarchy, there was a director, then a Program Manager, and finally two Project Managers, one of whom was my boss. Ted had gone to all of them and tried to get them to fire me, telling them the lie that I had given less than two-week notice. Never mind that none of them had seen a resignation letter from me, or that two-week notice is a courtesy. Virginia, where the company was headquartered and my office lay, was an at-will employment state. This meant companies could terminate staff without warning, and staff could quit without warning. Giving less than two-week notice was not a termination-worthy offense. Especially when I hadn't done it.

I had always liked and respected John. But then that had been true of Ted. Fortunately, John was more level-headed, and after Ted tried to get John to fire me, John had called Gary to see if he knew anything. And Gary had saved my ass, telling John none of it was true.

"Listen," Gary concluded to me back at the DOE, "just call John and tell him you haven't given notice. And in fact, you haven't even received an offer that would allow you to give notice. Anything else being said is not true and needs to come from you."

It sounded like excellent advice, but I just wanted to avoid all of it. "I'm not sure I really want to talk to him."

Gary nodded, as if understanding. "There's a way to make sure the call goes straight to voicemail. I'll tell you how."

"Really? I didn't know that." I was once again grateful for his help. He and Ted were heading in opposite directions of coolness. I accepted the offer and wondered what other tricks I didn't know. "Thanks, Gary. I don't know what I'd do without you."

"You'll be fine," he said, and I got the impression he didn't mean just about this situation, but in general.

I soon left the voice message for John and later went home, where I found the offer letter at last. Vast relief filled me. I had worried about finding myself unemployed. On checking my voice mail, I discovered a response from John saying he was relieved and knew I'd do the right thing. I felt guilty on hearing it, because I wasn't going to. Not anymore.

After what Ted had done, I wanted to get out of there. I could've told Tina to move my start date back, but I wasn't taking a chance on upsetting the new job when Ted had just burned the bridge at the old one before I had even crossed it, then tried to kick me into the chasm below. His assumption that I was giving one week notice became a self-fulfilling prophecy. When I told Gary my intention, he asked if I was sure I wanted to do that, a friendly warning, but I said yes, and he said he understood.

I called Tina and told her what had happened, hearing more apologies in a few minutes than in years. She offered to call Ted and explain that it was her fault, but I convinced her not to. Sometimes I've wondered if that was a mistake, but Ted had gone too far and I had no interest in salvaging that relationship. That he had even argued with Gary about it and not backed down told me it was already over.

Having never resigned from a corporate job before, I wasn't sure if I was supposed to tell anyone beyond my manager. Ted's sabotage had likely changed the rules, anyway. I had already written resignation letters that were in my desk at work because I had limited access to work email while at the DOE. My plan was to ask my old team's administrative assistant to get and distribute them for me immediately (she did when asked). Letters went to my Project Manager, the Program Manager above her, the Director Tim, and the VP John. But when I called the assistant, I told her to throw Ted's in the trash. Did the resignation's arrival the day after Ted claimed I had already given it undermine his credibility? Or did it confirm that he had been right about me giving less than customary notice?

To compensate for a six-workday notice instead of ten, I offered to work extra hours every weekday and a weekend, but they didn't acknowledge the offer. In fact, my resignation received no response at all. It was as if I had never sent it. It seemed that being unprofessional was contagious—Tina, Ted, me, then a bunch of executives. I'll admit to feeling like I was the only one with an excuse—wanting to escape a hostile work environment ASAP.

Even though no one approved it, I worked back at HQ both Saturday and Sunday to compensate, meaning that I was giving eight workdays' notice. My manager, who was the director Tim's wife, was in the building the whole time and ignored me. I spent my remaining days working at the DOE with Gary until halfway through my last day, when I returned to HQ for my belongings, the five-story building seeming squat due to the green roof and square shape. Having my resignation ignored had eliminated what little desire I might've once had to say goodbye to anyone, but I walked into the office of my Program Manager (Ted's counterpart in my division) because it was apparent that no one was going to say a word to me. She was polite and acted like there were no hard feelings, wishing me luck and saying she was surprised I hadn't resigned sooner because I was too good for the work they had me doing. I relaxed a little. Maybe they would be reasonable.

But then I walked into my Project Manager's office. She made her contempt known with a cold, flat, stiff expression. She asked nothing and hardly spoke to me, but she spoke volumes all the same. I lost any remaining respect for her, our Program Manager having just embarrassed her by contrast and she didn't even know it.

Then there was the other Project Manager, Liz, a tall, 40-something brunette with an irreverent attitude that came with a dark side I now saw for the first time. She accosted me in the hallway, snottily asking, "So you're leaving us in a lurch? You didn't fix my reports!"

I scowled, walking past her without stopping. "I fixed all but two and am not the one who broke them in the first place."

"You're unprofessional!" she snapped.

"So are you," I said under my breath, irritated with her "lurch" comment. My predecessor had built her a badly designed, inaccurate (and therefore useless) financial database in Microsoft Access. I had fixed all of it except two remaining items, and if she wanted them so badly, they could've accepted my offer of additional hours. I wasn't the one who'd left her in a lurch.

And what had they expected after Ted's behavior? Did they think I didn't know? That word had not reached me? I should have quit on the spot. Helping Gary was the only reason I hadn't. I doubted that they would've reacted any better if I'd proven Ted wrong and given the two weeks' notice. That I had made Ted look right about me didn't help my mood.

Cleaning out my desk didn't take long, and I soon stood beside my blue Dodge Shadow ES out front, the box of my stuff inside. I was about to open the driver's side door when my nemesis walked around the building's corner toward the front door I had just exited. My eyes and Ted's met across the distance, his gaunt, tall frame seeming more pathetic to me now, white wisps of hair blowing over his bald spot. Baleful red eyes gleamed from behind his large, frameless glasses, two horns jutting from his forehead as a sinuous, pointed tail flicked the air behind him; okay maybe I was only imagining that part. Then he opened his mouth.

CHAPTER TWO

The Maze to Freedom

I glared at Ted before pointedly turning my back, getting in, and driving away, denying him the chance to either accost me or apologize. Neither held any value to me. Part of me regrets not getting into it with him anyway, once I was a former employee, but his threat had me worried that he could do damage even after I was gone. Did reputations really follow you?

I never saw or heard from anyone at that company again, Ted's last words to me an empty threat. The difference between then and how we had met could not have been more stark, the journey to us becoming colleagues starting long before.

After high school, my love of composing and playing guitar for rock music led me to become a music major at Montgomery Community College in Rockville, Maryland. I wasn't the least bit serious about school at the time and haphazardly followed the curriculum, but I became a classical composition student. When I transferred to Catholic University to earn a Bachelor of Music, they forced me to change majors from composition to guitar for one semester. I accepted the switch and studied composing on my own, but the switch of majors caused a problem. I only had two years of school left and needed to acquire four years of classical guitar skill. Figuring it couldn't hurt to try, I heavily practiced and passed every performance test and recital to graduate Magna cum Laude.

But the severe tendonitis I had caused in both arms destroyed my life a year later, in 1996. Gone were my plans for a masters and doctorate degree, and a career teaching music in college while hopefully getting my compositions performed. I was so severely disabled that I couldn't even walk, sit still, or sleep without causing pain. I lost my friends, savings, and job. No guitar playing or writing fantasy fiction, as I couldn't type. I became an early adopter of dictation programs so I could try writing that way. I had to put the mouse on the floor and control it with my feet. Within two months, I had dropped off the face of the Earth, only leaving the house for physical therapy, severe depression my only friend. My memoir, *The Wine-Dark Sea*, recounts the story and the path to my interviews with Gary and Ted.

Therapy helped but at a snail's pace, and a year later, hardly anything had changed. It became clear I needed some way to make a living without needing my arms or they—and my life—would never recover. I started working ten hours a week for a wedding photographer named Becky, but my arms could hardly handle it. In late 1997, we realized she needed a database to track her photo orders. Having no idea what I was getting myself into, I volunteered to do it and got past every technical hurdle while creating her Print Orders system. I soon realized that being a database developer was the new career I'd been searching for. I could do all the work with my feet or the dictation program.

I searched the classifieds, but every Microsoft Access Developer job wanted me to know Visual Basic and to have two years' experience. The latter couldn't be helped, but that fall, I returned to Montgomery College to take a programming course in Pascal, to learn the fundamentals. My intention? Finish the semester and then find a job. That was a long shot, but I was desperate and determined. After the first day of class, something went wrong.

My physical therapist discovered another tendonitis injury to both arms despite me hardly using them; overuse causes the injury. Shocked and then angry, I watched two years of painfully slow recovery vanish as I went back to zero. I couldn't stand the waiting anymore. In fury, I went onto Monster.com and activated my resume so that recruiters would find it, hoping for a miracle. And that's when Ted and Gary entered the picture.

The first few recruiters who called got an enthusiastic response from me only to stop calling or returning messages. I had never worked with recruiters before and wasn't sure what to expect. Then one named Hunter reached out. He worked for ProSource and had the job working for Gary and Ted. He wanted me to interview with Gary, but first I had to meet Hunter at his Rockville Maryland office. I still lived with my parents thirty minutes east, but I had spent vast amounts of time in Rockville and knew it well.

We met in his small office several floors up in a glass building, one of the few I had ever entered; I never had a reason to unless a doctor's office was in one. I felt out of place, like this was where the adults were, and while I was twenty-eight, I didn't feel like an adult. When was I supposed to?

In his thirties and a little portly, Hunter had a balding head with buzz-cut hair on the sides. He wore a button-up shirt poorly tucked into khakis, as if he was too cool to wear it all "right." Having never worked in a place that required more than jeans, I had dusted off the nearest equivalent I had, plus a tie. Even while shaking my hand, he already acted slick and polished, a player and natural salesperson who seemed to enjoy his job. He acted like we were old friends at a bar, but rather than this masking the reality that we'd never met before, his demeanor brought this truth into stark relief and made him seem disingenuous. I felt slightly annoyed exactly because I immediately liked him, despite feeling that getting me to like him was part of his profession.

"So, you haven't done government contracting?" he asked, smirking. Papers, folders, and official-looking books on contracting cluttered the desk of his small office. Sports paraphernalia hung from the walls, a picture of him on a charter boat fishing on one wall. I suspected it was all for show.

I shook my head. "How is the government related to the job?"

"Okay, so here's the story, and this is true all over this area, not just this job. In this case, the Department of Labor has a project but not the people to do the work. They contracted it out so companies can bid on it. One called SysCorp won the contract, so they now have to do the work, but they don't have the staff either."

"Then why did they bid on the contract, or win it?"

He laughed. "Great question! That's how it's done around here. You win it, then go get the people to do the work, if you don't have them all."

"I guess that's where I come in."

"Exactly. SysCorp has its own recruiters, because they're a big company, tens of thousands of staff, but sometimes, like this time, they reach out to companies that specialize in recruiting. That's all we do here at ProSource. I'd be sending you to an interview with SysCorp. If you get the job, you work for ProSource, doing the work at SysCorp, though it's really for the Department of Labor. Make sense?"

I nodded. "Sounds complicated."

Hunter grinned again. "You'll get used to it."

"So this is why I'm interviewing with you here even though you said the job is actually in Alexandria." I had never been that far into Virginia, about forty-five minutes without traffic and inside "the beltway"—the roughly circular highway surrounding Washington, D.C.

"Right. I like to meet people before sending them to clients, so I make sure you don't have purple hair or something."

I deadpanned, "Good thing I dyed mine back to blond yesterday."

He laughed. "That's good. Be relaxed and you'll do fine with Gary. He's a nice guy. Like him a lot. Ted, too."

"Who's Ted? What's his role?"

"He's Gary's boss. Ted's the Program Manager. Remember that Labor project? It's really a 'program,' and Ted handles that program."

Trying to process that, I asked, "If it's a Department of Labor program, wouldn't they be the one managing it? Shouldn't the Program Manager be a federal guy, not a SysCorp one?"

He nodded. "Great point. And yes, you're right. The Department of Labor has someone who manages the contract on the government side, called a contracting officer. Ted's called the Program Manager, even though it's not a SysCorp program but a federal one. Some Program Managers manage more than one program, sometimes for different agencies. It's what they do for a living, managing the federal government's programs for them. Make sense?"

"Sort of."

Hunter waved it off. "Don't worry about it. It took me a while, too, and you don't have to worry about any of this. Ted does. He has to make the Department of Labor's contracting officer happy with the work that's being done on the program. The Department of Labor is SysCorp's client. SysCorp has lots of others, but they mostly do work for the federal government."

"I think that makes sense. Ted has a boss at SysCorp, too, right?"

"Yep. A Vice President, I believe."

"What's Gary?"

"Programmer, like you want to be. Believe he's also a contractor." Hunter noticed my confused look and added, "Ted is a SysCorp employee. Gary is not. He sits down the hall from Ted at SysCorp, like you would. He is independent, I believe. He has a contract with SysCorp, so he's a contractor. If SysCorp wants you, you would become an employee here at ProSource, and ProSource would have a contract with SysCorp as a result. To us you would be our employee, but to SysCorp, you would be a contractor."

This was all a little confusing, but my face fell for a different reason. I thought this was employment with a big company, not a little recruiting firm. "How does this work? I thought I was to be their employee."

"It's a six-month contract-to-hire position. For that time period, you work as our employee. After it's over, if SysCorp wants to hire you as *their* employee, they make you an offer, you accept, and you leave ProSource and become their guy. Make sense?"

I nodded slowly. "Why do they handle it that way?"

"Think of it like a test drive. Six months lets you decide if you like the job, and they decide if they like you. If not, you guys go your separate ways, though of course I'd be happy to help you find another position. If you both want to move forward together, you do. And I'm out of the picture."

My head was spinning, but I understood enough. "What do you get out of it?"

"Depends on how it's set up. Some companies like SysCorp pay a flat finder's fee, like ten grand. But for us on this one, it's an hourly thing. Every hour you work, you get paid, of course, but ProSource also gets paid. Let's say you'd get $25 an hour. We'd get slightly more. Maybe they pay ProSource $30 or $35 an hour for you. We give you $25 of that and we keep the rest."

I nodded but likely wore an expression that said, You're taking some of the money I'm earning. If I'd found the job without you, I'd make a lot more, so why don't I just do *that*?

As if knowing what I was thinking, he smiled and said, "That's how we make money. We know the companies who are looking for people like yourself, and we bring you to them. Lots of companies like this never put a job in the papers because they get swarmed with applicants. You can find a job like this directly, but it's hard. There's a reason we have full time staff who do nothing but cultivate these relationships with people like Ted, on the off chance that, one day, they'll need a recruiting firm and come to us. On that note, other companies have almost certainly approached Ted, so we compete with them. That's why you need to not have purple hair." He laughed.

I smiled, humoring him. I didn't want to belabor the point. "What about benefits?"

"None through us. Do you have any through your parents?"

"No, I have my own health insurance." I had stopped qualifying to be on theirs after I turned 23. I wasn't too thrilled with my HMO because they had denied most of the treatment I needed for tendonitis, so I looked forward to getting away from them.

"Good. So you're set for now. On the plus side, you only have to work seven hours but get paid for eight."

"Really?"

"Yeah. Not every contract does that. In fact, most don't, but this one does. We don't reimburse for mileage or parking, which is free there anyway, but you can deduct mileage on your taxes."

I nodded, not wanting to think about that.

The interview didn't last much longer, and I did well enough that he sent me to meet Gary a week later in Alexandria, VA. I lived in Silver Spring, MD, but saying so is misleading. There is downtown Silver Spring, and then there is a huge area north of it, and which has other towns. Driving up Route 29 from downtown might have me in Silver Spring, White Oak, Silver Spring again, Fairland, Silver Spring again, and Burtonsville, and that was just in one direction. My parent's house was in one of the suburbs in between these other towns. I was far enough away from Alexandria that the drive would be 45-minutes if no one crashed on the beltway. I felt reluctant despite my need for this.

And my need was strong. My entire life was waiting for it. My tendonitis-ridden arms were doing well enough that I could do things like cut my food without pain, but my father still did my laundry because I couldn't move the heavy, wet clothes to a dryer, or carry a basket back up the stairs to my second-floor room. Serious concerns existed about whether I could ever live on my own and do things like carry groceries home or take out the trash. I still relied on a dictation program to enter text into a computer, and a special foot mouse to control it. I wasn't sure if I could use these tools in an office, and it was on my mind as I drove to the interview.

Wearing a suit and tie with more familiarity than I wore mine, Gary met me in the lobby and immediately struck me as a low-pressure, laid-back guy, almost like someone's grandfather. He probably was, being in his 60s. He came across like he didn't care, his voice as soft as his demeanor, and something about him took away any nerves I might have felt. Unlike Hunter, he had me liking him without making any effort to do so.

Once at his small office several floors up, he sat behind a desk before a CRT monitor, a wired mouse, and a keyboard on the desk beside the desktop computer. I took a seat to one side of him instead of across, because there wasn't room there. Someone opening the door would hit the back of a chair if placed there. The room was mostly bare of decorations, unless you counted the scuff marks on the walls from attempts at moving furniture in and out.

He asked pointed questions about my experience, and I tried to be as forthcoming as I could, making a show of clarity because that is needed in programming, and I wanted to show my mind was clear. Maybe it would compensate for my thin experience. I had done no coding against Microsoft Access, only using the visual interface in it to create the system for Becky, so I had to show my other strengths. As part of that and showing initiative, I had brought a copy of the database on a floppy drive (remember those?). I also had a binder of screen shots in case he could not open the system on his computer, and he seemed pleased with me for having done these without being asked. They certainly gave the impression that I was not trying to hide anything, and I hoped that being this open would benefit me, as if my character could get me the job whereas my skills might cost me it. I was eager and wanted him to know it.

He opened the system and clicked through it as a user, with me trying to point out the reasons for the screens being laid out as they were. Graphical User Interface (GUI) design is a huge part of software and I again wanted to be clear that I had the user's interests in mind, repeatedly trying to show how I had made it easier. But he was moving a little too fast for me to say what I wanted to. I hoped he was "seeing enough" and didn't need more proof I had done a good job, but I felt frustrated that I couldn't show him more of what I brought to the job.

At some point, he looked behind the screens at the non-existent code, forcing me to admit that I hadn't done that yet. I pivoted to saying I was taking a course in Pascal to learn the fundamentals of programming, but he frowned and asked rhetorically how that was going to help. My heart sank. Pascal wasn't the coding language used in Microsoft Access, but an advisor at Montgomery College had suggested I take that to learn the concepts common to all software development. I replied to Gary that I was applying what I was learning to Access, but he didn't respond. I felt certain this wasn't going well anymore and can't say I was surprised. I really had no coding experience and was truly hoping for a miracle.

"So what's your situation?" he asked, handing me back the disk. "Hunter mentioned something about an injury, but I wasn't sure what he was getting at."

"My degree caused it," I began, before explaining about the switch of majors to classical guitar and passing my performance tests in half the years.

"You did it in only two years?" he asked, seeming impressed.

"Yeah. Seemed like a good idea at the time."

"A lot of programmers are trained musicians. They make good coders."

I nodded. "The music theory is pretty technical so you have to get all these things right, but fixing one thing can break another."

He smirked. "So it *is* like programming. What happened with the injury? Is there therapy you can get?"

"Yes, I've been doing it for over two years now, every week. It's a very slow recovery. I realized I needed a new career that doesn't rely on my arms, and working for

Becky made me realize this could be it. I enjoy it and feel like I'm good at it so far."

"Does that interfere with using a computer?" He waved one hand at his other forearm to indicate my injury.

Now I worried I was talking myself out of a job. "Yes, but there's a way around it. I have a foot mouse I use. It's a little challenging, but I can use the regular mouse, too. I just try to take much of the work off my arms."

"A foot mouse? I didn't even know they make such a thing."

"They'll never catch on," I joked, "but it works. I also use a dictation program for a lot of text. That was something I wanted to ask about, and if I could use it here. I just need to plug these into standard ports."

Seeming skeptical that these really worked, he nodded. "Yeah, that wouldn't be an issue."

We talked a little more about my situation, and I tried to show that I was not in a good one but that I wasn't wallowing in it, but trying to claw my way out using these devices and find a new career, and taking a class to help. When I came away from the interview, I really wanted to work with him. I needed a mentor, and someone as accepting, kind, and non-judgmental as he appeared to be was perfect. While I didn't know it yet, the conversation I'd just had with Gary would change my life. But as often happens, it wasn't so straightforward.

Afterward, Hunter called to see how it had gone and told me Gary was very interested, too, and impressed with my determination. He said I basically had the job but first had to interview with Ted, who would rubber stamp this. I couldn't believe it. My miracle had arrived! After two years of my life being ruined, I was finally going to escape and get on with, well, everything. I could not have been more excited.

A week later, I stood outside Ted's office door, at the building's corner, keyed up with positive enthusiasm. I had made it past the "technical" portion of the interview with Gary, where he examined my technical merits, so this should have been easy by comparison. I only had to impress upon Ted that I was a good guy, determined, and would be an asset. With Hunter assuring me I already had the job, I was not nervous but brimming with positivity.

The door opened and Ted stretched out a hand, which I shook. "Well, there's no job, but I wanted to meet you."

My heart stopped, my smile frozen on my face as he prattled on about me coming in, taking a seat, and whether I wanted a Coke or something, to which I muttered a stunned yes. He left to get one and I looked around the huge room with its nearly floor to ceiling windows, desk, bookcases, couch, and table with chairs, struggling to process what he'd just said.

There's no job? I thought, reeling. *Is he serious? What am I doing here?*

I was still standing there in stunned silence when he returned and shut the door, gesturing for me to take a seat at a round table near the windows, a more companionable place than across his desk from each other. I don't know if I appeared shocked into muteness, but he didn't seem to notice. It took every bit of acting talent I had to pretend I was calm, professional, and friendly, when anger, disbelief, and confusion roiled beneath my placid expression like a volcano waiting to blow. We did the usual things in an interview, such as talking about my situation and career plans, and what I'd been doing. What he most wanted to learn was how I'd gone from a degree in classical guitar to programming, so I explained only to have him interrupt, wanting to know when I started playing guitar.

"When I was at a private school in eighth grade," I began.

"Why a private school?" he asked.

For a moment, I stopped myself from admitting that I'm Learning Disabled but "gifted." I hadn't told anyone since high school, when I had it removed from my "permanent record" of education.

In grade school, my teachers had decided I was a troublemaker instead of someone needing extra help, and had punished me for struggling. Then I was diagnosed at the start of seventh grade and spent two years at the now-defunct Center School in Chevy Chase, Maryland. They specialized in such students and figured out the problem—I can't remember sequential information verbally given to me. They told me to write everything down as I heard it and I started getting As. Then I learned I was good at something—playing guitar—and my confidence really rebounded. But in high school, I was literally labeled a special student and given such cloying, patronizing, and unwanted help that I hated it. I had the label removed and swore I wouldn't tell anyone again. The story—and others—is detailed in another memoir, *Refusal to Engage*.

When Ted asked why I'd been at that private school, I opened my mouth to admit the truth, then shut it. A moment later, my lurking anger that he'd just taken away this job made me throw caution to the wind. There was no job to lose anyway, so I blurted out the truth.

"Really?" he said, leaning forward eagerly. "My son's Learning Disabled! That's great, that you've been so successful even with this. Very inspirational. How do you deal with it?"

Startled at the reaction, which was so much more positive than I'd expected, I almost wanted to laugh. All those years hiding it, and now my supposed liability had turned into an asset that had Ted on my side. We talked about it for a while, with him even asking if I'd be willing to talk to his son for some encouragement; he was suffering confidence problems like I had. The question surprised me, but I said yes, though that conversation never happened. We also discussed the accelerated classical guitar learning and that I graduated college with high honors despite being Learning Disabled. I clearly impressed him.

The interview went on for two hours, the longest I had ever been on—all for a job that didn't exist. I kept wondering how he had the time for this. We talked about so many things, including people I had known in the local music scene. It's a long story recounted in another memoir, *A Blast of Light*, but they had been awful people I finally walked away from, a fact Ted praised me for, citing my strength of character.

My troubles with those people had led me to become philosophical, and such comments are probably more common from me than I'm aware. Ted picked up on it and we had some talks about the nature of humanity, and whether or not people can rise above their demons. He admitted to having studied for the priesthood at some point and that he was always interested in this subject, so we bonded over this. In the end, I think he found me interesting, thoughtful, introspective, and of good character. This made his eventual behavior of trying to get managers to fire me as I departed the company even more shocking.

Toward the end of the interview, Ted told me they'd already hired someone else and asked if I'd like to meet him to see if he had any tips for me about this career. Not waiting for my answer, which was that I'd be happy to so I could push the guy down an empty elevator shaft and take his place, he led me out to meet the guy. He left me alone with him for an awful thirty minutes, during which the guy admitted he didn't even want the job and wanted to switch careers to something else. I hid my irritation that someone who didn't want it had taken the position from me when I was desperate for it.

After the interview, I got in the car and gave into all the cursing I'd been stifling since the moment Ted had ripped the job out from under me. I called Hunter and wasn't polite, feeling he'd lied to me. He said something about "don't bite the hand that feeds you" and I tried not to snap at him that all he'd fed me was a lie. Before long, after a few calls with Ted and Gary, he told me they really liked and respected me and wanted me for the job, but they felt I needed more experience. He claimed that Ted intended to create a position just for me. I didn't believe him anymore, and we parted ways, my job search resuming with other recruiters, few of whom called me back.

Meanwhile, my programming course was going well, and I crushed the assignments, doing every last extra credit question so that I routinely got more than a hundred percent on tests. My desperation and determination fueled my excellence. Ted had unwittingly lit a bigger fire under my ass.

Finally, in December, Hunter called to say that Ted wanted to send me to a training facility they wanted to evaluate, for a two-day course in Microsoft Access Intermediate programming, though there was no real coding. They would pay the $250 if I attended and wrote a report about the quality of the course, instructor, and training company. Being new to the corporate world, I had only some sense of just how peculiar this really was. When I asked if there was a catch, Hunter said no; I didn't believe him, but the whole thing was a positive sign, wasn't it? I did the course, which only covered things I already knew. Then I wrote the most detailed report imaginable, going so far as to describe the quality of the vending machines.

By this point, I was coding Becky's Print Orders system, adding a lot of functionality, now that I'd figured out how to do it. My confidence soared despite the lack of interest in my resume. I hadn't yet learned a trick with Monster.com: to update the resume every Sunday night even if I didn't make any actual changes. When recruiters searched the next day, mine showed up near the top of the list because it's sorted by "recently edited" or something similar. If I didn't do this, my resume slowly fell in the search results for candidates.

In January 1999, Hunter/Ted/Gary sent me to the advanced version of the course, which also proved too basic for me. What I didn't know at the time was that they'd also sent one of their employees, though he and I didn't meet despite only eight people being in the class; no one was chatty with each other. I did another report, and soon Hunter called again.

"They'd like you to take a weeklong course in Access programming. It's about $1400."

Surprised, I said, "Okay. There's really no catch to all of this? What if they never offer me a job and I take one somewhere else?"

In disapproval, he remarked, "That wouldn't be a good idea."

"Yeah, but I can't wait around forever."

"Understood, but you'd have to pay them back."

I stifled my annoyance. He had told me there was no catch, and I had known better. I hadn't signed anything with that condition in it, so it wasn't enforceable, but still. "That just makes me leery that they're spending this much."

"Oh no, this one would be on you."

I blanched and wondered why he hadn't said that up front. "Hunter, I can't afford that. I mean if there was a job for certain, then okay, but they're not offering one?"

"I totally get that, but they are determined to bring you onboard."

"I won't be able to pay the minimum on my card with that much being added." I was broke from a year of unemployment, followed by eighteen months of ten to twenty hours at minimum wage for Becky. I barely paid for my health insurance, car loan, and student loan, plus the minimum due on my credit card, despite the balance having only recently surpassed $1,000. Now Hunter wanted me to more than double it—for a job that didn't exist.

He said, "Well, think about it and let me know quick. The course is next week. They're thinking to bring you on in a couple months."

Shaking my head, I said okay and hung up. A couple months. That was March. That guy they'd hired had said he didn't want to do this job, and it was a six-month contract, after which, they could let him go if they were not happy with him.

He's not working out, I realized. *They want me to replace him.*

That was encouraging. Still, I couldn't afford this.

Was the course even worth it? The previous two hadn't been, and I didn't like potentially paying for courses they had chosen and which hadn't helped me. Those courses had focused on "power users" who did everything through the visual interface like I had done before. But I had moved beyond that now, my course in Pascal done. I had taught myself Access coding using a book. There was still a lot to learn, but the alterations I made to the system I designed for Becky were a strong step in the right direction. I now had some code to show. I looked into the new course they wanted me to take and saw that this time, it was the right kind of course—programming for Microsoft Access.

I had an idea and sent a carefully worded email to Hunter. I commented on how this was too expensive for me but that I appreciated their investment and continued interest in me, and that it was mutual. I suggested we each pay for half, or $700. This would tell me they were serious about bringing me on. It would also tell them I was serious about *waiting a couple months* (wink wink, nudge nudge). I tried to subtly let them know I understood the delay, that they were going to ditch my predecessor closer to the contract expiration.

To my surprise, a disgruntled Hunter agreed to it, giving me the impression that it was ProSource, not SysCorp, that was bearing the cost of these courses. I never learned who it was, but I only paid half. And that January I took the course, which proved beneficial. And I wrote another over-the-top, detailed report on it and what I had learned. There would be no doubting I wanted the job.

Despite this, I continued doing interviews with other companies for practice and in case Hunter didn't come through for me. If I had to repay them for over $1000 in courses to take a job making this kind of money somewhere else, that was better than zero. And that was the salary we were talking about, once converted to an hourly rate. It was more money than I'd ever seen by a long shot.

While this was happening, I realized Microsoft certifications that could provide companies some assurance that I was qualified, so I researched the one for Access. Microsoft had a website that told me which books to read and study for the exam, which cost over $100 to take. Figuring it would be worth it, and with me having surpassed 100% for my average score in Pascal last fall, I went for it. But as I sat there taking the computerized test of mostly multiple-choice answers, my determination turned to surprise, then disbelief, and increasingly frustration, confusion, and anger. The test bore no resemblance to the materials I had studied. I didn't know the answers.

I failed.

I didn't understand how this could have happened. At home, I double-checked the materials and the website's listing for the course. They matched. I had been lied to. And my faith in the ability to prepare for such a test lay in ruins. I felt duped, shocked, and manipulated. I swore I would never take another Microsoft certification exam again. I couldn't seem to catch a break.

And then it came. Hunter called in March 1999 and said his company would send me a written offer to start at SysCorp as a ProSource employee. Part of me didn't believe it until I got the actual letter. I was saved! I had watched 2.5 years of my life waste away from that tendonitis injury that still dominated me. But it was time to get on with everything. I had secured a new career that did not rely on my arms, which meant they could get the rest they needed to heal. Physical therapy, ice, heat, stretching, and anti-inflammatories only worked so well. Rest was the key. And I now had a potentially lucrative career ahead of me. In time, I could get back much of what I had lost in my life.

But there was a problem with the offer.

CHAPTER THREE

The Good Times

The letter from Hunter showed an hourly rate $7 fewer than he had been telling me since October. This was significant because it came in around $14k less per year.

"I explained this before," he said.

"You said it was $7 higher an hour."

"That's what we're getting paid. I told you we take a cut, and that's how we make money."

"Yeah, but you told me higher for me."

"No, you must have misheard me. Don't screw this up. I worked hard for this and it's a good deal for you."

I frowned at what I saw as attitude. "Not as good as it was supposed to be."

"You should be happy about this. It gets you in the door."

"This is not cool."

"Well look, get yourself in there and if it doesn't work out, you can go somewhere else and ask for that. It's only six months. Come on, man. I know you want this."

"Yeah, alright," I said, grumbling. I wondered if he was charging SysCorp more and was taking an even bigger cut now. Was he recouping the money spent on the training *they* had wanted me to take? Because it hadn't cost *that* much. If there had been a miscommunication, it had been his. The $7 higher number had come up repeatedly. The lower one never had. It mattered far more to me and wasn't something I would've screwed up. But I really didn't have other options, and we all knew it. I was certain he was screwing me. I tried to shrug it off and mostly did. This was still more money than I had ever made and the start of a promising new career, one that I had worked hard for. I was making $7 an hour, working 20 hours a week at most for Becky, who had been great to work for and was happy for me.

The rate issue didn't dampen my excitement for long. I had lost two-and-a-half years of my life to the injury, seldom leaving the house because there was nowhere to go and nothing to do when I got there, being unable to use my arms for much. By now, I could finally handle flossing my teeth without pain, or some handwriting if I paced myself. I had even resumed a little guitar playing, but it was only extremely easy stuff, just ninety minutes (including rests of several minutes) every other day. I was still a shell of my former self, especially musically, but I could get on with my life now. A long list of changes I wanted to make and made me feel keyed up about getting on with it. I would spend the next eighteen months on my transformation, detailed in *The Wine-Dark Sea*.

Gary told me to meet him in the lobby for my first day, at 8 AM, but on arrival, the doors were locked until 8:30, according to the lettering printed there. There I was, my whole life waiting on this job, and I couldn't get in. I laughed and mockingly banged my head on the door several times. Then I called him from a payphone. It was 1999 and not everyone had a cell phone, especially broke people like me. Gary sheepishly admitted to having forgotten the lobby wouldn't open until later, and the incident had the advantage of giving us both a laugh to start our working relationship with.

He led me to an office like his on the 6th floor, where a window overlooked parking lots and other office buildings that stood between two and eight stories. We logged me in and he loaded the system I was to work on, then announced he was leaving for the entire day to be at the DOE (where I eventually joined him as he retired). They left me unsupervised on my first day, and with nothing to do except poke around in the system. This all seemed odd to me. Had something about my behavior earned this much trust that I wouldn't spend all day on the internet? I decided to learn all that I could about the system, not wanting to betray that trust, should it exist. I was certain that my character had gotten me the job, not my skills, so it was time to ramp those up and not let them down. I initially found it odd that I didn't have to punch in or something, or tell people when I was going to lunch.

Sometimes I looked around in amazement that I even had the job. And then at the way my first day was going. I occasionally stepped up to my office door from within and stuck my head out, looking down the hallway in each direction. The building was a square with rounded corners, and I finally ventured out to look around. Along the way, I found Gary's office on another side of the building, then Ted's, but neither was in. I passed others who nodded hello, but of course no one knew who I was. This all seemed strange to me, just as odd as Ted spending two hours interviewing me for a job that didn't exist. I apparently had a lot to learn about the way the corporate world worked.

When I returned to my office, I found a middle-aged woman with greying black hair sliding my name tag into the door. She was slender except at her hips, which tight black pants covered. An open sweater lay atop her blouse, a tasteful number of bracelets, necklaces, and earrings adorning her. She struck me as someone's mother and re-minded me a little of mine, albeit thinner and younger.

"Hello," I said, deciding to wait for her to finish instead of trying to squeeze around her.

She turned. "Oh, I was just putting your name tag in. I'm Betty, the administrative assistant for Ted. Well, for everyone on our team."

Searching for something to say, I asked, "How big is the team?"

She smiled wryly. "They didn't introduce you to any-one, did they?"

"No one was in earlier and Gary had to leave for the day."

Betty took me around to meet a few people. The big surprise was Darryl, a twenty-something black man with a shaved head. I recognized him from the second training course I had taken, but decided not to say anything. He didn't seem to recognize me. He was the Project Manager on the Vetabase system they had hired me to work on, and he reported directly to Ted, whereas I reported to Gary, who reported to Ted. He was the main user, but we had a part-time intern that did data entry for him, too. And that was about it for people directly involved in it. A few other people worked on different projects, for which Ted was ultimately responsible as the Program Manager.

Some time that day, the admin responsible for the building's network, computers, and other hardware dropped by to see if I needed anything. Then he saw me using the foot mouse and made a face.

"What is *that?*"

"A foot mouse." I explained that I could plug the regu-lar mouse into it as well and use either, then answered his questions about why I needed it. "I also use a dictation program. I was hoping I could install it, but I get the im-pression there's no sound card."

"Yeah, none of the computers have one. Gotta cut corners somewhere. Everyone's always asking for one to play music or something, so there's a backlog."

My heart sank. It sounded like I was never getting one. He asked about the program, Dragon Dictate, a precursor to Dragon NaturallySpeaking, which is still around, and left me with the impression that I was screwed. But he came back later with one he'd removed from someone's computer, installing it in mine.

"You need it more," he said.

"Thanks man. I really appreciate that." And I meant it.

"Yeah, no sweat. One favor's all you get though!"

I could live with that.

But I soon realized I didn't need Dragon Dictate. In coding, programmers give objects like a button a name, such as "btnSave." To refer to that in code later, we can type the first letters and the auto-complete shows us the options. If I have three buttons that start with those letters and I type "btn," the list is restricted to those three. I could then choose one with the foot mouse, which became my real savior. I could double-click "btnSave," then copy the name and paste it somewhere else I needed it. This became my style of working, avoiding most typing.

Sometimes I freaked people out because they'd be looking at my computer screen and see things moving around while my hands were in my lap. I'd joke about using my Jedi mind powers to control the computer before revealing the foot mouse to a laugh and lots of questions about this and the injury. I also used a touch pad there, as it was easier on my arms than the regular hand mouse; both that and foot mouse worked without having to unplug one or the other. I had used the foot mouse since September, but until I got used to doing it eight hours a day, my legs were sore by day's end. This was one reason I got up to walk around every hour, a habit I kept long after I stopped needing to.

Soon Gary got me working for real on the Vetabase system that needed fixing. Under the Vetabase program, the Department of Labor required companies to report on how many veterans they employed. They had tracked this in an Excel spreadsheet, but this is a poor way to do that because the ability to show reports of specific information can be limited. When SysCorp won the contract, Gary imported the spreadsheet into Microsoft Access, and when I saw it, I couldn't help wondering what my predecessor had been doing. Because the "system" was crap.

A complete system should have four elements. The most important are the "tables," which come first. These are rows and columns of data. This might seem just like a spreadsheet, but there are differences in the way we lay them out. Without getting too technical, a spreadsheet might show a customer's name and their address on the same line, as shown in the picture.

Name	Street	City	State	Zip
John Doe	1 Main St.	New York	MD	10010
Homer Simpson	1 Ever Ter.	Springfield	NY	20878

Figure 1

What if the customer has two addresses? We would have two rows for them, and need to list their name twice, once for each address. This causes duplication of their name. This may not seem important, but duplicating data is a big issue because it causes redundancy and slows systems, especially very large ones like Amazon.com, where speed is important.

There is a way to solve this: a "database," meaning "tables," instead of a spreadsheet. Each table holds one type of data. In this example, we would need three: a customers table, an addresses table, and a state table, like this, with the fields of data found in each:

Figure 2

The "tbl" prefix is short for "table." There are other objects in a database, and each has a three-letter abbreviation like this to make it easier to tell what it is (in this case, a table). The Customers table is called "tblCustomers."

The lines connecting these tables show the relationships between them. TblCustomer's CustomerID is the same data as tblAddresses' CustomerID. In tblAddresses, the StateID field matches the StateID field in tblStates.

If we look at the customer table to see what data is in there, we would see this:

CustomerID	FirstName	LastName
1	John	Doe
2	Homer	Simpson

Figure 3

The addresses table would show this:

AddID	Cust ID	Street	City	State ID	Zip
1	1	1 Main St.	New York	MD	10010
2	2	1 Ever Ter.	Springfield	NY	20878

Figure 4

And the state table would show this:

StateID	StateName	StateAbbr
1	Maryland	MD
2	New York	NY

Figure 5

It is unlikely that the name of a state is going to change, but let's say it did, and the database is for Amazon.com, which likely has billions if not trillions of records. Maryland changes its name to Zinn. To change this in the system, we type "Zinn" into *one field* in tblStates, in the StateName field. And we change StateAbbreviation to "Zn" in *one field*. Two changes would take place in a nanosecond.

But what if we didn't separate data like this? What if "Maryland" was in a billion rows because Amazon had billions of orders that were sent to the state of Maryland, now called the state of Zinn. We would have to change "Maryland" to "Zinn" and "MD" to "Zn" a billion times. That would take a long time, even using program code to do it. And an enormous site like Amazon.com might crash while this was happening.

When I look at the addresses table, I cannot tell who the address belongs to. Well, I sort of can. "1 Main Street" belongs to CustomerID 1, whoever that is. So how do I tell who CustomerID 1 is? I look in tblCustomer. But this is tedious. Isn't there a way to see the customer's name and their address at the same time, even though the data is stored in two different places? Can't I make it *look* like a spreadsheet. Yes.

It's called a "query," a question. It is code that asks the database, "show me the customer's last name and first name from the Customers table, and their address from the Addresses table, at the same time. Use the CustomerID field, which is found in both tables, to match the records to each other." we find CustomerID 1 in tblCustomers and in tblAddresses. The result of the query looks just like a spreadsheet, but the data is *stored* differently to avoid redundancy.

First Name	Last Name	Street	City	State Abbr	Zip
John	Doe	1 Main St.	New York	MD	10010
Homer	Simpson	1 Ever Ter.	Springfield	NY	20878

Figure 6

If this makes little sense, the takeaway is this: data needs to be stored in discreet piles known as tables. Each table specializes in storing certain information. In order to see the information from multiple tables put back together so that we can make sense of it, we use a query, or question asked of the system, using code.

Queries are also the basis for another element: reports. This is just what it sounds like. If you're on Amazon and want to see a "report" of all orders you placed in the last six months, they expected this so you can click a button and get that result. The report fires off a query that asks the database, "give me all orders for this customer in the past six months. Sort the records by the newest orders first. And give me these fields from these tables, matching on these ID fields." And then it lists the items it wants. I'm guessing it is something like this:

tblProducts   –   ProductID,   ProductName, ProductDescription

tblOrders – OrderID, OrderDate, OrderStatusID, ProductID

tblOrderStatus – OrderStatusID, OrderStatus

tblPrices – PriceID, ProductID, PriceDate, Price

And so on. It can get complicated.

There is one last element to database systems: the user interface. This is sometimes called "forms" or "screens." When you're on Amazon, each webpage you see is one of these. They allow us to manipulate the data. We click on an item and see a product screen that is displaying data from the database. If we choose to order it, we are triggering code that adds the item to our cart. Every action we take on a site like this is through screens.

That brings us back to Microsoft Access, the software I was using in 1999. It is not an internet technology, but a "desktop" one, meaning it runs on our local computer, or the company network. Access is part of Microsoft Office and is designed for under a hundred people to use. At SysCorp, not even a half-dozen staff would be using the Vetabase system at once. Even so, it needed to be created correctly.

The last element I'll mention is that there is what's known as a "front end" and a "back end." The back are the tables, and sometimes the queries. The front are the screens and reports, and sometimes the queries. This matters because there are technologies that specialize in back or front end elements, and we can connect the front and back ends so they "talk" to each other. To a user, it all seems like one seamless system when there are unique pieces. But Access allows one to do everything. This might seem superior, but it's inferior because Access does not specialize in tables, queries, reports, or screens, which means it has limits. It also cannot handle large amounts of data or users.

I mention these details this one time so you can get a sense of what I did for a living, which is this: I built database driven applications. At the start of my career, it was in

Microsoft Access. I later switched to internet apps and other technologies, but the basic principles I just discussed are the same. A big takeaway is that the tables are everything. Queries, reports, and screens all refer to them, so the tables come first. And the tables make little sense if looked at by themselves. The users need the other pieces to make sense of it all.

Which leads me to the state of Vetabase when I took it over from Gary and my predecessor. It was tables. That was it. There were no queries, screens, or reports. It was not a complete system, but a shambles. The basic table design was okay, but I quickly learned something startling—there were over forty copies of the most important table. It took me a while to figure out why. When the Project Manager, Darryl, needed a report, my predecessor did not give him an actual report. Instead, he duplicated the table with only the data he needed to show. And then he just left these duplicate versions of the table sitting there, creating a mess. And it was my job to clean this up. I initially thought my predecessor was responsible for this mess, and while that was true, Gary had told him to do it that way! This was the first sign that I was better at Access than either of them, to my surprise.

I began to frequently work with Darryl, who I liked. And at meetings with him, Gary, and Ted, we discussed the state of the system and what I felt needed to be done to make it usable. The Department of Labor occasionally wanted a report with little warning, and it wasn't easy to meet their deadlines unless I created actual reports that, with the click of a button, would produce the desired result. I could give Darryl a button to run them at once, instead of it taking me a day to create it. The client was sometimes not too happy about our delays.

As the months rolled by, the system grew in functionality. Gary complimented me on my work and how quickly I adapted, and no longer worried if I wasn't cut out for the job. He shrugged off any mention of trouble I was having, and I typically got past it without his help. Gary didn't work on it at all, being at the Department of Energy except a couple half days. Hunter sometimes called to say he was only hearing positive things from Ted and Gary. He occasionally swung by and took me to lunch on him. Everything seemed to be going great.

As I gained a reputation for knowing what I was doing, more work came my way. I rebuilt an inventory system that I was just supposed to fix. Gary was the culprit again. He knew coding better, but I knew database design and screen layout concepts better and thought farther ahead. I had a better mind for details, creating few bugs while fixing those he created. He didn't have an ego about it and appreciated my diligence. So did Ted and the coworkers for whom I finished building a working Vetabase system full of the screens and reports they needed to do their jobs. I had the respect of my co-workers and enjoyed it and the easy banter we shared. The good rapport came in handy when I needed Ted's help with something.

Over 60,000 companies needed to submit Vetabase reports. The ones doing so electronically had to do so in a format that my new system accepted, so Ted asked me to re-write the now out-of-date instructions for clients to follow. I did, but when the submissions came in, I found mistakes in 115 of them. Ted had me write letters to the affected companies detailing which mistakes they'd made and how to fix them. The problem was that my name and contact information were going on them. I knocked on Ted's door one afternoon to talk about it.

"You don't want your name on the letters?" he asked after my opening salvo.

"Well, I do, just not *that* name."

"What's wrong with it?" he asked, smirking.

I humored him with a smile. "It's about to change." Seeing his perplexed look, I launched into the explanation I'd been mulling over. "I was going to change my name later this summer. The whole thing. But by the time I do, companies will call for David and, well, I won't be known by that anymore. I figured my new name should go on the letters, even though I haven't filed the paperwork to make it official."

He leaned forward. "Really? That's interesting! I changed my name when I was thirty." Ted was full of surprises, but he didn't elaborate. "What's your family think of this?"

"Haven't told them yet. In fact, you're the first. This thing with the letter sort of accelerated it."

"Sure. What's the new name?"

"Randy Zinn."

"Family name or something?"

I shook my head. "It's my pseudonym. Or I intended it to be. You know I write fantasy books outside of work, so it was supposed to be for that. It means nothing. I just wanted a clean name. It almost doesn't really matter what my new name is. The goal is to get rid of my birth name, and since I've already thought of myself as Randy Zinn as an author for about ten years, it's the obvious thing to change my name to."

"Why? Mind if I ask?"

I'd expected this question but would not tell the truth to most people. Ted was different, since we'd already talked about very personal things in my life during my job interview. He'd proven himself a conscientious listener who respected what I had to say for myself, and we'd had the occasional philosophical conversation since. I wouldn't quite say he was like a father to me, but someone who had taken an interest in what was happening in my life and trying to help me succeed at work. So far, it had worked out for both of us, with me improving the Vetabase system to where he and Darryl could now easily meet the client's expectations.

"Well," I began, "it's a long story, but I had speech problems from the time I was in third grade until just a few years ago."

"Really? Could've fooled me."

"Thanks," I ruefully replied, gauging his sincerity. He seemed to mean it. "I was really quiet for about twenty years because of it, and my relationships were unpleasant as a result."

"Do you mean those friends you used to hang out with in your late teens?"

I nodded, pleased he remembered. "Partly, but even before that. The thing is, when you're quiet, people can use you like a blank screen they project character traits onto. Usually nasty ones. Then they give you an attitude for supposedly being some jerk they've made you out to be. Anyway, I always felt like everyone had me wrong, like I was being mistaken for someone else, and they referred to that fictional person by my birth name. I eventually decided that if he's not me, then I must have another name."

"That's a very powerful thing you've just said." He clearly approved. "I noticed you've been making some other changes, like the teeth whitening."

"Yeah, I've been busy," I said, not sure how much to admit. It had surprised me others noticed that. My teeth had gotten *that* much whiter. "I think the big thing with the name change is getting people to go along with it."

He grew stern. "Don't worry about that. I'll make sure everyone does or they'll have to answer to me. We can definitely use your new name in the letters. We just have to make the change for everything here. Your badge, login, all of that."

I hadn't thought of that. "Okay. Thanks Ted. I appreciate that."

"Sure. Randy," he added, smiling.

I grinned. No one had called me that yet. But I'd been dreaming of it and all that it meant, leaving behind a false identity that had dogged me since childhood. During the two-and-a-half years tendonitis had dominated my life, I had finally gotten past the speech problems. It was the other reason I wanted to reinvent myself. Tendonitis had destroyed my life so that I needed to start it over again, anyway. And then I overcame the speech issues and could talk and act like a normal person for the first time in forever. The job gave me the means and opportunities to make the changes I wanted, and I was plowing my way through them one by one.

The real me was getting stronger every day and appearing more and more in my behavior as I changed how I conducted myself. Showing initiative in my interview with Gary months earlier had been part of it. Like most people, I wanted to be accepted for who I really was, not play some charade, especially when it wasn't of my choosing. When you don't speak well, people are cruel to you about it, and you hide your difficulties, and that leads people to make assumptions about why you talk little. Those conclusions are seldom good and include crap like thinking you're too good to talk to other people. They were right that I had an ego problem, but it was crushing insecurity, not too much confidence. It was all behind me now, but I was still trying to act like my authentic self and not give in to old behaviors. I had come a long way and had more to go. The name change would be a big step.

Within a week, it happened at work, including the sign on my office door changing. Ted made everything happen quickly, and I experienced no backlash, just curious questions I mostly dodged. Most of them struggled to stop calling me Dave but were quick to correct themselves. My family had little to say about it nor did Hunter, who dropped by without warning about five months into the six-month contract.

"Let's go to lunch," he said, gesturing for me to follow. I glanced at the lunch I'd brought in a container and figured I'd put it in the fridge when I got back. We chatted about random stuff on the way down to his blue convertible BMW sports car. He seemed to be showing off, and I wryly wondered to myself if this was where the rest of my promised salary had gone. Which part of the car was mine? The last month of my six-month contract was approaching, and I was looking forward to being hired at the higher rate stated in my contract, ProSource no longer taking a cut. I knew this lunch was about discussing the future, so it came as no surprise when he got down to business after we ordered food.

"So listen," he began, eyeing a waitress like the player he no doubt was, "Ted and Gary say you're doing fine and have made it clear they would be happy if you were to stay on."

I cocked an eyebrow. "If" I was to stay on? I had already told Hunter I wanted to stay, so the "if" was on their side. He also normally said I was doing great, not just fine. Had something gone wrong that I didn't know about? Or was I being too sensitive? "That's good to hear," I said, pretending to ignore that.

"I want to make sure I'm involved in any plans of yours."

"Sure." My alarm rose. If SysCorp hired me, Hunter was out of the picture, so why would he need to be involved in plans unless they weren't bringing me on board?

"Sometimes we can't tell where things are headed, but I think there's about an 85% chance they'll bring you on."

Only 85%? "What's causing the missing 15%? Why don't they already know?"

"Well, when they won this contract with the Department of Labor a year ago, they didn't know they were getting this bullshit system you had to redesign. We brought on that guy before you and he was incompetent, so that wasted a lot of money. I mean, we booted him a month early. Should've been way before that."

"I don't think the guy ever did anything. I mean, I designed an entire system in less than five months and there wasn't shit after he had the same time."

"Yeah, I know. Gary hated him. Loves you though. We should've hired you in the first place."

I could have told them that. "He's been great."

"Yeah. So listen, the problem is that your position wasn't in the budget. SysCorp won the contract based partly on how much money they could do it for. Then they needed to hire you and the other guy to fix that system. Ted did the right thing, but the fact is they can't afford you. He's trying to figure out a way to keep you on."

Shit. "I guess that's why he's been having me do more and more work for other contracts." On my timesheet, I had to charge my time to more than one, not just the original contract.

"Exactly. The thing is, you've automated the system like they needed you to do, so now they don't need you to run reports or anything."

I almost laughed. "So I programmed myself out of a good job?"

He chuckled. "Maybe. I still think they want to keep you on, just maybe not on that contract. Ted is looking around."

I deadpanned, "I can always go back to the office and screw the system up so they need me again."

He laughed loud. "Not the way to handle it, Rand!"

It seemed like either way, I was out of a job. They had known this when hiring me on a contract-to-hire basis for a job that wouldn't be able to afford me after six months, regardless of how well I did. They had lied me to. First the money. Now this. And with only five months' official experience (I knew some places would ignore my time coding for Becky), I was suddenly not in a great position, my future once again threatened. Lunch left a foul taste in my mouth.

Weeks later, Hunter changed the 85% chance of being hired to 0%, saying I would be gone in weeks.

CHAPTER FOUR

The Outsider

Ted confirmed I would no longer be working for him and apologized. Then he asked for an updated resume and began trying to get me a job working for someone else, anyone else, within the company. I didn't ask him to because it never occurred to me that someone would.

But he bungled this, telling them I wanted to be a software developer, not that I already was. In doing so, he undercut confidence in me, and two groups in other buildings passed on hiring me partly because of it. I could tell because they repeated "you want to be a programmer?" back to me, forcing me to counter it that I was already a professional coder. They took Ted's word over mine and dissed my resume. First impressions matter and Ted had doomed me with them by accident.

I appreciated the effort and felt certain Ted did it mostly out of respect. But I also wondered if guilt drove him to it. He had almost certainly known all along that my contract-to-hire position was a sham. I didn't think he owed me, but maybe *he* thought that. He made one last effort with a group one floor below us in our building, doing work for the Environmental Protection Agency (EPA). He didn't think it was a good fit, but it was better than the unemployment line. I did a round of interviews with several managers, then the division director Tim, who made me an offer.

And lowballed me.

He made the verbal offer at the same rate that Hunter was paying me through ProSource, even though this middleman would be gone. I had expected a $7 an hour increase, so I objected, and he came to my office to discuss it.

Tim sat down and slung one leg over the chair's arm, a casualness I hadn't expected from a director. Unlike most senior people, he wasn't wearing a tie or button-up shirt, just khakis, sneakers, and a polo. He was handsome and could have passed for a dashing pirate with his black mustache and tiny goatee, slightly curly hair close-cropped so that it had almost no chance to curl. Average height, slender, and moving briskly as if athletic, he seemed like he was in his thirties and thought he owned the place.

I said, "The rate was supposed to be $14k higher a year."

"Yeah, but this has benefits. You have none now."

"Are you saying those benefits cost the company fourteen grand a year?"

Smirking, he dodged that. "You have no computer science degree and no real experience."

I frowned. I had six months full time and a year of part-time work designing systems for two businesses. While I knew some would ignore this, saying it to my face was rude. "Then why are you hiring me?"

He chuckled. "Listen, we're gonna send you to SAS training, so that's part of why the offer is what it is."

I had never heard of the technology, but I let that pass. "That doesn't change this offer being way below what I was expecting."

"We know you don't have any other offers."

Did he just admit to lowballing me? And how did he know that? Ted. Jesus. That was the only way he could have known, because I had occasionally spoken with Ted about my job search. Unintentionally or not, Ted had helped Tim lowball me. Why might he do it on purpose? To save his buddy Tim money on the EPA contract. I was wondering just how much help Ted really was.

Tim hadn't stopped smiling. "Well, think about it."

I hadn't stopped frowning. "Yeah. Sure."

I knew I had no choice and resented Tim knowing this and using it against me. I consoled myself knowing that while I'd have training and full benefits, they weren't worth $14k. As a result, I began my new position with a chip on my shoulder, one eye already on the door.

I still worked under the same Vice President as before, named John. Tim reported to him and was a director. Under Tim was a female Program Manager like Ted. And under her were two women project managers, one being my boss, whom I soon learned was Tim's wife. The other project manager was Liz. My new team was over twenty budding scientists who, except for those managers, were mostly five years younger than me, fresh out of college. They were a clique who gave me my first experience of being shunned at work. They were not friendly and didn't interact with me, or even acknowledge my existence unless they needed to, which was rare and only applied to one or two of them.

At first, the work was decent as I created a database to calculate scientific data, which proved arduous. Then a young, attractive blonde woman wanted me to fix another system, prompting several guys to point out how lucky I was to work with her on anything. She was my first friendly coworker there until I met Alexa, another blonde woman who initially drove me crazy. She wanted help on another database, but her unrestrained Attention Deficit

Hyperactivity Disorder (ADHD) caused such rapid talking and subject changing that she was a bit much to handle. She knew it and made self-deprecating comments about it, sensing that I was both amused and exasperated. Somehow we became work friends, and I taught her how to change things in the Access system she had inherited.

Before long, Liz asked me to help with a financial database that was broken. When I looked into it, I realized they did not design it right and it would never produce accurate data due to structural flaws. With her approval, I began redesigning it and had it working more every week. She became a big supporter of mine at work and even read a few short stories I had written on learning I wrote fantasy books.

I now worked on the fifth floor instead of the sixth, but I sometimes went back to visit my old coworkers. This usually resulted in a surprised, "What are *you* doing up here?" It wasn't said in a mean way, but with repetition, I had the impression I wasn't particularly welcome, as if the previous friendliness had come with an expiration date I had exceeded. Even Ted and Gary reacted that way.

Just when I thought to stop coming by, several of them (not including those two) invited me to lunch. They admitted they went to lunch together once a week and had been doing so for years. I had worked with them for six months and never gotten the invite. Was it because I was a contractor? Or not actually liked despite how they acted? Or was this a private thing no one got invited to? I went with them once or twice. They invited me for the Tuesday before Thanksgiving, but when I went up early to meet them, they were gone despite me waiting around for a while and asking about them. I ended up going to eat by myself somewhere. I dropped by that afternoon to ask about it and learned they had left early without telling me, ditching me before the holiday, saying with amusement, "Better luck next time!" After that, I stopped dropping by. I never saw any of them again.

Not long after, someone gave me an update about Ted's group. He had cost SysCorp the Vetabase contract by going over budget—presumably on me. Another firm now had the contract. As often happens, the new company subcontracted the work out to the SysCorp people who'd been working on it. SysCorp had lost the contract to Acme Consulting, but then Acme Consulting offered SysCorp a subcontract to continue doing the actual work—for less money. This resulted in a few terminations and pay cuts. Acme Consulting hired one SysCorp guy, Darryl, who had reported to Ted. They made Darryl their Program Manager instead of Ted, who now answered to Darryl!

I had, in effect, made all of this happen by fixing, automating, and finishing the Vetabase system. This meant they needed fewer people to do the work, allowing Acme Consulting to underbid SysCorp. And the money SysCorp spent on me fixing the system made them go over budget and cost them the contract in the first place. I couldn't help but wonder if this had given Ted a chip on his shoulder about me, or caused my old team to ditch me for lunch the one time. But I had done my job.

Around that time, my group did a bunch of layoffs, which I survived, but Alexa didn't. To my disbelief, she got a job at Verizon as a Software Engineer when she knew nothing about this except for what little I had taught her. But the kicker was her salary: $6,000 more than what I was making. By now, Tim had repeatedly reneged on the SAS training I'd been promised and then said it wasn't going to happen at all. The work was already getting lame and unfulfilling. The job had no future for me. And my only friend, Alexa, was gone. I'd had enough.

I began looking for a job, telling recruiters a salary expectation, which was $14k above what I was currently making, though I didn't admit this. It was the salary Hunter and I had originally discussed. I couldn't get the number out of my head. I wanted it and updated my resume on Monster.com, blocking SysCorp from seeing it by using a feature provided for that. I'd heard that companies sometimes fire staff who are looking to leave.

One day, a recruiter named Tina called. She worked for a recruiting company called SmartTech and had a job at United Systems, a huge defense contractor who had buildings all over, including in Aspen Hill, Maryland, about twenty minutes from my parent's house, where I still lived. I knew the area well from passing through it and even hanging out there for a year or two after high school with some friends; we had called ourselves a gang, "Nitemare," but we were no such thing, just a bunch of metal heads goofing around. My days of having long hair ended in 1997.

"Before I can send you on the interview," Tina said over the phone, "I need two references."

"Oh. Well, I think my best ones are where I am now, but they don't know I'm leaving." I also suspected that I needed to ask their permission again even now though both Ted and Gary had already done it.

"Sure. I understand. I only need them on file. I don't actually have to call them yet."

That made little sense to me, but I wanted to clarify. "When would you call them?"

"You'd give them to me now. I would schedule the interview. If United Systems wants to hire you, we would send you an offer letter, and once you accept, we would check your references."

"Oh really? I thought you would check before an offer."

"Nope."

I wanted to ask what happened if my references trashed me but didn't. Because they wouldn't. "If we get to the point of an offer, I need to have it before I can resign and ask them to be a reference again."

"Not a problem. We do that all the time."

"Great." I gave her the info.

For salary, I didn't want to admit what I was making for fear that a company would just stick me with the same thing. It had already happened once. Employers always ask this question and have a space on the job application for it, and of course we're all encouraged to never lie or hide things, but the truth can be used against us. Being new to my career, I wasn't sure what I could get away with and reluctantly admitted my current salary and the expected new one that was over $14,000 higher. Tina asked about the difference, and I admitted I knew I could get this (or at least, I thought I knew that) and that my current employer was underpaying me. She wasn't sure she could get me that, but felt certain we could at least split the difference, getting me halfway there.

Before long, I did the uneventful interview at United Systems with the guy who would be my manager if they hired me. I brought that binder showing updated screen shots and code of the Vetabase system, but he wasn't much interested in it. The interview was pretty easy, and I left feeling confident.

Days later, on Wednesday, I was rollerblading in Rock Creek Park when I had a really nasty fall on rough asphalt, while not wearing knee or elbow pads. An ambulance took me to the hospital. I had ripped skin from one forearm and the opposite knee, gouging out a deep hole. It was excruciating, and I couldn't use that arm for weeks. I could also hardly walk, limping badly from a knee I couldn't bend much (or straighten) and which was as heavily bandaged as my dominant arm.

The night of the accident, Tina called with good news: United Systems wanted to hire me and they could meet my entire salary request. I was thrilled, especially when my painkillers finally kicked in. For the job, I would need a security clearance but could start work before that was completed, as it can take over a year. The arrangement would be just like with ProSource, a contract-to-hire position as a SmartTech employee for six months before United Systems hired me as their employee. My year-long stint at SysCorp, six months as a contractor, then six months as an employee, was ending.

I missed the rest of the week at work while recuperating. My director Tim called the next day, but not to see how I was doing. Apparently, my old boss Gary had resigned for retirement and wanted my help to close out his work at the DOE in D.C. Ted had gone to his VP, John, and gotten permission to borrow me from Tim, with Tim's approval. I noticed no one had asked me what I thought of this. I would have gladly helped Gary, but my injuries were a problem.

I could hardly drive because getting my injured left leg in or out of the car was very difficult. Being 6' 3", I couldn't bend it much, especially bandaged and with dress pants fabric painfully pulling down on the wound. I had to drive with one hand. Getting to work was difficult, but getting to the DOE would be worse, driving to the metro, and limping around and on stairs, and being jostled by crowds, my wounds repeatedly struck. Stairs were so difficult that I slipped at home one day and fell, landing hard on my injured arm.

When I was back at work for a few days before starting with Gary, people almost ran into me several times in the hallways from barreling around a corner or charging out of their office. Seeing me limping, they sometimes asked why, and it became apparent that no one knew about my accident or hospitalization because my manager and the Program Manager I had emailed told no one. Tim hadn't mentioned it despite being married to my boss. Surprised, I emailed and included my old team on it, asking if anyone was going out to lunch and would be willing to pick up something for me because it was so hard to get around. I received no response, even from Ted. My only friend Alexa was gone, and the clique was more apparent than ever. Around 2pm and having gone without lunch, my old team's administrative assistant finally asked me if anyone had done it, then got something for me that day and the next, with my heartfelt thanks.

I now thoroughly hated my job and looked forward to resigning.

My mood worsened as I started the work for Gary and dealing with that awful commute. Passing the same D.C. bum who cursed at me every morning didn't help my mood; I couldn't limp away from him fast enough. While I liked Gary, the work sucked, and I chafed at the delay in my offer letter from SmartTech. Tina had told me I'd get it on a given Monday. Based on this, we had agreed on a start date two Mondays later so I could give two weeks' notice. But the offer was late.

And then Gary walked in one day and told me Ted was mad at me, resulting in the phone call where I learned Tina had violated our agreement and called him for a reference check before I had received my offer letter, given notice, or verified Ted would still be a reference. He threatened to badmouth me to Tina, hung up on me, and went to my Project Manager, my Program Manager, my Director Tim, and my Vice President John, trying to get one of them to fire me. But John had called Gary, who told him I had not given notice, nor received an offer letter that would allow me to do so. And Gary told me how to call John and make it go straight to voice mail so John would hear it from me, but I didn't have to talk to him.

And when I got home, I found the offer letter. I called my old team's administrative assistant and asked her to distribute the sealed resignation letters in my desk drawer but to throw Ted's in the trash. She called back and verified having done it. I worked at HQ that weekend and my Project Manager was present and ignored me, not making eye contact if we saw each other in the hall. I spent the next week with Gary until Friday, when I cleared out my desk at HQ, where Liz accused me of leaving them in a lurch, my current Program Manager was the only polite person, and I exchanged a hate-filled glare with Ted before driving away and never seeing any of them again.

Gary had said he didn't know what had gotten into Ted to make him act this way. Neither did I. I did not work for him anymore and hadn't in about six months; it didn't count that I was doing him a favor helping Gary close things out. He was outside my chain of command, which was precisely why he couldn't fire me and had to get someone else to do it. That should have told him something about the appropriateness of what he was attempting.

Ted had said I owed him personally and professionally. I didn't agree on either. Personally, the closest he had was supporting my name change at work, but that was still a professional thing, and he would have been wrong to interfere with it or support other people doing so. I didn't owe him for that.

As for professionally, there could have been merit there. Either SysCorp or Hunter (and my gut says it was ProSource, trying to please their client) had paid for the first two courses, but that had been their idea, lying that there were no strings attached. They paid half of the next, more expensive course, but the course was again their idea and they wanted me to pay it all without a promise of a job offer, so that was asking a lot of me. They knew it and agreed to pay half when I asked, so we each asked something of the other and we each did it. Were we square? Maybe.

But even if we hadn't been and I owed them, they violated the agreed upon salary discussed prior to my first interview. They lowballed me and cost me $7000 during the six months I worked for them. They also lied that it was contract-to-hire when they probably knew it wasn't. And I had done an excellent job for them, a kind of repayment. We were square.

Then Ted tried to get me a job in the company, but he screwed it up for me in two ways. First, he told them I was a wanna-be programmer, undercutting me. Then, even when he got me the job with Tim's EPA group, he told them I had no other offers, and a salary figure that he had gotten from Hunter, because only Hunter and I knew what he was charging them and paying me. This was none of Ted's business to tell Tim my salary expectation, especially when the number was wrong. This made it easy for Tim to lowball me. So, on one hand, Ted helped get me the interview with Tim's group, but he also set in motion my departure from day one with the salary issue. In my mind, I had lost another $7k in the six months working for Tim's group. Ted complained I hadn't gotten his permission to use him as a reference. When did he get my permission to discuss either my salary expectations or job hunt status with others? We weren't square because Ted owed me for that.

I asked him the day he threatened me, did he think I had to stay in an unfulfilling, underpaying job just because he helped me get it? He said yes. He was wrong. I didn't owe anyone that. All of his anger about the call with Tina was her fault and then his because he wouldn't let me clear up the misunderstanding. And what he did after that was unforgivable. One of us owed the other, and it was him owing me an apology.

In retrospect, Ted had taken an uncommon interest in me personally from the start because people at work seldom have much interest in peers at all and he'd wanted my life story. I can only speculate that my departure felt like a betrayal to him, even though it had nothing to do with him. Maybe he had expected me to come to him about the job if it wasn't working out, but that wouldn't have been appropriate because I would've been pitting him against my new managers, who would've seen this as going over their heads, regardless of who outranked who. I had done nothing wrong until I made his false accusation of less than two weeks' notice a self-fulfilling prophecy. But he had turned my job into a hostile work environment when it wasn't exactly cordial to begin with. I should have quit immediately.

CHAPTER FIVE

Dealt with and Corrected

Aspen Hill is a small town halfway between Rockville and where I grew up. I had driven through it countless times and even hung out there for two years around high school graduation, even though there isn't much to see, just strip malls, a Home Depot, and a long, rectangular building that was my new job. After my first day, I walked over to the nearest strip mall, wanting to catch a movie for old time's sake. Four years earlier, when tendonitis destroyed my life, I had gone to the movies there once or twice a week for months because the dilapidated theater gave me $1 off ticket, good for seven days, and the movies were priced at $2 instead of the usual $10 anyway. But now the theater was gone (not surprising). Disappointed, I still felt good about the contrast between then and now, my life in shambles vs. being rebuilt, with great prospects ahead

I was two thirds of the way through my personal transformation. I had just had a rhinoplasty to fix a breathing problem, then grew a mustache and goatee I would have for decades before adding a beard. I was buying a Suzuki Katana sport bike at a motorcycle shop in Aspen Hill. Approaching age 29, I was now apartment hunting, the injury having delayed being on my own. My arms had recovered more, and I felt confident they could handle bringing home groceries, taking out the trash, and doing my laundry.

Besides the salary I had expected a year earlier, the new job gave me something a secret security clearance. Having one not only makes it easier to get jobs that require one, but could raise my salary by five figures. United Systems was a large military contractor for the Department of Defense, with buildings all over the United States and internationally. My new team wrote software that ran on the nuclear submarines in the U.S. Navy. The company would "sponsor" me for the clearance. You cannot get one on your own, or "hold it" active. A company with a government contract, one that requires staff to have a security clearance, must do that.

Gaining a clearance meant significant paperwork detailing past residences and jobs, an FBI agent interviewing those who'd known me and checking items like driving records and credit card usage. Bad character, or being susceptible to foreign coercion (having a lot of debt they can help you with), causes a clearance denial. Having a clearance wouldn't mean I knew anything classified (and over the next twenty years, I never did), because there's still a "need to know" element. If I didn't need to know that information, I wouldn't see it. When an investigation starts, an interim clearance is often granted so I could begin working.

I reported to Willy, a Section Manager. He supervised the software development team of eight people. His unruffled demeanor reminded me of Gary, but he was average in height, with hunched shoulders, a shaggy mustache, and grey hair. He seemed out of place in a corporate environment and more like he should run a general store in the country, or sit on a rocking chair in front of it, sipping beer and being unimpressed with everything. He was strictly professional with me, never chitchatting, and while pleasant, kept a cool distance.

I worked at one end of the long building's second floor. Our Group Manager, whom Willy reported to, had the corner office, but everyone else had a cube. Our group occupied part of one wall overlooking the parking lot facing a Dunkin Donuts, gas stations, and the movie theater strip mall in the distance. These were giant, four-person cubes, each person in a corner, the cube against the window. At its other side stood another cube. The pair filled the space between the window and the hallway at the building's center. Row after row of these filled the building interior and the eight programmers in our section occupied two of them. There was no room for me, the ninth programmer. Next to our Group Manager's office sat an empty set of these double cubes against a different wall. And that's where they placed me and Aayush, another new guy.

He also worked through SmartTech on a contract-to-hire basis and started days after I did. Iranian, portly, and short, he was reasonable, relaxed, and casual about work troubles, the first of which lasted over a month—neither of us had a computer. Willy gave us a huge stack of documentation about the system we would work on. The smartphone hadn't been invented (it was May 2000) and Aayush and I had nothing to do.

This often continued after we got our computers because the company was CMMI and ISO-9000 certified. If a company has documented procedures for software development, this supposedly ensures a high reliability that the software will meet its objectives. There are institutions that invented ways of measuring these practices, and a company like United Systems invites them to come in and evaluate them. They give out ratings, like CMMI Level 1 up to Level 5. With each level, the documentation and formality increases exponentially, and in theory, the quality of the software does. But all of it takes considerable time. The result is that the coders sometimes had little to nothing to do for six months as part of the process cycle; I believe United Systems, or our group in it, was Level 3 and going for the next tier. The job could be damn slow.

At SysCorp, I had used Microsoft Access for all four elements of the system: the back-end (tables and queries) and front-end (screens and reports). But I had made a significant step up with the job switch: the front-end screens were now developed in a fuller programming language called Microsoft Visual Basic (Access used a simplified version of this), with Crystal Reports. Aayush and I finally got computers and were brought onto the project—NavSec, a suite of programs used by nuclear submarines to log maintenance and a parts inventory. The system had been in place for a while and just needed updates. Much of the team was friendly and ten years older than us, having been there a decade or more.

Everything was going fine until my first incident with someone about three months into the job. Aayush and I had to fill out paper timesheets every week, then fax them back to SmartTech, who we kept in contact with, usually through our account rep James; he was married to Tina, the recruiter. But he had an assistant named Susan, with whom I was exchanging trivial emails about something. At the end of one, she signed off and concluded with a reminder to fill out and submit a weekly report, which I'll call a TPS report in homage to the movie *Office Space*. I wrote her back.

Randy: TPS report? What's that?
Susan: The client requires you to fill that out every week.

I had no idea what she was talking about and was months into the job.

R: This is the first I've heard of it.

S: You and Aayush haven't been doing your TPS reports?

I turned to my cube mate. "Hey Aayush, have you ever heard of a TPS report?"

He looked over one shoulder. "No."

"Me either."

R: He's never heard of one either.

S: I am reporting this to your manager! If you are found to be in violation of corporate policy, you will be dealt with and corrected!

My eyebrows shot up. "What the hell? Holy shit!"

"What?" Aayush asked, probably surprised by my language.

"Hold on." I forwarded the email to James and told him I'd call in a few minutes. Then I related Susan's threat to Aayush, whose eyes widened before he smiled. The phrase "dealt with and corrected" amused both of us. We weren't the only ones. Five minutes later, I called James. When he answered, the first thing I heard was laughter.

"Hey Rand."

Relaxing at his tone, I said, "I assume you've seen Susan's email."

"Yeah, man. Don't worry."

"What's up with this?"

"Some of our other clients need that report, but not United Systems."

I looked over at Aayush, who laughed when I asked, "So we aren't going to be dealt with and corrected?"

His non-stop laughter increased. "Not unless you want to be."

"Part of me was sort of looking forward to it. Is Susan really young or something? Right out of college?"

Dryly, he asked, "How could you tell?"

"She seems flush with newfound power to destroy."

"I could tell you stories, man. I don't think she'll be around much longer."

"Not the first time? Can you imagine what her boyfriend must be like?"

"Very obedient, I'm sure."

We laughed and hung up.

Susan was indeed gone before long. She's probably doing stand up comedy somewhere. Or working as a dominatrix.

The phrase "dealt with and corrected" entered my vocabulary for years. I hadn't met my wife yet, but once I did and told her this story, anytime I was upset with her for her stalling on a task, I would jokingly say, "If you don't take care of this now, you will be dealt with and corrected!" And we would both laugh.

I met my wife months later that fall, through Alexa from my last job. Alexa suggested I join her and a few friends for playing pool one night. I wasn't feeling social but went and met one of her new coworkers, Sofia, a woman from Russia who had been living in the U.S. since her teens. She was about five years younger than me, and we quickly fell into flirting. We were nearly inseparable within a week. Alexa would eventually play a role in the end of that relationship, too, as detailed in *A Storm of Lies*.

Around that time I met Sofia, United Systems offered both Aayush and me employment and we transitioned from SmartTech, a largely uneventful affair that had us as contractors for one additional month while the paperwork went through. I settled in and moved into my Gaithersburg apartment, a little north of Rockville and Aspen Hill, but a year later, Aayush moved back to Iran. Coincidentally, my troubles at work began in earnest. All the programmers in our group reported to Willy, our Section Manager, and worked on one system, NavSec. I was pulled off NavSec to head up another project with a Jamaican woman, Gabrielle. They decided not to distract Willy with the project and have another Section Manager, Hank, be in charge.

Hank oversaw work on the mini-network, SubNet, running on the nuclear subs, and the documentation and coordination for that. Ex-military, he was short, spunky, had spiked brown hair and several forearm tattoos, was bow-legged, and fit the stereotype of the not-too-bright, former jock. In his case, he was a former running back for a college football team. His job entailed coordinating the work of others, not doing anything himself, as far as I could tell. He sat just outside our Group Manager's door near me and the group's administrative assistant.

The new Financial Management System (FMS) project was not for the Navy but a group inside our company, on the first floor, and since United Systems was documentation heavy, we had to write a formal requirements document. Doing this requires programmers repeatedly meeting with the client and learning what they *think* they want. We ask a lot of questions, including things they haven't thought to voluntarily tell us. It's like being an investigator, and I was good at not only hearing what they haven't told us, but asking clarifying questions and then documenting the system's needs. This would result in a Requirements Document and Software Design Document, plus Test Plans, storyboards, and flowcharts. I hadn't needed to do these before.

Like many companies, our programming group had templates to use for these documents. They defined the structure, style, and type of content to write within it. No one knew who had developed the templates, but we all thought they sucked. Much of what we were supposed to write in them made little sense, was redundant to another area of the doc, or just didn't apply. So without being asked to, I invented new versions, with input from Gabrielle, to use on FMS. I tied the documents together with a numbering system so that requirement 5.3.1 matched flowchart 5.3.1 and storyboard 5.3.1. Gabrielle and Hank both loved it, and I felt great about being appreciated.

Then a smiling Hank walked into my cube one day. "Randy, I have good news and bad news."

I swiveled around in my chair, leaning back. "I'll take the good first."

"I'm your new supervisor."

My eyebrows shot up, having heard nothing of this and concerned about implications, but I just smirked. "I said I'd take the *good* news first."

Laughing, he sat on the edge of the desk. "Since you're working with me on FMS and sit near me, they moved you."

I frowned, fearing I wouldn't work on the NavSec app anymore. And changing my supervisor just because of where I sat didn't seem smart. "Doesn't that mean I'm the only programmer under you?"

"Yeah."

"Gabrielle isn't moving?"

"No."

"So this is because of where I sit?"

He laughed. "Not really. I was kidding."

I wasn't so sure about that. "What's the bad news?"

"They killed FMS."

My project was dead? Part of me wasn't surprised because the internal client we'd been meeting with had been very negative about the system, which would have changed her process, presumably for the better, but she relentlessly harped on this at every meeting. Her boss had been behind FMS, not her, and after months of ironing out how the system would work, she'd apparently convinced her boss to kill it.

I asked, "When did that happen?"

"Yesterday. It's a done deal."

"So why are you my supervisor then?"

"The change was already done before that."

"Might as well put me back on NavSec and with the other developers."

He shrugged and got up to leave, smacking me in the shoulder. "Nah, they're already in the next development cycle. We'll find something for you to do."

It proved a popular refrain he would say to me many times in the future, but Hank's short stint into managing a software development project was over. And so were my days programming at United Systems, a fact which increasingly soured me. I slid into a black hole of meaningless work. Often, even that didn't exist. I spent my days playing computer games, planning vacations, and researching equipment I needed to build a music studio at home. At times it was great, all that free time, but other times I chafed about my newfound uselessness. When the next cycle of development on NavSec started, they again left me out despite pleas to be put back.

One of the many "busy work" assignments Hank gave me was coordinating documents between us and other military contracting companies that were working on Sub-Net. They required everyone to comment on any new doc, officially signing off on it. I had to take their comments and update the document with suggestions, coordinating a dozen different people's status on a range of formal documents. This was really Hank's job, which he pawned off on me. Paperwork is part of being a programmer, but I was increasingly becoming *only* a paperwork guy, never coding.

On September 11, 2001, Hank forced me to go to a meeting in Crystal City, Virginia, which is so close to Pentagon City that it's a mystery why they are considered two different cities. They named the latter for the Pentagon, which it overlooks. The meeting included people from the companies working on SubNet. Hank wanted me to be the one standing up and commenting on who had responded to documentation requests. Exasperated, I reluctantly went to a meeting I considered an utter waste of my time, which I was perfectly capable of wasting back at the office.

The meeting took place in a high-rise conference room big enough for forty people to sit at the long, rectangular table, cushioned swivel chairs all around it, a projector showing Microsoft PowerPoint slides on a wall. Everyone present was former military, which I gleaned from their idle talk, tattoos, and comments about the project in real-world situations that showed they'd served on a nuclear sub or in the Navy, like Hank.

I was the one standing before the others, doing my part of the presentation, when a female administrative assistant, with long black hair and wearing a blue business suit, came to the door and discreetly tried to get the attention of Joe, who ran the meeting.

"What is it?" he finally asked her.

"I just wanted to say," she began timidly, "that reports indicate a plane has crashed into the World Trade Center in New York."

Wow, I thought, seeing surprised expressions on everyone's faces. No one said anything for several seconds.

"Well," began Joe, rather casually, "everyone who flew in from up north needs to make reservations for tonight. No one's flying that way."

I frowned, thinking that made little sense. Why would one plane crash cause air space in the entire northeast to be closed? Others nodded in agreement, being wiser than me, apparently, and Joe called for a ten-minute break for people to make hotel reservations. Without me having a computer there and it being years before smartphones, I didn't know that during the break, a second plane crashed into the other World Trade Center Building.

When we resumed the meeting, we hadn't been at it another few minutes, with me again standing before the others, when the same woman raced into the room, this time not bothering to wait for Joe's permission to speak.

"Oh my God!" she began breathlessly. "Something just blew up at the Pentagon and you can see the smoke from here!"

A moment of stunned silence followed that. Then everyone stormed up from the table and toward a door. I followed them across the hall as they filed into various empty offices lining that side of the building. Across the way, through the window, an absolutely enormous cloud of thick, dense, black smoke hurtled into the sky.

"Holy shit!" I said, astonished. That something massive had exploded made a deep impression. Awed silence and muttered astonishment filled the rooms.

"This is not a coincidence," said Joe.

"We're under attack," Hank stated.

The truth of it struck me, but seemed too bizarre to accept.

After a while of everyone staring, Joe urged us back to the conference room and said we'd take a longer break. Hank, myself, and another guy from United Systems went down to the building's foyer and outside, where they smoked a cigarette and I tried to glimpse what was happening on the TV screens of a restaurant that had opened early for lunch. But I couldn't see anything, and we soon started back upstairs even as a blaring announcement showed the building was being evacuated. I barely had time to grab my stuff before being forced out. I assumed we were leaving for good, but to my amazement, Joe made everyone go to an outdoor courtyard on the second level, which was accessible via steps outside, to continue the meeting.

"Is he serious?" I asked Hank, who smirked.

"Got somewhere else to go?" he responded, gesturing at the roads visible nearby, where traffic already choked them.

We had little information, but obviously something major was happening and I couldn't believe their business-as-usual attitude. I was the last person to sit down, unsure if I could get away with just leaving. By now, I'd learned that the Pentagon metro station had been closed and I couldn't get home on the train that went through there. How was I supposed to get to my car at the metro station near my parent's house?

As we sat there for the next hour, I kept trying to call my fiancé Sofia (our wedding was in a month, just a year after dating), but couldn't get through. The lines were jammed. I was desperate for information. Every few minutes, an F-16 fighter jet flew overhead, visible between the high rises, and each time it happened, I looked at Joe, thinking none of us gave a crap about this meeting anymore except him.

He finally seemed to get the message and let everyone leave, but the damage to our ability to get home was done. I asked the other United Systems employee there if I could get a ride from him, and he agreed. But we soon sat stuck in traffic that wasn't going anywhere fast. I finally got through to my fiancé, who worked in Arlington, not too far away. She and her work friends had escaped to one of their houses nearby. We hatched a plan for me to hike to another metro station and head away from D.C. to another metro stop, where they picked me up. Not until 3pm did I finally reach her friend's house.

The day was surreal for many of us. For me, it was knowing something huge was happening but having no information for so many hours. By the time I finally sat before a T.V., trying to take in all the footage from New York and elsewhere, those in the room with me had heard it all before and I had to ask them to be quiet so I could catch up. On seeing news reports about the Pentagon, I was surprised that the only video footage showed just a small tendril of smoke curling into the sky, nothing like the black column, half a block wide, that I had seen.

A month later, a half-dozen coworkers attended my wedding, including our Group Manager, and this increased the feeling that I had found a real home at work. But for the rest of 2001 and much of 2002, Hank refused to give me any actual work to do despite me repeatedly asking for that or to return to NavSec. At one point, when Chrissy, the group administrative assistant who sat near me, went on maternity leave, he even made me take over her duties. Worse, our group hired another programmer who was also given to Hank, who immediately assigned her development duties as I looked on in amazement.

I objected to this only to have Hank go around asking people if they could think of a system they needed. That means they didn't need one, of course, but some of them suggested something. When I tried to meet with them about it to get requirements, they kept blowing me off. I slowly stopped sending meeting requests about the crap projects. They fell through because no one really wanted them to begin with. Hank gave me shit about me having nothing to do, as if that was my fault.

My frustration grew, as did my attitude. I increasingly wanted to quit, but a recession struck and many people in the area were losing their jobs. I felt lucky to still have mine, especially considering that I was now being deprived of programming experience so that my resume had less to show. I finally got a hint of what the problem with Hank was.

One perk at United Systems was mandatory training at Learning Tree International for weeklong courses. I returned from one of these to find a note on my desk from Hank. They had asked everyone to rate their skill level for database system development. Since I was absent, Hank had helpfully assessed me for myself and suggested that if I disagreed, to submit a correction. The options were from one to five stars, with higher being better, and I was astonished and offended to see that he'd rated me as one to two stars on everything.

Now I know why he won't give me any programming work! I thought.

"Hank," I said, approaching his desk with paper in hand, "what's with the ratings you assigned me on this?"

He looked up innocently. "Oh that? It's no big deal. If you disagree, just give it to Chrissy with corrections."

"Yeah, I will. But why did you rate me so low?"

He laughed and turned back to his computer. "I thought I was on target."

I scowled, insulted anew. "Are you kidding?"

"Don't get mad. Just fix it if you don't like it."

"Is this why you don't give me coding projects? You know I'm already a programmer, right?"

"Whatever."

"Whatever?" There's nothing quite like hearing your boss dismiss what you do for a living, or are supposed to be doing were it not for them.

He glared at me. "Just fix it. Jesus, Randy. Don't be such a crybaby." He turned back to his desk, dismissing me.

For the first time, I thought he was a dick.

By the summer of 2002, I volunteered for a different project, to develop coding standards. This means everyone should follow certain guidelines. For example, every screen that has a "save" button should have a similar name, such as "btnSave." You don't want one coder to call that button "SaveButton" on his screen, another to call it "ButtonSave" on his, and a third to call it "btnSave" on his screen. That makes it harder to work together because everyone's style is different. To avoid that, companies sometimes use coding standards, so we all do it the same.

I was just one of the team members, and someone who'd been pushing for the standards, but I ended up taking over the project when the leader made it clear he didn't care, wanted nothing to do with it, and wouldn't make decisions. I took on more of the role and finally asked if he wanted me to take over, aware that he could be offended. But he wasn't and eagerly turned it over to me. After a few months, we'd finished the project. I felt good that I'd finally accomplished something, even though it was more documentation. I hadn't launched Visual Basic or Microsoft Access on my computer in over a year, which was a significant dent in my coding experience. Hank was destroying my career and there was nothing I could do about it unless I quit. But with so much less experience than I should've had, I was worried I wouldn't find another employer.

I've often joked that I lost my soul at this job, by which I mean my work ethic. I could only spend so many hours of the week, month after month, with little to do before I started screwing off all the time. This wasn't done *instead* of work, but because I didn't *have* any.

My concerns about Hank's opinion of my coding were justified. Before long, they transitioned three programmers from another group into ours. Hank became supervisor for all three and immediately assigned them to a new project that came up. I only found out because one coder, an Asian woman named Sukiya, sat near me. And Hank and she had a meeting about it in her cube, where I couldn't help but overhear. In disbelief, I approached him at his desk afterward.

"Hank," I began, "what's this RDT project you and Sukiya were talking about?"

With his usual casualness, he remarked, "Oh, that's a new thing for the Navy. Sukiya's in charge of it."

I stiffened. Not only did three new people get on the project, but one was in charge when I had seniority? And why had three coders been transferred to our group when I was sitting right there, practically begging for coding work?

"Is it something I can work on?" I asked. He turned, the blatant surprise on his face showing he hadn't even considered it. *Asshole*, I thought.

"Yeah. We need some documentation."

What the fuck did you just say to me?, I thought. I stifled a curse and forced my tone to be even. "Not for that, Hank. For *coding*."

"Oh! Um, yeah, I *guess*."

Well, don't sound so goddamn excited.

Before long, I joined the project as an actual programmer. It was a miracle. The project was to create a database-driven website using ColdFusion for the front end and Microsoft SQL Server for the back end. Sukiya insisted that me and two other guys, both of whom were in their mid-20s, were her equals despite her being in charge of it, and yet she soon made it clear with her behavior that she wanted to do everything personally.

"Since I'm the only one who knows ColdFusion," she began cheerily at our first meeting, "I'll start creating the front-end basics."

I nodded. I didn't know the first thing about ColdFusion, but was willing to add to my skill set. "Once you get the architecture in place, and create a couple screens, the rest of us can use those screens to see how you're doing it and model our work on that."

"Yeah," agreed Anthony, "that should work. I can load ColdFusion on my computer and start playing with it."

"Me, too," said Matt.

"Why don't I design the database?" I suggested, then couldn't help pointing out, in case they didn't know, "I have years of experience with it." Technically, I was new to using SQL Server instead of Access, but the basics of database design don't change with the technology. I had also taken a SQL Server course, used it on the cancelled FMS project, and had otherwise experimented with it out of boredom if for no other reason.

"Great!" said Sukiya, beaming. "Since we all know where to get started, I guess I'll see you tomorrow!"

We split up, and I left for the day within the hour. I already had some ideas on how the database design needed to be laid out and was eager to do something technical for once. But when I arrived at my desk the next day, I found a completed database design printout lying on my keyboard. In Sukiya's handwriting was a note, which read, "I had an idea after we talked yesterday and just threw this together!"

I scowled at the paper. *She did my work for me?* As my eyes poured over it, my scowl deepened, for it was perfect, not something just thrown together. An hour later, she breezed past me on the way to her desk. I got up and went over to her.

"Sukiya," I began patiently, "I thought we agreed I'd do the database design."

"Oh we did!" She always spoke with this incredible cheerfulness, coming across as ultra-polite, nice, and helpful. This already seemed fake and passive aggressive. "I just wanted to work on it and stayed late to finish it."

Giving into a frown, I said, "I was wondering how you finished it so fast."

"You can still do one!"

"What's the point? There's nothing wrong with this one."

"You can do one anyway and then we'll compare."

"Sukiya, there's nothing left to do on it."

"I'm sure I missed something."

"You didn't. You know, you kind of stepped on my toes, doing my work like that."

She giggled dismissively. "I was just trying to help, Randy! Geez!"

"Well, now I have nothing to do on it." After all that time waiting for technical work, she took mine right out from under me and giggled about it. I couldn't help thinking that her entire existence in our group was more of the same.

She sighed in exasperation and I walked away before I said something rude. I was the first one she did it to, but by no means the last.

As the weeks passed, she continued agreeing with me, Matt, and Anthony about who was doing what. And then she did parts or all of our work for us by staying late and then leaving cheerful notes about how she was just trying to help, she was having fun, to let us know what we thought, and to have a nice day. What she didn't understand—or ignored—is that there's a big difference between asking to contribute to, or help with, or review someone's work, and just doing it, which implies you think they can't. It is therefore insulting.

Me and the other two repeatedly discussed Sukiya's toe-stepping marathon with each other and with her. She always laughed gaily, like we were just silly little boys not to be taken seriously. She either couldn't or wouldn't see that she was upsetting all of us. Besides doing our work, she failed to do her part on the ColdFusion front end. This prevented any of us from working on it.

We would ask her why we were choosing who would do what when she was just going to do all of it, anyway. Her response was always the same giggling, passive aggressive jollity that just made it worse. Matt and Anthony were more polite about it than me, maybe because they were eyeing the door. One of them soon quit United Systems altogether, then the other, both privately citing to me that Sukiya was a major reason. They didn't want to be on a team like this. Neither did I.

I approached Hank at his desk one day, hoping for relief.

CHAPTER SIX

Snipers and Bomb Threats

Hank turned to me in his chair and said in annoyance, "Randy, grow up.".

"Excuse me?"

"You need to learn how to be part of a team."

"*I* need to? You should say that to *her*."

"All I hear from her is that you never do any work."

My jaw fell open. I didn't know which was worse, her badmouthing me behind my back to Hank or doing my work all the time and then complaining that I never did anything. "*That's* rich."

"You're a grown man," Hank continued dismissively. "Learn how to deal with her and quit whining."

He turned back to his computer. I stifled telling him to fuck off.

In the weeks that followed, I stopped trying to do any work with Sukiya. There was no point. We met and agreed what we would work on. Then I went back to my desk and played computer games or something. When she asked how the work was going, I told her it was great to put her off, even though I had done nothing. She expressed exasperation, and in this I took some satisfaction. After all, I had cracked that passive aggressive demeanor and finally got her to show an attitude. I took it as a victory of sorts. But it was one that would come with a price.

I worked from 8 AM to 4 PM at that job, seldom taking a lunch break. On the morning of October 3rd, 2002, at my apartment, I started my car and saw the gas meter low. The dashboard clock read 7:40 AM, meaning I might be a minute or two later than 8 AM if I got gas before work, but I didn't have a clock to punch in. I decided to get it done now and fill up near my apartment.

Almost thirty minutes later, I approached work and the stoplight where three gas stations filled four of the intersection's corners. One Shell station stood to the left, another Shell one lay to the right, and the third (Mobil) was also on the right past the light. The one closest on the right was the one I used if filling up near work, but with that already taken care of, I left the road before going that far, pulling into United Systems' parking lot on the right.

My stomach growled at the sight of the Dunkin' Donuts building between me and Shell station, but I decided against it and went inside to my job, having noticed it was now 8:10 AM. Up the elevators I went, then down the long hallway to one end. As I stepped into our area of cubicles, Chrissy came out of the office of Paul, our Group Manager.

"Hey, did you hear gunshots outside?" she asked, eyes intense. She was short and plump, with straight black hair that was already turning a little grey even though she seemed to be in her early thirties. I had always liked her for being down to earth. She was kind, instantly likable, and pleasant, all of which made the intensity in her expression stand out.

My eyebrows went up. "Do you always start conversations this way?"

She chuckled. "Paul has a police scanner and just heard that a shot was fired at the Mobil station across the street."

I blanched. I had just been out there. In fact, if I'd gotten gas at the Shell station, it's possible I would've still been there when that happened. Any shots must've happened in between me entering the building and getting to my desk. I learned later that someone reported it at 8:12 AM.

"I didn't hear anything," I admitted to Chrissy.

"That's strange."

I nodded and went to Hank's desk, glancing out the nearest window there. No cops yet. Shootings didn't happen around this suburban area and I figured it was a mistake, and that I'd never hear more about it, but not long after, Chrissy hurried to me at my desk.

"I just heard there was another shooting at Leisure World!" she excitedly revealed. The retirement community was just up the road. I passed it every day.

"That can't be a coincidence."

"People are saying it's an escaped mental patient."

"Escaped from where? I don't think there's an institution around here. Except maybe *this* place," I joked, though I wasn't smiling.

She smiled. "There are cops out at the Mobil station now. They're blocking off our parking lot."

As the morning continued, rumors ran wild inside United Systems. Several people, including myself, wondered if the shooter had something to do with our company, as we were the only thing around except a Home Depot and a decrepit department store, and we had tons of former military there. Was it a disgruntled ex-employee? The building went on high alert. Nearly two hours after the initial shooting by us, Paul's scanner picked up a report of another shooting twenty minutes away in Kensington, across the street from my doctor's office, at a different gas station.

By noon, cop cars and news trucks packed the parking lot of our building, which became the place from where the national news broadcast about the shooting spree took place. The Beltway Snipers, as they were soon dubbed, had shot and killed three people that we knew of that morning, including a cab driver who had been murdered while filling up his car across the street at the Mobil station. If I had been out at the Shell station filling my car up, I could've been one of the victims. We hadn't heard about the first of what were really four victims. They murdered a fifth person that night near the D.C. border.

As the days passed, more shootings took place, many at gas stations, causing myself and others to hide behind a pillar or inside our cars while filling up. I'd stand there scanning the area for places where a sniper could shoot me from, not scared but in disbelief that I had to do so. Other shootings took place at shopping centers, sometimes in Virginia. Police extolled us to walk in a zigzag pattern because they knew a sniper was doing it and this would make it harder to be shot dead. I followed the advice. Everyone was on the lookout for a white box truck that had been seen leaving one crime scene. Suddenly, they seemed to be everywhere. Reports came in of drivers of those being pulled over repeatedly in the space of minutes by different cops.

As I now did every day while eating yogurt or a bagel before heading to work, I turned on the TV with two questions on my mind. Did they catch whoever was doing this? And was there another shooting? It was now three weeks after it started, and I saw a reporter with a very familiar-looking scene behind him, with a Wendy's and a line of trees. He was talking about another shooting that had just happened.

Where is that? I know I recognize it.

And then realization struck.

Every day when I left the parking lot at work, I turned left and immediately waited at a stop light to turn left again. The resulting view matched what my TV now showed, the cameraman standing on the median strip with the reporter. The angle slowly widened, confirming it. Another murder had taken place in Aspen Hill, just down the street from work, barely an hour ago. Realizing traffic would be snarled, I went to work late. It proved to be the final shooting, as the snipers, John Allen Muhammad and Lee Boyd Malvo, were captured two days later far to the north inside their Caprice, which had doubled as a getaway car and mobile sniper perch. The teenage Malvo assassinated people from within the trunk, firing through a hole above the license plate. He's in prison for life. They executed Muhammad.

It wasn't the only time violence hovered around the job. On Veteran's Day in November, I sat at my desk around 10 a.m. when Chrissy once again approached with disturbing news.

"Randy," she said, "the building's being evacuated."

I turned in surprise, as I hadn't heard a fire drill and or announcement. "Really? Why?"

"Bomb threat." Her face was serious.

"You're kidding."

"No. Come on. Let's go."

I grabbed my phone, jacket, and started following her and the mass exodus of people heading for the stairs. We made it outside and soon mingled with annoyed co-workers in the chilly air. Most of them weren't wearing coats, a fact that became more bothersome as they made us stand there until 1pm while bomb-sniffing dogs went through the building and cleared it. When I left work at 4pm, fire trucks, an ambulance, and police cars were at the shopping center across the street. Inside one store there, someone had placed boxes that would look like bombs on x-ray machines. The police blew up one box and discovered another at a nearby store.

The next day, I tried to leave work for an appointment only to discover police cars blocking off both driveways at work again. I approached one officer, who wore the typical gun, handcuffs, and other gear.

"Is it possible to get out?" I asked.

"Yes sir, but we'll be closing it until 12:30."

That was ninety minutes, and I expected to be back before then, but I could always park elsewhere and walk over. "Do you know what's going on?"

"Bomb threat."

"Again?"

"You can come through right here," he said, gesturing at his car, which he got into as I left for mine.

When I returned later, I discovered a swarm of news trucks lining the street outside the parking lot, which the cops wouldn't let them enter. They kept me out, too, and I parked at a shopping center. On my walk back, I saw a familiar face from the local NBC news station. Matt Collins was middle-aged, portly, and delivered his reports with such melodrama that my mother had always declared how much she hated him the minute he started talking.

"Hi Matt," I said, falling in beside him on the sidewalk, where he was plodding. "What's the story?"

He nodded at me, looking typically taciturn. "A woman called in a bomb threat."

I hadn't known the gender, which surprised me. "They don't know who?"

"Not yet."

"I work in the building. This isn't the first time."

"I know." He said little else, and I felt surprised that he didn't ask what those at United Systems thought of everything. I left him behind and discovered that the building was being closed indefinitely, so I went home. The bomb threats continued for a month, stopped, and then resumed the following spring for a few months. We never found out who was doing it, why, or if they got caught.

Sometimes it seemed like bombs were going off at work anyway, directed at me. Hank alternated between giving me nothing to do and dumping a ton of crap projects on me at once. One day he gave me seven of them, and when I emailed him asking which ones were priority so I could start on them first, he told me to stop being a cryaby and just do them. He had an increasingly big attitude toward me, and it was becoming mutual. Sukiya was not the only coder hired into the group, usually reporting to Hank, and immediately given meaningful coding work while Hank consistently bypassed me. Over the course of three years, no less than ten programmers were hired, and I was powerless to do more than object and ask for such work and be transferred back into the NavSec team under Willy, only to have Hank call me a crybaby. Sometimes one of them quit and they gave a new hire their coding project instead of me. I had a huge chip on my shoulder.

Around this time, the training coordinator referred to me as a "constant critic" in an email to all the managers. The reason? He required me to enter training requests into his system, which had frequent bugs, like requiring me to fill out a field that Hank, not me, needed to do. If I didn't write something in it, I couldn't submit the request, so I wrote in the field that it shouldn't be required at this point, letting him know of the error. I always pointed out system errors so the coders (whoever they were) could fix them; otherwise, hundreds of people would deal with the bugs. If he had been mature, he might have thanked me or apologized for the trouble. Instead, he criticized me to my managers. I wasn't sure if he meant it in a bad way and I shrugged it off, but the next day, as I passed him in the lobby, he removed any doubt from me.

He said, "Why don't you just use the system like everyone else instead of bitching all the time? You're the only one whining about it."

Startled, I stopped myself from saying, "Fuck off," and instead said, "If you don't want people pointing out your mistakes, why don't you stop making them? You should thank me for telling you about the bugs before dozens of other people find out what a shitty job you're doing. As it is, only I know. You're welcome."

He gave me the finger. I knew he and Hank were buddies and had no doubt my manager was badmouthing me to the other Section Manager and Paul, the Group Manager above them. The chip on my shoulder grew.

Like many companies, United Systems did annual performance reviews, where each supervisor writes a standardized, fill-in-the-blanks form about the work of each person they manage. Despite the spotty work they had given me since Hank became my manager two years earlier, these had gone well enough. But not this time. He accused me of never doing anything and had written a review so bad that I wondered if he was going to fire me. It actually said, in writing, that I hadn't done any work, which was a lie.

"What about the Access database I created for Alan?" I asked, feeling defensive. "That took me two months, and he said he loves it."

He nodded in realization. "I forgot about that."

"You forgot? I send you a weekly report on everything I'm doing."

"Don't get snide."

I wasn't sure what to say about that. He was an imbecile *and* an asshole. "I also programmed that system for Bill's group."

"Oh yeah. I remember now."

I stifled frustration. For the next five minutes, I reminded him of one project after another, some of them documentation ones. The list of completed work was quite large, partly because most of the projects had been small. His negative attitude toward me lightened as it increasingly became apparent I had done quite a bit of work. He began to laugh, and the tension disappeared until I asked a question.

"How long will it take to redo the review?"

Surprised, he chuckled. "What? I'm not redoing it."

I scowled. "Why? It's wrong. We just covered everything I did and none of it is reflected on the review."

"Paul already signed off on it."

I didn't see what that had to do with anything. "So?"

"I'm not redoing it, Randy. Just sign the review and we can get out of here."

"I'm not signing that. It's all wrong, and we just went over exactly why."

"You have to sign it, Randy."

"No, I don't. Signing is like agreeing and I'm not endorsing such a negative, and wrong, performance review."

"Don't be a pain in the ass."

I was sick of him talking to me like that. "That's really not appropriate, Hank."

"Look, if you have a problem with it, you can write a rebuttal and we will include it with your file, but you still have to sign it that I went over it with you."

A moment of tense silence followed. "I want to talk to HR about it first."

He glared at me. "Goddamn it, Randy, stop being a crybaby all the time."

"And while I'm at it, I'm going to address you calling me names like that all the time."

"Sign it!"

I got up and walked out instead, leaving him cursing at me behind my back. I walked to a big corner office that had several offices within it. One was our HR woman, who confirmed I could write a rebuttal, but that I had to sign Hank's review. I ended up not addressing Hank's name calling, trying not to rock the boat any more than necessary, and I regretted it. I wasn't happy that I was repeatedly being labeled a crybaby, critic, or some other insulting thing, and it belatedly occurred to me that Hank had stopped me from complaining about him by characterizing me that way ahead of time. He was a manipulative little shit. I did write a long rebuttal, and nothing came of it. I'm not sure if Hank or our Group Manager ever saw it, but it eventually became clear that it didn't matter.

Fortunately, I was finally getting a break from Hank, but in a way I never expected. That summer, they promoted our Group Manager Paul to a Department Head position, and for his backfill, he actually chose Hank as our new Group Manager. I couldn't believe it. What could he have done to possibly warrant a promotion? Hank promoted another guy to take his place and for several months, I answered to that guy, but then I was switched to a different boss for a few months. Neither of them had any actual work for me to do and clearly didn't know what to do with me. Maybe it explained why they kept bouncing me around. And it happened one more time.

While this was happening, my original Section Manager Willy retired, and it was now Hank's job to choose a replacement. We all wondered who the new software development manager would be and none of us could imagine Hank's choice until it happened—Sukiya. The woman who was always sucking up to Hank. The person who had the least seniority in our group. The coder who everyone loathed because, during the past few years, she had taken her step-on-your-toes approach to everyone. Many of them had approached me before this to say they now understood why I hated her because they did, too. And now they all reported to her.

As if this couldn't get any worse, after several years of failing to get myself transferred back into Willy's group, now run by Sukiya, it finally happened. This meant Sukiya was now my boss. I thought Hank did it to get back at me for complaining about her, his pet. Even before this, many had discreetly speculated that he and Sukiya were having sex, the way they were always laughing together and sometimes going to lunch.

They moved Sukiya into Willy's old desk, and finally, after 3.5 years of me working at the company, they switched my seat to that section to sit with most of the other coders. It would have been a relief were it not for Sukiya, but our days of having run-ins with each other were over. She was now too busy to do anyone's work for them, and everyone knew I disliked her, so if I needed to talk to her, someone in my team would voluntarily do it for me, if possible. It became a running joke. Maybe things were working out after all.

But that summer, the company installed a new Vice President above us. He spent the first week randomly walking around and observing people at work, and he didn't like what he saw—people reading a newspaper, playing internet games, and one even napping. Hank declared what many of us thought of as martial law—he outlawed flex time, where people could get their 40 hours a week however they needed to, such as working two extra hours one day and taking off two hours early the next. Beyond this making everyone mad, it wouldn't fix the problem, either, making the decision even dumber. He had just proven to everyone what I had been telling them for years—he was a horrible manager.

I don't think Hank knew just how much people disliked him now. And one of the reasons was that I hated him and most of the coders liked and respected me, and I had more experience with him than anyone but Sukiya, who they also hated. In other words, just as Hank had likely ruined my reputation with managers, I had ruined his with everyone else.

The new VP also announced that he was going to decide if the company was a software development one. We clearly weren't, so this did not bode well, especially when he announced layoffs were coming, but none of them were big. His rationale was that laying off 10-15 people at a time wasn't a big layoff, even if he followed it with so many similar ones that he reached 500. Laying off 500 at once is a big layoff. Doing a few every week until you reach 500 is not. According to him. Some people like to have their cake and eat it, too.

But then something happened that I felt certain would finish changing my fortunes for the better. They finally gave me a significant software development project to co-lead with Zhang Li, a short, middle-aged Asian woman I had always liked despite her not being very friendly. She had a kind soul, and we always got along well. Long before we worked together, we had been in the same Microsoft Access programming course, the one that SysCorp had agreed to pay half the cost for. She had remembered me because I used the foot mouse during class and when I first started at United Systems, she saw me using it there and recognized me, though my use of it had largely stopped. My arms were doing much better, as was my life.

But this was no ordinary system. Before they had hired me, the only system our group designed was NavSec, which was a Windows desktop app running on the nuclear submarines. Now they tasked Zhang Li and me with creating a web-based version of it. She and I were the technical leads, and given that our entire group ultimately supported this app, I had suddenly become one of the most prominent people. After three years of languishing in Hank's wasteland of bullshit projects, I had somehow been catapulted into this position.

And I knew why. With all of my downtime at work, I had taken training courses and also taught myself a newer way of doing things—using Microsoft ASP.NET, a web-based technology, for the front-end, instead of the older and soon-to-be-unsupported Microsoft Visual Basic. The web was a significant shift in thinking from designing desktop apps like NavSec. I also learned Microsoft SQL Server, a far more robust and capable database platform for the back-end than Microsoft Access. We were to use both. They had given Zhang Li and me the task of modernizing NavSec, and no one else in the group knew as much as I did about these technologies, including Zhang Li. The other staff would have to go to training. I already had. Sukiya and Hank had little choice but to assign me to the project in a senior position, and I was certain they were upset about it.

After our first meeting with just the two of us, Zhang Li mentioned a new documentation system that Willy's team had been using for two years and which they mostly loved, but she had some questions about how to use it and remembered how good I was at understanding such things. When she showed it to me, I initially felt pleased. The documentation system was mine, the one I had invented on the FMS project, and I was glad that the software development team had been using it. I was also a little irritated that no one had told me. I had some resentment that I was only doing useless work for Hank, and now I learned they had deprived me of two years of satisfaction that I had contributed something worthwhile to my job. Caught between pleasure and frustration, I had only seconds to enjoy the positive part.

"Interesting," I began, recognizing my document templates, "I didn't know you guys have been using my system all this time."

"Hank designed this."

My eyes widened in disbelief. "What?"

"Yeah, I was surprised. His system is a really good one. We were all surprised he came up with it when he gave it to Willy."

I picked my jaw up off the floor. "He did *not* design this. *I* did."

She laughed. "Come on, Randy. It was Hank."

I shot a nasty look in Hank's direction, but he wasn't there. Chrissy overheard this and started watching. She knew I loathed Hank and agreed with all of my reasons for it. She thought he was an asshole, too. "I designed this while working on that FMS system years ago. Ask Gabrielle."

"Well, it doesn't matter."

"Yes, it does. He's taking credit for my work." I suddenly wondered how much Hank's taking credit for this contributed to him being promoted. And he then promoting Sukiya to Section Manager. "Do you really think he came up with this? He couldn't plan his way out of a cardboard box with four of the sides already open."

Chrissy laughed.

"Well," began Zhang Li.

"I'm serious. The whole reason you're here asking me about it is how good I am at documentation. Everyone knows it. It's the only useful thing I've done at this job. I even took over the Coding Standards team because no one wanted to do it."

That seemed to register on her. "Okay, okay. I will ask Gabrielle. It's okay."

I felt a little guilty. "Sorry. I'm not mad at you. Just him."

She laughed a little and things had smoothed over. But I got upset again after she asked me her questions about how the documentation system worked, saying some of it didn't make sense. When she showed me what was wrong, I discovered that Hank had also told them how to use it wrong, adding insult to injury. The one good thing I had done, he had both screwed up and taken credit for.

When I told Zhang Li how it all fit together, the audible and visible reactions of "getting it" were impossible to miss. She finally patted my arm and said she should have known it was me all along. Word quickly spread that Hank had done all of this. I told people. Chrissy told people. Zhang Li and Gabrielle told people. They all knew about the tension between me and Hank, or me and Sukiya, and everyone increasingly hated both of them. Word reached Hank, who decided to put me in my place, approaching me at my desk.

"Randy," he said, tone unfriendly, "are you whining that no one knew you did that documentation system?"

"Hank," I said, mimicking his tone, "why does it bother you that everyone now knows it was me?"

"Get a life, Randy. I'm tired of your attitude." He turned away without waiting for a response, which allowed me to give him the finger behind his back. Since he was the Group Manager, I didn't have to directly deal with him anymore and seldom did. Chrissy had once remarked to me that Hank had his favorites, and he wasn't shy about it.

My prominence quickly rose, which felt like revenge for all the sidelining and interference. While Zhang Li and I were co-leads, I was the obvious expert in the documentation due to it being my system. I was also the one who had led the Coding Standards team and produced the User Acceptance document we had to use. My English was also better than Zhang Li's. I had to repeatedly fix grammar issues in her documentation, and she was gracious enough to ask me to, or I did it during a peer review where such alterations are expected. This stood in dark contrast to Sukiya's approach to "team work." Generally, the coders had no ego, except the know-it-all, Sukiya.

As for the project, I had a better sense of user interface design than Zhang Li and worked faster. The result was that I finished my pieces of architecture or initial screens faster and helped her with hers at her request. She wanted me to review her work, clearly looking to me for guidance. I didn't get a big ego about this because I respected the other programmers, who I had often felt had more experience than me in Visual Basic at least, and they had helped me get up to speed years earlier when I started. As other programmers in our section joined the team, I found myself leading the meetings more than Zhang Li, who tended to be quiet. She wanted my help to present her work to the others because I explained it better. And I taught those who needed help what to do, or Zhang Li tried and ended up grabbing me to assist. Everyone needed to present their work to the team at meetings, but when people repeatedly showed up unprepared to do so, I created a checklist; I wrote everything that needed to be done and then followed up on later.

I quietly relished my sudden dominance, because while Zhang Li and I were technically equals, I was the unofficial lead programmer and project lead. This was a come-from-behind victory if ever I had one at work. I was happy there for the first time in years.

And then came my next performance review that April 2004, four years into working there. I had reported to four different managers in the previous twelve months, each for roughly a season. First Hank, then his replacement, then someone who ran another group that had no programmers at all, and finally in the Willy/Sukiya section. I had apparently reported to Hank's replacement one month longer than anyone else, and Hank chose him to write my review. The time with him as my manager was to represent the entire year, an act of unfairness in waiting.

And like Hank, who was his best friend and who had undoubtedly badmouthed me to him for years, he'd had no use for me. He had also been busy learning Hank's job and shown zero interest in assigning me projects. And like Hank, he had made it clear that I was expected to find myself work rather than have my manager assign it to me. Both seemed to think I had the right to walk into any meeting and announce that I was joining a team or project and taking over various tasks, like it or not. And I would just bill the client on my timesheet. And my manager would just approve the timesheet even though they had never said I could work on that. It was all a load of crap. Someone needed to tell them that managers find work for their staff, not tell staff to find something to do. The irony was that I had often suggested I join a project, only to be told no.

And so the unsurprising verdict was that I did nothing. I didn't bother objecting. Instead, I did what I had done the year before—I wrote a long rebuttal detailing my actual work and including copies of my status reports to each manager, proving that the review was a lie and that my managers were incompetent.

One Monday not long after, Hank asked to see me in Paul's office, which had never happened before. Despite both having been promoted, neither's seat had changed. I followed Hank in there to see Paul sitting at a table with a manilla envelope on it as Hank closed the door behind us.

"Well," began Paul, his demeanor pleasant as I approached a chair in his office, Hank sauntering over behind me for another, "there's no easy way to do this."

CHAPTER SEVEN

The Pentagon

Wearing a resigned smile, Paul shoved the envelope toward me across the table and stopped talking, so I opened it to find a layoff notice. He didn't even have the balls to say it aloud. This was how my four years of working there would end.

I glared at him. "You came to my *wedding*."

"Look, Randy," began Paul, "it's not personal. There are budget cuts going around and we've been laying off staff for a year. You're just the first one in our group."

"You just hired two programmers a month ago. Why not them?"

"We have to look at who is contributing where."

I did a double-take. "Seriously? I invented the documentation system that Hank here took credit for and we are using on NavSec. Did he tell you that? And I'm the co-lead on the new NavSec, but I lead all the meetings and everyone comes to me, not Zhang Li, for help with coding and paperwork, and you're saying I'm not contributing? What programmer in this group is more prominent than me right now?"

He waved a dismissive hand. "There's a common idea in business that if someone gets two bad performance reviews in a row, they need to be let go."

I swore under my breath and pointed at Hank. "Did this guy tell you he knows that review last year was all bullshit and he and HR made me sign it, anyway? All because you had already seen it and he didn't want you to know he'd screwed it up. He forgot everything I had done for other groups, forcing me to write that rebuttal. He tried to make me look bad instead of him, and I can see it worked. And then you had someone else do a review from four months to represent the entire year, when he was so busy learning Hank's job that he never gave me any work. Now you're firing me over it."

"Let's not rehash stuff."

I bristled more, feeling like everything I had ever done had been ignored. "Oh, like I have ever had a chance to tell my side of what's going on and have it considered. You obviously ignored the proof of my work in my performance review rebuttals, neither of which I should have had to make. And it's not rehashing when you finally get to say it. This is all based on lies."

Paul laughed a little. "Look, I have made the decision. Your last day is Friday and we're giving you two weeks' severance."

"Am I supposed to be happy about that? Where is Sukiya, anyway? Isn't this something she is supposed to be doing, or is someone finally doing *her* work for *her*?" I thought that was a pretty good dig.

With a smirk, Hank replied, "She's on vacation this week."

"Well, that's convenient."

"We didn't want a scene," he added.

"You know you're her manager and that means that if she's not doing this, you should be. Do you ever do anything?"

Laughing, he said, "I could ask you the same question."

"Watch it." The asshole had set me up for forever. I turned to Paul, who seemed amused by the obvious dislike between Hank and I. "Anything else?"

"No."

I left before I said anything worse, not that it would've mattered much, but they could always change "laid off" to "fired."

Hank and I had been bad for each other. And it was mostly Hank's fault. Before he became my manager, I had a promising career as a software developer. Now I was leaving a job four years later with so few projects to my name that my resume could only sum that up with a vague, "Coded various projects" kind of line. They had badly compromised my ability to land another programming job. Before it all started, Hank had been well liked, but now he was disliked and disrespected, principally because of his poor treatment of me when the programmers who formed the heart of our group liked and respected me. And then there was his fawning over Sukiya, the only person more hated than him.

I had badly overstayed my welcome. And that's why my wife and I were all grins that night when discussing my layoff. I had just bought my first truly nice car, a maroon Acura TL, and now had no job to make payments. But I was thrilled. There was no question I had a chip on my shoulder at United Systems. That it was warranted is never an excuse. The awful thing about the timing was that I was finally able to not only lose that attitude, but move on to a more "rightful place." And then they terminated me. I had snatched defeat from the jaws of victory. It's also lame when the best thing you can say about a programming job is that you became an expert in documentation and you got to wear jeans to work for four years.

The next day, as word of my termination spread, I learned my coworkers were furious. The two programmers hired into our group a month earlier were to remain as I was laid off for supposed budget cuts. This caused significant outrage. I had more seniority than half the team now, and of course I was the lead on the most important coding project. Gabrielle remarked, I think without meaning to, that she should have been laid off instead.

Everyone wanted to know why this was happening, and I wasn't shy about airing my opinion, partly because I could "read the room." They hated Hank more than ever. Most of them had some idea of the bullshit from him toward me over the years, but I now made sure they heard every last detail. Management would have been smarter to escort me out than give me the time to speak the truth.

Even my final week was not without drama. They told me of the layoff on Monday and that Friday was my last day, and that I would get two weeks' severance, meaning paid for two more weeks after that. On Wednesday, Hank told me with an amused grin that every day I worked after being told of the layoff was one day less of compensation I would receive. Rather than being paid for the last week of work and then two more as severance, the severance had begun immediately. I could have walked out the door Monday and never returned, being paid for two weeks. Put another way, I had effectively just worked two days for free. This was bizarre and unprofessionally handled, but what else was new?

By the time I knew, I had a farewell lunch planned for Thursday because the programmers wanted to do it. Chrissy normally planned these but was gone until Wednesday, when she learned of my layoff, and everything associated with it, and eagerly took over. Before long, an outraged Chrissy told me that when Hank learned of the lunch that everyone else wanted to do, he tried to talk her out of planning it, claiming that my layoff was not a positive thing and a farewell would seem like a celebration. Was he tipping his hand? I had no doubt that was exactly how he felt. And I have always wondered how much of a price he and Sukiya paid in loathing for all of it. I left immediately after the farewell lunch Thursday and never saw any of them again, though a few coders stayed in touch, one being a fan of my music; I was months away from my first CD release.

On the day I finished writing this account in 2021, I was near the old building in Aspen Hill, so I drove by to fill up my car at that old Shell gas station next to the Dunkin Donuts. To my surprise, United Systems had vacated in 2010. The building sat empty for some time before being demolished. As I write this, the lot is still empty, blocked off with chain link fencing, and overgrown with weeds. With any luck, the same happened to Hank and Sukiya.

I had not been to a job fair before, but tried one along with activating my resume on job boards and responding to postings. For the latter, I seldom received a response and felt I was wasting my time. How many people applied to those jobs? Was it so many that recruiters just ignored people? The ones I applied to fit my skill set and yet I seldom heard back and didn't get an interview. Not once.

So I headed to my first job fair, in a hotel conference room. This fair held more promise than some because it was for "cleared professionals" only, meaning people with security clearances. In theory, this limited the market, but the place was full, anyway. Wearing a suit and tie, I held a leather folder from SmartTech with resumes inside as I stopped at a table to check-in; I had needed to register and provide enough information for them to verify my clearance. An attractive young woman handed me a name tag to slap on my chest, immediately making me feel like a dork at a party where I knew no one.

I stepped into the conference room, seeing booth after makeshift booth along the walls and in the center, scores of similarly dressed job hunters moving between them. Each booth consisted of a table filled with pens, cups, frisbees, pads, bags, and various other stuff, all branded with company logos. At each table stood one or two people from the company and, behind them, some sort of sign (or two) announcing their firm. Women outnumbered men working at these stations, while men were almost exclusively the candidates.

I made the rounds, getting familiar with the routine of it. A grinning woman would greet me, welcome me by name, and ask what kind of work I was looking for. After my answer, I'd get the question about why I was looking and if I had a resume. Most told me I could just submit one online, making me wonder why I was bothering to be here, but the answer appeared to be grabbing the paraphernalia on the table. That's when I noticed other guys had a bag, into which they stuffed one or two items per table.

I received a range of responses to them learning my degree was in classical guitar. A few said such people make talented programmers. One told me my Bachelors had no value. Others wanted to know why I had made the switch. Most said they did not have a position that fit my skill set but that they would add me to their database, and I excused myself. Two or three of them did a quick interview, writing notes on my resume and saying they would be in touch. But I never heard from anyone at this or other fairs and stopped doing them.

This was the day I learned that having a secret clearance impressed no one in the world of cleared professionals. Most of the companies wanted me to have a top secret or higher, such as a TS with polygraph or SCI, two even more invasive dives into who you are, because their government contracts required them. The "public trust" clearance is less impressive than secret, but you wouldn't have known it from the dismissive reactions I received to my clearance level. I quickly lost faith in being there at all.

Outside of the fairs, I went on several interviews, some for jobs I wasn't that interested in. I needed to switch technologies. I had been doing Microsoft Visual Basic for front-end development for years, but that creates programs that runs on Microsoft Windows. Since Al Gore created the internet, desktop software was the past and web-based software was the future. Microsoft had already come out with a replacement for Visual Basic called ASP .NET, or .NET for short. The heart, or core, of the language differed because the internet differs. The web is a "stateless" environment, meaning a web page that code produced is just as lifeless as one with no code in it. By the time the user sees the page, the code is no longer running. It already did its job—it produced that webpage.

This differs from Windows, where any program is still held in memory and therefore running. The code is active. If I want to store "x = 125" in memory and then later multiply x times two, I'm referring to a value (x) that has already been set. It therefore works.

This is not possible on the internet because "x" has no "state." It stopped existing after the page was created and wrote "x = 125" on the page as text. Multiplying x times two results in an error because x doesn't exist anymore as a value a coder can use.

If you've ever seen a URL with a bunch of "gunk" on the end, you are seeing one way that web coders go around this. You might see something like www.url.com?x=125. We have stored the value of x in the URL "query string" because it's not in the page anymore as an item that can be manipulated with code. But a coder can grab it from the URL and use it.

This is just one of many ways in which writing web-based software is a very different paradigm and ways of thinking.

Moving from Windows to the web wasn't the only change I sought. Microsoft had released Visual Studio ASP .NET, a replacement for older coding environments. Two different languages could be used within it: C# or Visual Basic .NET, which differed slightly from its predecessor Visual Basic (that was being retired).

The other change was switching databases from Microsoft Access to Microsoft SQL Server, a far more robust and sophisticated database platform that was significantly different in capabilities and usage. I only had a little experience with all of this at the end of my time with United Systems. I was still a novice despite being the one helping my peers get going on it. All the coding work we had done was not the final software, but the basics of getting familiar with it, like test projects. I had not worked on a "real" application with it. But this was where I wanted to go, and I badly needed a job that would help me get there or I might get stuck in the past (Visual Basic). Most of the interviews I did were focused on this past because I had experience.

But a month after leaving United Systems, I went on an interview for a job at RCS using these newer technologies. And the work was for the Army; sometimes would I be at the Pentagon, the Department of Defense headquarters for the U.S. military. I had never been inside it. I hadn't been near it since the September 11th attacks, when terrorists crashed a plane into the side of a building. The United States was still technically at work because of the attacks that day, and I would work inside the Army Operation Center (AOC). All of this intrigued me, especially on learning RCS would upgrade my security clearance to top secret. It looked like a significant step up from United Systems.

The interview took place at a small Northern Virginia (NoVA) office with desks, all of them empty, for less than a dozen people in an open room. My interviewer, Matt, was my intended manager. He was a few years younger than me (I later learned he was 25), average height, slender, and handsome, with sharp brown eyes and short, spiky brown hair. He carried himself with a subtle swagger, like he had something to prove. But he gave the impression that he had already done so and felt good about himself over it. He seemed capable of being very charming, but during most of our talk he seemed bored, like he wanted to be somewhere else.

"So what's your experience with .NET and SQL Server?" he asked, leaning back in a chair at the worn brown desk.

I had been afraid of this question. Or I should say the answer. "I've taken classes in both at Learning Tree."

"Good cookies," he interrupted, not showing any pleasure at the memory. It was almost as if he didn't think they were good but had heard that others thought so, and he was telling me something he thought I would react to.

"Yeah. I've been working on prototyping a system at my last job, but I still need to work on a more substantial project. I wanted to be honest about that because it's where I want to go, but I would need a bit of help."

He waved that off. "That's not a problem. I can teach you it."

I felt dubious but glad to hear it. "That would be great. If there's an example screen and I need to create more of them, I can pick it up fast from that."

He seemed unfazed, to my relief. "We've got other guys, so we can all help as needed. Don't worry about it."

Now I felt more invested in the opportunity and looked around the empty room. "How many are on the project?"

"The company only has eight people. That includes the owner, Rick, and his wife, Nancy. She does all the admin stuff. Not everyone is on the same project, but it's all the same client."

I nodded. Nancy was the recruiter who had called me. I hadn't known she was the owner's wife. "So, is this where you work? This office?"

"Only a few days a week, so we would both split between here and the Pentagon."

"Where is everyone?"

"Out for lunch. Some are at the Pentagon."

"How long have you worked here?"

"Couple years. I'll be gone in a year, but you never heard me say that." He flashed a smile. "I want to head to Florida. You or another guy we're hiring would likely take over for me."

Did he think that would appeal to my ambition? Because it worked. But I was already interested. "Nancy didn't get into benefits much."

He nodded and jumped in. "It's all the usual shit, health dental, vision, short and long term, AD&D, that kind of stuff. We get a Christmas bonus. Rick throws cool parties, especially in the summer. He likes to show off his money. He buys a new car for a hundred grand and drives it a few months before selling it at a tremendous loss from depreciation."

Rick sounded like an idiot, but I said as if envious, "Must be rolling in it. What's it like at the Pentagon?"

"A fucking maze, dude," he said, startling me. I hadn't heard an f-bomb during an interview before. "It's cool though. Most people can't park there, but we're more important, so we get parking passes. I'll help you figure out where. The lots are restricted. The client is generals and colonels in the Army and they're all pretty cool. They have to wear military dress because we're technically at war. The women are pissed." He smirked.

I smiled to commiserate. "I bet."

"Until you get your interim clearance, you'll have to be escorted everywhere in the AOC, but not the rest of the building. You'll get lost, though. I'll show you around. It's not bad once you know the way, but trying to find something without being shown is impossible."

We chatted a little more, and I came away feeling good about my prospects. His indifference to my inexperience and repeated offers to help me had me convinced he would be a good manager to work for. I wasn't sure how to read him and took him at face value, meaning helpful and laid back, not someone to make an issue out of anything. I needed that after the last job. Within days, I had the written offer of a salary a couple thousand more than before. I would be out of work five weeks total and considered myself very lucky.

I reported to the Pentagon in May 2004, taking a long metro ride to the station beneath the enormous building. The station looked no different from anywhere else until I ascended the escalator to the surface, concrete paving all around me. I took a moment to look around, having never been so close before. Parking lots stretched for long distances in the morning sun, lines of people streaming toward the grey, concrete building behind me. Armed guards reminiscent of police stood around, with machine guns over shoulders, visible bulletproof vests of black over their blue shirts and dark pants, communication gear in their ears, and strapped to their vests. They provided a sober reminder that this was the headquarters of the U.S. military, and we were technically at war with terrorism. Amid the civilians, men and women wearing various uniforms strode by. In time, I would learn the difference between

Army, Navy, Air Force, and Marine fatigues, which seemed mostly subtle color variations and finer points of style.

To avoid attracting attention by gawking, I moved toward the tall, wooden doors, making eye contact with guards and smiling. One directed me to the visitor's area, from where I called Rick, the company owner, to come get me. In the meantime, I presented the identification I'd been told to bring and listed my new employer as the contact. The attendant looked me up in the system and verified I wasn't a tourist but new staff, giving me a temporary ID and advising me to wait for Rick, who arrived after a long wait. I don't recall how he identified me, but we finally came face-to-face.

Rick stood nearly as tall as me but had packed fifty pounds onto this torso, suggesting his gluttony ran to more than expensive cars. He had average length, black, slightly curly hair. He wore dress pants and a white button-up shirt with no tie, similar to me, except I almost never wore white shirts. As we walked, he kept close to a wall in the ultra-wide corridors, with one hand's fingers reaching out to slide along it as he went. His demeanor seemed content and distracted, as if I didn't really warrant that much attention and our conversation was something he felt needed to happen but which held no actual interest for him. I sensed I was nothing more than a guy doing a job he needed done, and as long as I did it, he would pay me little attention. I didn't especially like him.

He advised me to watch closely as we went along halls that reminded me of a museum with their polished tile floors and occasional glass displays along the walls, a statue or bust here and there. Pictures and sometimes a large mural decorated walls in between signs telling you which area and concentric ring you were in. The Pentagon was like five pentagons, each with another inside it. The innermost ring was A-Ring near the center courtyard, the outermost being E-Ring. While there were stairs and escalators throughout, we headed down a ramp enormous in width and length.

"For the first few days," Rick said, "one of us will probably need to come get you because finding your way down to the AOC isn't easy."

I nodded, already feeling a little lost just two minutes into our walk. Trying to connect with him, I joked, "Any chance I get an office with a window?"

He didn't react at all other than to say, "It's in the basement in a bunker, so no one does. You won't see the sun until you leave for the day."

"Nice."

"You'll have to leave your phone outside at the guard station. You wouldn't get a signal anyway, but they don't allow cameras or recording devices inside."

I frowned, but shook it off. This was long before the smartphone took off and I hardly used mine, anyway. "Matt said I had to start here 5-days a week before working out of the McLean office two or three days a week. How soon–"

"No, you're here every day."

I did a double-take, not sure I heard the implication right. "I can't work out of that office at all?"

"No. No one does. The information is too sensitive. He wouldn't have told you that."

I stifled a frown at the confirmation—and the suggestion that I was lying. "Nancy said it, too."

He shook his head. "No, she definitely knows better. That's my wife, by the way."

"I know." Was he implying that I called his wife a liar? Getting off to a good start already. But I hadn't heard incorrectly. Both of them had lied to me and the job had already taken a turn for the worse. The commute was longer, unpleasant, and I hated public transportation. "Matt also said we can get parking permits?"

"Yeah, that's true. I can start paperwork today, but you might find it better to come in on the metro. I met Nancy on the train. She was hot and I just sat down and started talking to her. She probably thought I was a creep, but we're married. Got a couple kids."

I wasn't sure what to say about that. "I met mine through a work friend. No kids. Still busy doing music stuff outside of work. I'm about to release my first album."

He finally perked up. "Yeah, I saw that on your website. I graduated from GIT."

That surprised me. He didn't seem like a rock guitarist at all, not to mention someone who had gone to the Guitar Institute of Technology in L.A. We chatted about this the rest of the way through the maze or corridors, some of them under construction, with jackhammers blasting away and clear tarps hanging from the ceiling to separate us from it, as if it helped.

With years of rest, physical therapy I had finally stopped, exercises and arm stretches, and tons of over-the-counter anti-inflammatories, my arms had recovered from tendonitis enough that I no longer used the foot mouse. I seldom used the dictation program at home, either. My guitar playing had recovered enough for me to record my first album, featuring only my music. I still had limits on my playing time, like only doing it every other day for no more than two hours at a time, but I could play all of my own material again. With a modest home recording studio I had built, I wrote, performed, and engineered the entire album, playing all guitars and bass, and making the mistake of using a drum machine instead of getting a live drummer. But I hadn't realized this mistake yet and was five weeks from releasing the album on my own so-called record label. The time off from work had helped me set the release in motion with a press release and authoring multiple articles for guitar-related websites.

"Bring in a copy," said Rick about the album. "I'd love to hear it."

"Sure." Few people had shown much interest in my music over the years, so this was a pleasant change.

"The Colonel we work for might love it, too. He's into that kind of stuff. I'll introduce you to him and everyone else in a minute."

We soon stopped at what looked like a reception desk with an armed guard behind it. I signed in with Rick, both of us handing over our turned off phones to the guard, who put them into a set of wall cubbies set aside for it. Then he buzzed us through a thick door. The Army Operation Center (AOC) inside wasn't huge and was unremarkable except for one room that reminded me of a set from movies. It had an enormous wall full of monitors. Several rows of built-in tables with computers faced that wall, various personnel manning them. I wasn't allowed in there and only rarely got a peek through the door if someone else was coming or going as I walked by. The air in the AOC smelled musty and old, and since visitors didn't come down here, minimal upkeep occurred so that worn and torn, thin carpet lay underfoot, and the cubicles were cramped.

Rick finally led me to mine, which was beside Matt's against a wall to the right of the floor. Across the way to the left were two cubes for other staff of theirs. Straight ahead, the tight corridor made two immediate right turns into Rick's small office, outside of which sat another cubicle where Don sat.

Don was the most senior programmer there but worked on other projects, so we wouldn't be working together. He was Rick's height, middle-aged, quiet but friendly, laid back, and had short blond hair and a small gut. I liked him but grew wary of him because I was insecure about my coding knowledge of the new technologies, and he knew quite a bit. He routinely dropped by my cube to ask me technical questions that gave me the impression he was trying to find out how much—or how little—I really knew. And that was the very thing I wanted to hide from him. I groaned every time he came over.

Rick soon delivered another unwelcome surprise; with these accumulating, I was getting my first taste of a bait-and-switch, when you're told things to get you on board and none of them are true. He said the contract required me to take a 30-minute lunch break and my hours had to be 8:30-5pm, meaning I was always commuting in the height of rush hour and have no say over my schedule. The lunch requirement had existed at other jobs but not been enforced, and I didn't do it because I ate quickly and while working at my desk. The day provided enough minor breaks that this was unnecessary, but Rick enforced it.

Between the job location, work schedule, and lunch break, I was losing about five additional hours of my personal life every week. There was nothing to do during the lunch breaks except give myself tours of the building, which I did, finding the 9/11 memorial and paying my respects. Sometimes I went to lunch in the cafeteria with Matt and two of the other coders, or we went to the open-air courtyard at the Pentagon's center and the food trucks there, sometimes standing in long lines. I hadn't expected the presence of a McDonald's, Subway, and other franchises in the food court.

The first day, Matt got me set up with my computer, where SQL Server and ASP .NET were already installed. He surprised me by saying they were using the C# programming language instead of Visual Basic (VB). This alarmed me because I had seen a few examples of C#, enough to know that it was quite different. It raised the stress, and when I said I hadn't used that before, he told me not to worry about it.

Then he dumped two coding books on my desk, which would prove to be the only help he would ever give me. Not once would he answer a question, just put me off and tell me to Google it. He didn't seem to care that I wasn't making much progress, creating the impression of low urgency. This was a relief, taking pressure off me, but I found the work to be difficult because he kept giving me bugs to fix. It meant a coder who knew more than me had written the code but gotten something wrong and he expected someone with hardly any real world experience in the technologies to fix it. This was not realistic.

I felt frustrated and confused. These were old feelings. I am Learning Disabled and had struggled in grade school, my teachers assuming I could do the work when I didn't understand it. Instead of helping, they were often scornful, deciding I was a troublemaker and punishing me. While Matt hadn't snapped at me to stop being lazy like they so often did, I still sensed the specter of my childhood hanging over my head and half-expected a rebuke. I was unhappy and felt unsupported.

Until I got my upgraded interim clearance, I had to be always escorted within the AOC, another reality I hadn't been warned about. This included every time I needed to come and go, or use the bathroom inside the AOC. Someone had to have eyes on me at all times except in the bathroom (thank God for small miracles). This grew awkward if I needed to use the toilet for longer, adding a kind of pressure to do my business quickly even if my anatomy wasn't cooperating. In the meantime, my escort, usually Matt, had to wait for me. Sometimes Matt needed to go, and no one was near our desks to watch me, so I had to follow him into the men's room. At least he didn't make me enter the stall with him.

I got the parking pass within days. Traffic down I-270 and over the notorious American Legion Bridge was awful, but it usually improved along the GW Parkway except at bottlenecks. I traveled the entire length of it to reach work. The parking lot and Pentagon were so enormous that it took a full fifteen minutes to go from my car to my desk at a brisk walk, but the commute was still faster—and more pleasant—than the metro's crowds, noise, jostling, and rushing to avoid a missed train and the resulting wait for another. The odds of being slightly late to work were good, but Matt soon made it clear that he was casual about it.

That first week, Rick called me to his office. I said hello to Don on my way in and then sat. "What's up?"

Rick handed me a fingerprint card with some info written on it in blue ink. "The sooner you get fingerprinted, the better. Did you already complete your clearance questionnaire?"

"Yeah. They don't do fingerprints here?"

"No. Go to a local police station. It's like fifteen bucks."

I noticed he didn't say if they covered that. "Do you reimburse for that?"

He looked startled and laughed. "No."

So he bought hundred thousand dollar sports cars and then sold them within months for a tremendous loss, and yet couldn't cover $15 for his staff? When I asked Matt about taking off early to get this done, since it was work related and the police station only did it when I was at work, he said yes.

"Any time you need to split early," he concluded, "just go."

Was he really that cool? He acted like he thought so. "Really?"

"Yeah. I don't care. Neither does Rick."

I found that hard to believe and would not test it, but Matt actually made me leave early the first two weeks I was there, making me nervous that I would lose my job over it, but he was manager and making me do it. Did that make it okay? His excuse was that he was leaving for the day and didn't want to find someone else to watch me because they would have to sit at his desk or mine to do so, or I would have to go wait in their cube; I could not be out of sight. This only lasted two weeks because they granted my interim clearance at light-speed, freeing me from the escorts inside the AOC.

For Memorial Day weekend, Rick threw a daytime party at his house, where he showed off expensive cars like a dodge Viper, showing up a surly Matt and his less expensive BMW M3. The Colonel revealed the history of RCS, that Rick had been a coder who had created some application the Colonel liked. The Colonel set up a contract just for Rick to win, and RCS was born. Rick had gotten lucky and was no businessman and had never even been a manager. The Colonel had awarded all of his subsequent contracts, so at every chance, Rick cozied up to the man who had changed his life.

The Colonel was okay, but I much preferred a Major who was the military guy I interacted with the most. Gunner had the stereotypical Army buzz-cut and was average height. Like all the military at the time, he only had two outfits—boots and Army fatigues with a hat and without. Gunner's drawl revealed he was a southerner, and he seemed like the "good ole' boy" cliché of not being too educated but down-to-earth and sincere, where character mattered. He radiated a kind of goodness that made me like him despite an apparent lack of personality. I told myself he was just all business while in the service and showed nothing else on purpose.

As if to confirm his directness, he once slammed his fist down on a table and chastised a female Captain, who was being flippant and dismissive toward him during a meeting. He outranked her and put her in her place, receiving an immediate "Yes, sir." Part of me just thought it was unprofessional, but the rest of me wished I could do the same to someone being rude to me and get away with it.

By late June, a month into the job, I noticed that both Matt and Rick would talk shit about staff members who weren't around. The comments were both personal and professional, usually dismissive about how dumb they were with coding, life choices, or whatever. Irony lay here because doing this was stupid of an owner and manager. I knew that if I ever did something they didn't respect, they would do it to me if they weren't already. Did Rick know that Matt only worked five or six hours a day, coming in after me and then leaving before me? Could Rick check our badge records and see when we swiped in and out of the AOC? I doubted it because that was government-held information. It didn't occur to me then that he could request it from his butt buddy, the Colonel, and likely get it, especially if the point was that he had another terrible employee like the one I replaced.

I learned my predecessor's fate from a coworker. The FBI had arrested the guy for having sex with a minor. Not only had this ended his clearance and therefore his job, but some of the relationship had taken place from his government email account. The FBI had seized the computer. The Pentagon monitored phone calls and emails, and probably everything else we did inside the building, but after this, additional scrutiny had fallen on RCS. We all had two computers, "low side" and "high side." One system and network had more security on it than the other. My monitors, keyboard, and mouse were connected to a switch box that let me go back and forth. The work happened on the high security side while email and the internet were on the lower. Both were being watched, but I wasn't worried about it. I had too much to do because it took so long to figure it out on my own.

Matt continued not helping me like he'd promised during the interview. Each time I asked a question, he'd say, "in a minute," or something similar, and that minute was never coming. I began to ask other coworkers while trying to also hide my degree of ignorance for fear of it costing me my job. While Matt had acted like the inexperience wasn't an issue, the owner Rick might not have agreed. And Matt's indifference to my skills had been predicated on his help, now denied. I felt vulnerable and in over my head. And frustrated. I made progress and got work done, but I knew it was slower than expected even if no one told me so; I had been a programmer long enough to sense how long something should take. But no one said anything, and I tried not to worry about it while simultaneously working my butt off. I spent a lot of time in programming forums to get a question answered.

I seldom saw Matt do any actual work; we could see each other's screens with a turn of our heads, our backs partially turned to each other. He wasted much time on websites with upgrades for his car, or looking at web design tools for his personal use. He wanted to get into game design. There was an online gaming site and its forums, where he also spent hours, and several subordinates of his played one game online with him after hours. For all of these, he would get other coworkers up from their desk to look at what he was doing. Since Matt showed excitement about it, they played along, crowing about how cool it was. The fawning was embarrassing and I wouldn't do it. Maybe that had something to do with what was to come.

One day he was going on about something and when I asked what he was talking about, he came over to my computer, moved me out of the way, switched me from high side to low side, and then typed in the URL to bring up the page. It was a stereo upgrade for his car. He excused himself and I closed the web page. Five minutes later, Rick emailed all of us, admonishing us not to use the internet except for work-related items. Matt returned seconds later and this time I noticed he had come from the direction of Rick's office.

A coworker asked him, "Was that about anything in particular?"

"Yes," answered Matt, stepping into our cubes. He looked right at me as he sat. "It's not about you, dude."

I hadn't thought that it was. Did he think I would wonder? What would make him think I would? I felt ambivalent about him saying it, the reassurance not reassuring me. But I didn't use the internet much for anything personal and had been surprised how often the other guys did. Being unaware of the monitoring wasn't possible because every email had a warning automatically added to it. The phone had one written on it. The message was everywhere—you are being watched.

One day during my lunch break, and with my sub sandwich still half-eaten in one hand, I sat looking at a sample database schematic that Microsoft Access shipped with. We didn't use Access there, just SQL Server, but they installed it with the Microsoft Office suite. I was trying to figure out how to handle arranging some tables for something I was doing at home, though the concept still related to work. I just didn't need to implement something of that sort right now. I realized Matt saw it on my screen when he asked about it.

"Whatcha working on there, Rand?"

I turned to him and saw a "gotcha" sort of smirk I didn't get. I explained I was trying to understand a table layout design.

Still grinning weirdly, he asked, "What for? All the systems you work on already have one."

"I know. It's just something I was thinking about because I was doing some stuff at home."

He didn't say anything, but got up and left. His disapproving demeanor surprised me, given his own activities, but I shrugged it off. Then I checked my personal email from the website browser and saw a note from my local newspaper in Gaithersburg. I had told them of my CD release that week and a reporter had responded, wanting to do an interview about my tendonitis injury and my triumph over it to release the album. She had a tight deadline and wanted to schedule something soon, and asked me to call her, so I did. The conversation veered into the kinds of things she wanted to cover. She asked if I could address them, so I spent two minutes telling her a little about the injury's cause, treatment, and my prognosis.

As I was doing this, Rick walked up behind me and stood looming over my shoulder, casting a literal shadow from the overhead lights. Finally, he loudly snapped at my back, "*What* does this have to do with your *job?*"

Startled, then angry at being spoken to like that, I feigned politeness as I asked into the phone, "Can I call you back after work?" She said yes, and I hung up. Then I turned around and glared at Rick, who I was certain had said that loudly so the person I was talking to would hear it, trying to embarrass me.

CHAPTER EIGHT

Machinations

Rick glared at me and snapped, "I want to see you in my office."

I sensed I was about to be fired, but being spoken to like that did not agree with me and I did not soften any anger in my eyes as I rose and followed him. Instead of turning toward his room, he went the other way, to the AOC exit, into the rest of the Pentagon.

"Let's do this outside," he said, walking ahead of me. "I don't want anyone else hearing what I'm going to say to you."

Silently following, I glowered at the threat, especially for him saying it within earshot of coworkers. I would not listen to a bunch of attitude thrown at me, if that's what he had in mind, and he clearly did. Being an adult in my early 30s had me unaccustomed to being spoken to like a brat. He was going to moderate his tone or the conversation would end when I said it did, not him. After United Systems, I was not inclined to take a lot of shit for long. I had no idea what he was so angry about, but felt ready to defend myself. By purposely walking slower than him, I forced him to slow down and look back repeatedly as we went, his frustration at this amusing me. We soon stepped into the courtyard with the hot, humid summer air pounding down on us and rising from the concrete. The food trucks were doing brisk business, some people leaving with their purchase and others sitting on a bench to eat or doing so while walking around. We began doing laps around the exterior as he started in on me.

His first words were, "I'm going to fire you if you don't step up your productivity."

I stiffened in shock on hearing the most loaded word from my employer. I felt ambushed and broadsided. "*That's* what this is about? My productivity?"

"No, it's about a lot of things, but the client has noticed how slow you are. So have we, and they want you gone. I'm thinking of agreeing."

Cold anger swept over me. A lot of things? I hadn't been told about a single issue. On the job disapproval scale from 1 to 10, "you're fired" is #10. The suggestion of firing is #9. In theory, we should be told there's an issue long before arriving at that end of the scale, and given a chance to improve. He undoubtedly included Matt in that "we" and I wondered who "they" were. I had seen nothing but friendly behavior toward me. Now I would always wonder who wanted me fired, and this, by itself, made this a hostile work environment that my asshole employer had just willfully created. Was Rick lying? Why would he? And what had Matt said about me to Rick, but not to me? A manager is supposed to have your back and help you stay out of trouble, not say nothing and badmouth you to his boss. Was that how I leaped to #9 without warning? Something was going on behind my back.

"If this is such an issue," I began, "then why has it taken so long to bring it up?"

"We were giving you a chance to shape up."

"Thanks for that," I dryly interrupted. "You have to tell me you think there's a problem in order for me to fix it."

"What do you think I'm doing right now?"

I didn't hide my disapproval. "Threatening to *fire* me."

"Well, there is no excuse for you not getting more done. You are spending way too much time on the internet."

My anger returned. "Matt knew I had little experience with .NET and SQL Server and so did you. It's hardly on my resume and I was upfront with him. That and him refusing to help me is causing any delays, not screwing around on the internet. Check my traffic logs."

"I will," he said defiantly, not seeming to realize this statement was an admission that he hadn't already done it and therefore didn't know what he was talking about. I caught him. "You also shouldn't be making personal calls."

I frowned. "It was less than five minutes, and I was on my forced lunch break, which you interrupted, by the way. I even still had a sandwich in my hand."

"I know you were talking to a reporter," he said, startling me that he knew this. "We're working in the Army Operation Center at the Pentagon while we're at war, and you call a fucking reporter. How do you think that looks?"

I flushed a little, feeling stupid. He was right, but only because of appearances. My predecessor using Pentagon computers to arrange sex with a minor seemed to rear its head. Rick was undoubtedly still upset about it and I was to take the brunt of this. My call had nothing to do with spilling military secrets or work at all, but that seemed to be his other point.

I asked, "Are you saying I can't do personal things while I'm on the personal break your contract forces me to take?"

"Just stop screwing around and get your work done."

"It's a valid question and you aren't answering."

"Why do I have to spell it out for you?"

"Because that's what good managers do." I wondered if he was being vague so that I couldn't follow a rule he refused to say and then fire me for not getting it right.

"Just stick to work-related websites."

"Even on break?"

"It doesn't matter when you do it. You're making us look like shit."

No, you're doing that all on your own, you asshole, I thought, resenting his statement. There had to be some reason wouldn't say it, so I persisted, partly because I could tell doing so irritated him. "So can I do personal things on my personal break or not?"

"Get back to work."

"Yes or no."

"Get back to work."

I wasn't spending any additional time with this asshole and wasn't walking back with him. "I'm still on break, so are you ordering me to violate the terms of your contract? Or is that another simple question you can't or won't answer? I'll finish my break here and find my own way back."

He shot me an annoyed look and walked away, disappearing into the building. I was furious and was quitting this job as soon as I found another. I was tempted to quit right then. Rick had left no doubt that he was a total asshole. The question now was Matt. I knew he had lied to me about the job location, helping me, and the benefits, some of which didn't exist at all.

But he repeatedly acted like he was on my side, encouraging me to leave early with it not being a big deal, or telling me, without prompting, that Rick's email about internet usage was not about me. Was Rick making a general accusation that he wanted to throw at all of his staff or had Matt lied that the email was indeed supposedly about me? I wasn't sure what to believe and didn't like feeling people were pulling bullshit behind my back. I had enemies, apparently. Rick was certainly one of them. And "they" implied at least two people in the Army. Maybe Matt. I wanted out, a feeling that grew exponentially over the next week.

In what seemed like a purposeful attempt at creating a hostile work environment, Rick began asking several times a day what I was working on and when it would be done. The tone of it all was *stop screwing around.* He also began dumping tons of work on me with a deadline that I couldn't possibly meet. He was setting me up for failure. But the worst moment was the day he sent me an email, CCing all of my coworkers and the Army staff, saying he was leaving early and he expected me to be seen working hard the whole time and have something completed and sent back to him by COB. He almost literally told them all to spy on me and report on me to him. The passive aggressive stunt floored me. And I was pissed.

"That's messed up," said Matt in response.

I turned and saw the email on his screen, too, feeling surprised that he commiserated. "Does he always do stuff like this?"

"No. He's a fucking dumb ass. Don't worry about it. I'll have one of the other guys help you."

"Thanks," I said, further surprised. So maybe only Rick was an asshole?

One of the others helped me get the assignments done and in the days that followed, I began peppering them with questions any time I got stuck on something. It was faster than researching anything or figuring it out for myself. I no longer cared if anyone knew of my ignorance because I was quitting, anyway.

Don continued dropping by to subtly probe my knowledge, and while I liked him, I wanted to tell him to knock it off, that I didn't know what the fuck I was doing, and to stop poking me like a lab rat. He now sometimes blatantly walked into my cube and looked at my screen, then asked me what was on it, what it did, and how it worked. He wasn't being subtle about trying to catch me on the internet. I was being massively spied on for 8.5 hours a day, five days a week, and the tension was thick and oppressive. I knew I couldn't complain to HR because that was Nancy, Rick's wife! Despite Rick dumping shit on me constantly, I started getting things done faster, and he had no excuse to fire me. But I hated working there.

I soon did my interview with the reporter, who sent a photographer to my house to take photos of me with my guitars. I received the equivalent of a full-page story in the local paper and felt good about this. My album release was a bit underwhelming in that I only sold one hundred copies over the next year, falling far short of my hopes. But I was successful in gaining an endorsement with three companies: Peavey, whose amps I used; Morley Pedals, makers of effect pedals; and Alvarez Guitars, whose acoustics I used. I also had minor radio play on a few obscure stations. I was learning that the instrumental guitar genre doesn't sell well, even for those who get coverage in major guitar magazines, which I hadn't.

For July 4th, Rick did another event, and I badly wanted to skip it but ended up going. He rented a go-kart place in Virginia for several hours. I spent almost all of my time with Don, who I couldn't quite figure out. I got the impression he thought things about me he wasn't saying. Had he figured out I was clueless and told Rick? Because Rick thought I knew everything and was refusing to do it; he was so sure that confessing got me nowhere. Was Don playing some game of his own? I couldn't imagine what it would be. He seemed somehow sympathetic toward me, and during those moments of him dropping in at my cube seemed almost reluctant, as if had been told to go do it and then did a poor job of trying to catch me on the internet.

He had been CC'd on Rick's nasty email, so maybe that was it. Regardless, he seemed to befriend me at the event and even let me take his Harley Davidson for a ride.

My job search sped up with phone calls and emails from recruiters, and Rick had me go for a walk in the courtyard once again. He informed me he had requested all of my badging records for when I entered and left the AOC going back to my first day. He had added up all the times, revealing that on any days when I hadn't been there 8.5 hours, I had usually only been five minutes late or left five minutes early. Rather than seeing this as proof I was putting in a full day, he said he was deducting the accumulated four hours of time from my vacation balance and once again brought up firing me, this time for falsifying work records, as he put it. I actually had nothing to say about this because it was so petty and fucked up that I was speechless. And to think Matt had made me leave early the first two weeks. Matt, that guy who was only putting in five to six hours a day. That a double-standard existed was impossible to miss. I was being targeted. I at least knew by who—Rick.

The following week, Matt asked me to update something with a SQL Server database, but he didn't tell me how to reach it or what the username and password were to access it. Moreover, he did not tell me what needed to be done. Database tables and their relationships can be quite complicated, and I needed specific details on how to ensure I updated the right records using criteria he should have given me. But none of that really mattered because he didn't tell me how to even get into the database, saying Rick would give me that info. When I asked Rick for it, he said Matt had it. Back and forth they went for the rest of the week.

Meanwhile, the Army Major Gunner came to me each day asking for a status update because his superior officers needed the update done. Matt had told him I was doing this for him. I told Gunner I didn't have the access yet, then went to Rick or Matt only to have them repeat all of this. Gunner returned. I told him I had no access. Matt and Rick put me off. Gunner returned...

Finally, the Major had enough. "Goddamn it, Randy!" he yelled. "I need that update *now*."

Spreading my hands in futility, "I know. There's nothing I can do about it. Matt and Rick won't give me the information to login to the server. I don't even know which one it is. Rick says Matt has that info and Matt says Rick has it. They've been doing this all week."

"Goddamn those two," he muttered, turning away. Then he stopped and turned back. "Sorry for losing my temper."

"Yeah. No worries. Sorry I couldn't be of more help."

He walked away. This was on Thursday and Rick was never in on Fridays. On Monday, he came to my cube first thing and, for the third time, made me take a walk to the courtyard with him.

"If I was Matt, I would want to kick your ass," he began.

I cocked an eyebrow, not understanding why he said this. The idea of Matt beating me up almost made me want to laugh. I was probably eight or nine inches taller, which meant I had "reach." But Matt wasn't exactly intimidating and gave the impression of never being in a fist fight because he would back down. I never had and had won all of mine, not that I was macho, because I wasn't. I just had excellent eye-hand coordination, knew how to throw a punch, and could tell if someone was formidable that way or not. Matt was the sort to say anything to get out of a fight, then go back to airing his chip on his shoulder about you behind your back. I was the sort to be eager to clobber someone who had it coming if they gave me the chance by taking a swing at me first, making my punch self-defense. I had once stood up to nearly a dozen guys in high school and come away unscathed.

Oh please let Matt or you try to kick my ass, I thought. *Make my day.*

"What's he upset about?" I asked, my tone bored on purpose to show I wasn't exactly worried about Matt attacking me, a stunningly inappropriate sentiment at work, casually delivered by the company owner.

"You made him look like shit to Gunner."

I suspected it was about the database thing and said, "I think he can do that on his own."

"He already has."

"What?" I asked in surprise.

"He's been on a kind of probation here. Gunner has repeatedly questioned Matt's leadership or management style, and you just added fuel to the fire. If he's your supervisor and can't get you the database information, then obviously there's a problem with him. That's what Gunner thinks."

"He's not wrong," I said, amused. I had gotten Matt in trouble with the truth. He had it coming for refusing to help me all this time. And to think he had been on probation for being incompetent. I felt no surprise, only regret I hadn't known this sooner.

"I had to put out fires with Gunner over this and you made RCS look bad in front of the client."

He was right, but it was his own damn fault. And I wasn't holding back. The asshole could fire me if he didn't like what I had to say about it. "Maybe you guys should have stopped jerking me around and just given me the information from the start or the half dozen times I asked for it. What did you *think* was going to happen?"

"Look, I don't want the Major thinking he can come to you to get rocks to throw at my company."

Now there's a great idea. Don't go putting thoughts into my head.

The conversation didn't last much longer, and I went for a walk so I could laugh and grin without peers wondering why. A week later, they finally gave me the database information I needed to complete the work. Another week!

By that time, in August, I tried to interview at a company called USAIS for a job with exactly the same technologies, and the company had 5000 staff, full benefits, and could hold my clearance. But when I arrived for the interview and stepped out of the elevator in one of the building's two towers, the place was deserted, the doors all open. Wandering amid an apparent zombie apocalypse that would explain the lack of people, I found the office door of the guy who was supposed to interview me and knocked, but no one answered, so I called the number and the phone on the other side rang. Mystified, I had little choice but to go home, frustrated. This was years before the iPhone revolution, so while I could text, I could tell my interviewer could not (that was a land line ringing—remember those?), and I had no email without a computer. The interviewer, Jack, laughed and apologized, saying the company had moved from that tower to the other and he forgot to tell me. We rescheduled for the next day, and I still went because he seemed very cool on the phone, and working with someone who wasn't an asshole held a special appeal.

This time I found the right place, a beautiful and newly redone floor of a building that stood at least ten stories tall, higher than any I had worked in before. It stood right beside the beltway in NoVA and would be a fairly easy commute, being one of the fastest buildings in NoVA that I could reach from my house. A parking pass to the adjacent garage came with the job, a small food court with seating off to the lobby.

Jack seemed between five and eight years older than me, balding, with very short brown hair and an equally short, stubble beard. He wore corduroy trousers and a tight, untucked, plain sweater that did nothing to hide a prodigious beer belly. Big-boned and an inch shorter than me, he gave the impression of having once been fit and a jock, and he had worked in logistics for the U.S. Navy. His demeanor was that of an old friend and drinking buddy—laid back, jovial, devil-may-care, and unfazed. He acted as if we hit it off immediately, even though I didn't really think so, but I did like him. I wasn't expecting such a personality to greet me for an interview where I was prepared for seriousness, but he was anything but, and he made the guys at the Pentagon look incredibly uptight. Maybe this was exactly what I needed. At some point, he asked with a big laugh if I wanted a job, meaning I had it, with him being fine with teaching me what I needed to know about the technology.

There was a catch. They wanted it to be contract-to-hire, so no benefits at first, but I could get most of it through my wife. We agreed on a conversion salary a few thousand above my current one. I had learned my lesson from ProSource and SysCorp and made sure I worked this out and in writing. Jack started me on paperwork and then suggested I take it home and send it via FedEx, so I left.

But I dropped it off the next day instead of sending it because I had an interview a few minutes away at the infamous "toilet bowl" building (google this!). The structure has a giant standing ring at the front and it reminds people of a toilet seat, hence the nickname. I had never heard of it, to the surprise of the recruiter. The problem with the job was that it was for Microsoft Access, a step backward. I had wanted to cancel the interview after meeting Jack, but I would have felt bad and went, did well, and got a second job offer in two days, this one for $5k more. But they only had 75 staff, and I was now leery of a small company thanks to RCS. When I hesitated, they threw another $5k at me and 1000 shares of their stock, worth $1 a piece.

I decided to politely tell Jack this, and he said he could come up another $5k but would still be $5k behind them. So I declined the other company's offer, and they responded with another $3k and a $1k signing bonus. I had always thought having two firms competing for me would be fun, but it kind of wasn't because the job I considered a dead-end had more money than the job of my future. Jack confirmed he couldn't go any higher and even suggested I take the other job, but I said if he could get me the number we'd agreed on, I was still interested. He had to get approval, and the waiting game started.

Around this time, another recruiter called about a job at the White House, and while it sounded cool to do this, I knew it came with intense scrutiny and I just couldn't take any more of that after how I was being spied on by RCS. I refused to even do an interview over it, to the surprise of the recruiter. I printed out a resignation letter and left it in my work desk, eager to hand it to Rick once I had an offer from USAIS and Jack.

Having left early several days in a row, with permission, for several "doctor appointments" when I showed no sign of being sick, I wondered if they knew I was interviewing. And I didn't care. Matt had sometimes bitched about how much he hated Rick, the Pentagon, and everything about his job. I had seldom said much, but he suddenly ramped this up, talking about how great it had been to work on the beach in Florida with his feet in the sand. He wanted to become a game programmer. He talked so often about this that I finally commiserated and admitted to my hatred of the Pentagon, too.

"Are you interviewing?" he asked, as the two of us and other coworkers walked to the food court. It was now early September. "I knew those weren't doctor appointments, several in a row like that."

I smiled, not surprised he had figured it out. He was too smart. I no longer gave a shit. "Yeah."

As if befriending me, he said, "You should get out of here. Rick treats you like shit."

"I know. He's an asshole. I have a job all lined up, but they're dicking around with an official offer. Once I get it, I'm out of here."

He laughed. "Cool. I'd be right behind you if I could."

On Monday, late in the afternoon, Rick handed a piece of paper to every staff member except me. Then he took one coworker into his office for ten minutes, and when that guy returned, he told me Rick wanted to see me in his office. I sensed what was coming and Rick wasted no time after I shut the door at his suggestion.

With a pleasant demeanor, he said, "I'm firing you for unsatisfactory job performance." He handed me a termination letter that I immediately noticed was dated two months earlier.

"Why is the date so long ago?"

"I've been meaning to fire you for months," he admitted, "and have been putting it off."

And I almost laughed. The letter's date was right after he threatened to fire me the first time and then dumped a ton of work on me, with me getting it all done, anyway. And even that had not been enough to change his mind. I succeeded at all of it despite the nasty attitude surrounding me, and he had still intended to fire me. Then I realized that by getting the work done, I might have validated that I could have done other tasks sooner before that. In a way, it was true, but only because I stopped hiding my ignorance, or trying to get things done on my own, and started asking someone other than Matt for help. It wasn't because I had been screwing off and stopped. Rick had been telegraphing this termination for two months, which made his next statement all the more stupid.

"One reason I'm firing you is your attitude."

"*My* attitude?" I said in disbelief, nearly laughing again at the absurdity. "What part of that conversation in June where you threatened to fire me was supposed to result in a good attitude? Or telling people to spy on me and report back to you, and then them *doing* it?"

Ducking the question, he looked smug as he admitted, "I never wanted to hire you in the first place because I didn't think you had the skill set. I only did it because Matt wanted you."

I scowled. "That's rich. I've been telling you for months that I was new to the tech and that's why I was slower than the others, and you've been refusing to believe me, and now you claim you knew it all along?"

Rick smirked in a way that suggested he thought he was too smart to be lied to successfully, and that lying was what I was doing. "Matt told me you knew it all cold and he just couldn't get you to do anything because you were always screwing around on the internet and leaving early. He also told me you have a job lined up, so that's why I'm finally firing you."

My jaw went straight through the floor. From the growing smirk on Rick's face, he seemed to think my stunned reaction was that he had caught me so utterly that I was speechless. That wasn't it.

It was Matt. This whole time, Rick had been coming down hard on me and I thought he was the asshole—and he was—but Matt was behind it. All of it.

Matt had tricked me. He had noticed my absences for interviews that I claimed were doctor appointments, with him suspicious about their true nature. I suspect he formed a plan to get me to admit it. He ramped up his complaining about work to get me to do the same. Then he claimed he was looking to quit and do interviews to make me think we agreed, so when he had asked me if I had interviewed, I stupidly admitted it to my wolf in sheep's clothing boss. He told Rick and finally got me fired. It appeared he had been trying to get me fired for a long time, long before the bullshit with the database issue that got him into more trouble with Gunner. And I realized why later that night.

Rick had previously told me that Matt was on probation for mismanagement mistakes. For still-unknown reasons, Matt had wanted to hire me over Rick's objections, but it was a mistake. The Army wanted someone who could hit the ground running. And that wasn't me. I didn't know why, but Matt had refused to help me as he had promised and the result was slower results from me. The client noticed and complained to him and Rick but said nothing to me (still true). Matt had a choice then—admit he had hired someone not fully qualified and made another management mistake, or claim I knew exactly what I was doing and was refusing to do anything because I was screwing around in various ways. He had been setting me up almost since I started. It all made sense now.

Matt didn't want me to know he was setting me up all the time, of course. He would do something like make me get on the internet to look at car stuff that *he* had been looking at and then go tell Rick I was surfing websites again. Minutes later, when Rick emailed staff admonishing all of us for internet use, Matt explicitly told me it wasn't about me. This was some next level evil shit. Almost everything that had happened had been Matt beefing up his lie that I knew the tech and refused to do my work, rather than admitting I didn't and needed help, and he had screwed up again by hiring me. He not only never complained about my work or speed, but hid from me all complaints about it because he was the principal one making them behind my back while telling me I was doing fine.

Matt had played Rick and me against each other. Rick was just as much Matt's victim as I was, but only I now knew it, and the grin on Rick's face had shown that he was an even bigger fool to trust Matt than I was. Matt was an evil little son of a bitch.

Rick fired me on Monday and said my last day would be Friday. After months of being nasty, he remained very smug and gloating for the rest of the week, during which I did my revenge tour.

On Tuesday, Don stopped by my desk while Matt was gone. Looking resigned and slightly sympathetic, he said, "Well, I heard you're leaving us Friday."

Not sure who else had been knifing me in the back, I kept my face neutral. I also didn't want to seem like I was sad to be leaving, or more importantly to my pride, that I felt Rick and Matt had gotten the better of me. There is an inherent disapproval involved in being fired, but I wouldn't let it look like I was a victim or someone who had it coming. But I also wasn't getting into explanations.

I replied, "I have a job lined up, which is why he fired me, so not worried about it."

"That's good. This can be a harsh place to work. Unforgiving and not realistic about the work we do."

Curious what he'd say and having nothing to lose, I replied, "Rick said two government people wanted me fired." The idea still stung, not knowing who was being nice to my face while doing this behind my back.

Don nodded. "One was probably Barbara. She tried to get me fired three different times."

That surprised me, but I wasn't sure if I should believe anything he said. Everyone was two-faced except Rick, who was at least obvious about the aggression. I had seen no attitude from the government or Army staff at all, so two of them wanting me fired still mystified me. I felt betrayed by virtually everyone. Oddly, the lone person I could trust to be honest was Rick, but he was an overbearing and ignorant asshole.

I said, "The only one who I know wanted me fired, besides Rick, was Matt."

Don gave me the most genuine smile I had seen from him. Was it because I finally figured this out? "He's been trying to get you fired for months."

I held his gaze, encouraged by my suspicions being increasingly confirmed. "You know something, don't you?"

He nodded. "Yeah. I sit outside Rick's office, so every time Matt went in there and threw you under the bus to him, I heard everything he said."

Well, this was getting interesting. "Like what?"

"Like claiming you were an expert in .NET when I could tell you weren't."

I exchanged a knowing look with him. "I knew you were not-so-discreetly testing my knowledge when you dropped by all the time."

He smiled. "I knew you could tell. Matt is full of shit. Always has been. Quite a bastard, too. The government people hate him, but Rick likes him because he doesn't know the games Matt plays with people like you."

It wouldn't have surprised me in the least if Matt had done something like this before. He was quite good at it, I must admit, like some sort of Grand Master at fucking with people. "But you do."

"Yeah."

"And you say nothing."

He shrugged. "It's not really my place."

I stifled condemnation. "You let him get me fired."

He pursed his lips. "Yeah, I guess I can't argue with that. It's for the best, though. Let me know if you need a reference."

I tried not to roll my eyes. "You remind me of an expression. Friendship like yours can be had anywhere."

He shrugged slightly at my rebuke and smiled. "We aren't friends."

"No shit. Get out of my cube."

His smile grew, and he walked away. No one in this place could be trusted. Why was trust even an issue at work? It shouldn't be a factor at all. And yet we all had top secret (or better) security clearances, granted by a Department of Defense during war as we worked in the Army Operation Center. The irony. Those around me could be trusted with state secrets, but not with simple decency. This was the most corrupt place I had ever been.

My statement about having a job lined up wasn't entirely accurate. Jack still hadn't sent me a written offer. Telling him they had fired me wasn't smart because he might change his mind. I had already declined the other job twice. After Friday, I either had to continue waiting on Jack, or find another job and admit to them I had been fired when asked why I was looking, assuming I was honest, as companies always stress we must be. I had pressure. Fortunately, I also had a plan.

From the Pentagon courtyard, I called Jack on Tuesday.

"Hey bud," he said.

"Hey man. Any word on an offer?"

"Not yet. Still trying."

"Okay, well, I wanted to ask you something. I have a feeling that my job knows I'm looking and they might fire me."

He jumped in before I could say what I was getting at, mostly because he knew. "If that happens, I can have you in here the next day."

"Okay, great, because I would really like to work there with you but would have no choice but to look at other places."

"Right. Just keep me in the loop."

"Awesome. Thank you."

I hung up, feeling that went better than expected. The next call would be Thursday, telling him my fear had been realized—they found I was looking and fired me. If Jack was right, that would provide a day for paperwork and, with any luck, I could start the next Monday. Matt wasn't the only one who could play games.

I spent much of the week wandering around the Pentagon's halls, figuring it might be the last time I was in there. I sometimes discreetly tagged along with an organized tour that someone was giving visitors, if I happened to wander across one; they had been occurring throughout my tenure.

On Wednesday, they had schedule a work barbecue at Fort Myer, a tiny base close to the Pentagon. Low, old buildings that were barracks dominated it and there didn't look to be much to see. I drove through the security gate after showing my Pentagon badge to the armed guards. Like most such places, the speed limit is very low, the roads narrow, and stop signs control traffic flow at the considerable number of cross streets. The barbecue took place at a picnic pavilion beside a green lawn, with old trees looming overhead. Everything about the place seemed old because it dated from the 1800s.

Both RCS and Army staff were present. I hadn't wanted to go, but I was bored and wanted to visit another place I normally couldn't get into. This would also be a chance to assess the Army personnel to see if I could figure out who had wanted me fired, but I had no luck. Everyone smiled just like they always had. Was it now a grin of satisfaction? Did they find it funny I attended a social event with people who knew of my supposedly humiliating firing? They said nothing, of course, because people who talked badly about me behind my back and smiled to my face populated the AOC.

Matt was there, of course, and gave me a big handshake that seemed peculiar for its unusualness; no one else shook my hand, nor did he usually. It was phony and meant to continue the charade that we were best buddies. I wanted to punch him in the face. He chatted me up more than ever, often grinning hugely at me, pouring on the charm and acting like was a swell guy. He had not mentioned my impending departure, nor had I said anything, because I wanted to see if the little shit could even admit it had happened. But he didn't. Not a word. Everyone acted as if they did not know. I left early, knowing that by doing so, I might open the floodgates of badmouthing me, but whatever.

I was about to have an epic Thursday.

CHAPTER NINE

Two Can Play Games

In the morning, while Matt wasn't there, Gunner dropped by my desk at the Pentagon with his usual southern, folksy demeanor lending sincerity to what he had to say. He would be the only non-RCS person to acknowledge my departure, which he admitted to knowing about. Gunner said he was sorry to see me go and asked if I had anything lined up. He seemed genuinely glad when I said that I did, and then came a moment I had been thinking about for days.

I looked Gunner in the eye, trying to project quiet confidence and some gravitas. "I can give you an earful about what's really been going on around here if you have a minute."

He looked startled. Then he considered my offer, a spark of quiet delight barely hidden. "I think I have a few minutes. Let's go to my office."

"Great."

I followed him, a smile growing. In the aftermath of the database fiasco that made Matt and Rick look bad, Rick had said he didn't want Gunner thinking he could come to me to find rocks to throw at them. Well, sometimes we shouldn't put an idea in someone's head. Gunner's small, windowless office had room for and a lone chair I occupied and his desk, behind which he soon sat. For the next forty-five minutes, I threw Rick, Matt, and everyone who had done something bad at RCS, including the knowledge-withholding Don, under the bus as gloriously as anyone has ever done. I was honest about everything, including my lack of qualifications and the result. Gunner nodded over and over, like the pieces of a puzzle were clicking into place, and he asked questions I had answers for. I loved him for this conversation if for no other reason than I could tell he believed everything I told him, and we were two men of integrity in a sea of deceit. He was like a breath of fresh air filling my sails as I sailed away, and I could tell he felt the same.

"We both know they fired me," I said toward the end, "so you could think this is just revenge, and you would be right. I'm not gonna lie. I hate those guys. But I don't want you to take my word for a thing. I've given you the information you need to verify much of this, and I would strongly encourage you to look into all of it. I can almost guarantee that this kind of bullshit will continue long after I'm gone."

He nodded. "It's been going on since before you started."

"The kicker for me is that this is the Army Operation Center in the Department of Defense. We are technically at war. I may not be military, but things like honor, integrity, and truth matter to me. The Army and our country deserve far better than these dishonorable assholes screwing around like this."

His eyes lit up. "Absolutely! Absolutely."

"I felt it was really important for someone here to know the truth about them, and you seem like the only decent person here besides me." I smirked. "Sorry to be leaving you on your own. I've enjoyed working with you."

He laughed. "No worries, Rand. No worries. Same here. I really appreciate you taking the time. This has been very helpful. Eye-opening. I hope your new job goes a lot better."

"Thank you. Can't go much worse," I said, laughing.

I rose to leave, and he gave me one of those crushing, military guy handshakes, unlike the weak and pathetic one Matt delivered the day before. I opened the door to step out, and as I did so, the door across the hall opened. It was the door into the entire AOC, and none other than Rick, followed by Matt, were stepping into the hall at the same moment I was exiting Major Gunner's office. The look of alarm on their faces was priceless. That I was exiting a closed-door meeting with the Major could not be missed, and given the history, they had to be appalled at what I might have told him. I reveled in the moment, grinning hugely at them. Was it petty? Yes. Satisfying? Also yes.

"Hello boys!" I cheerfully said, then exited the AOC and went for a walk, laughing all the way to the Pentagon's courtyard, where I called Jack.

"Hey man," I began, "it looks like I was right. They found out I'm looking to leave and just fired me. My last day is tomorrow."

"We will get you in here Monday."

"Awesome." Maybe I should have tried this weeks earlier.

"I already ran it by my boss and he's on board, so no worries. Can you come by tomorrow to do any remaining paperwork?"

"Absolutely. Just tell me when."

"Great. I'll send you an email by COB."

I hung up, taking a victory lap or two before returning to my desk. Then I did something else I had been considering. One of my tasks had been to retrieve information from a database for Barbara, the woman Don said had tried to get him fired three times. I had used code to generate this information for her, but technically, I had never been asked to create code to do it, just to get the result. So I deleted all of my code for that. Let them figure it out themselves next time. Petty? Yes. Satisfying? Also yes.

At lunchtime, I went up to my favorite food truck in the courtyard by myself and took my time. Then I called my wife for a bit, updating her on the USAIS job with Jack. The phone call distracted me so that I did not at first notice Rick across the courtyard. He was speaking with a black man I hadn't seen before. The bald man wore a suit and tie and held the same sort of leather binder that I had taken to job fairs. I was already certain that this was a candidate to replace me, and I began watching, my sunglasses hiding my eyes. Nonetheless, Rick looked directly at me at one point, and grinned in a way that I found smug. When they shook hands, this seemed to confirm my suspicion that this was my potential replacement. That Rick was interviewing him instead of Matt told me the latter's trustworthiness had fallen. May it drop straight into Hell. I also didn't appreciate Rick doing it where I might see it, like he was rubbing it in my face, that obscene smile now causing cold anger.

As Rick and the candidate began walking away, I saw an opportunity for more revenge and wasn't passing it up. I hung up with my wife and followed, knowing where they were going. The guy likely didn't have a badge and needed escorting, so despite that farewell handshake, they were staying together as Rick took him on the five-minute walk to the front security gate. I'd had an idea and knew the route back. The odds of Rick looking behind him weren't good, but without being obvious that I was tailing someone in the Department of Defense Headquarters, I kept my distance and hid behind others walking ahead of me, or kept to one side to duck behind a pillar, display case, or into an adjoining hallway. But Rick never looked back.

They made it to the entrance, which posed a problem. It stood two stories, with us on the upper floor. The space was wide open. Two escalators on the nearer side went down. Twenty feet away, two on the other side went up, nearer the security screening area at the bottom with its armed guards. Ahead on the lower floor were multiple double wooden doors to the outside. There was nowhere to hide on either level. By the time I reached the escalator top, Rick and the candidate were at the bottom and shaking hands, then going their separate ways. The man went through the doors to the outside. Rick turned to the ascending escalators and boarded one even as I stepped onto one of the descending ones twenty feet from me. All he had to do was turn his head and he would see me, not that I really cared. What was he going to do? Fire me?

Don't turn your head, I thought, staring at the side of his face. *Don't turn your head, don't turn your head, don't turn your head.*

Then I was farther down than him and I stopped looking at him until after getting off the escalator, in case he happened to finally look over and he would only see the back of my head, unsure if it was me? I was a last step before the doors before I glanced back once and saw him walking away at the top, oblivious. Then I exited the Pentagon into the sunlight, my eyes darting for the candidate. To the left was mostly grass before a steep drop over a wall to asphalt, where buses careered around the sharp corner. Ahead in the distance were more buses at the bus terminals, beyond them part of the vast parking lot surrounding the massive building on nearly every side. To the right was a hundred yards of concrete sidewalk leading to more parking spaces in the distance, and off to one side and close to me, the metro station canopy, beneath which lay escalators. My prey was halfway to it. I took off at a run and caught up just as he was about to turn around and step onto the descending escalator.

"Hey man," I said, getting his attention, "did you just interview with Rick at RCS?"

He looked startled and stopped feet from the escalator. "Yes."

"Trust me. You don't want to work here."

I then did almost the same thing as I had just done with Gunner, giving the guy an earful. He kept looking at me in amazement and, like I was a nut job, so I finally said, "Look, I'll be the first to admit that they fired me and I'm biased against them. And you're my potential replacement and maybe in theory I could resent you, but it's not your fault and I have no ill will toward you at all. Quite the contrary. If you take this job, you will have my sympathy. You can doubt everything I'm telling you, but ask yourself how much I must loathe these guys to follow you all the way from the courtyard to tell you these things."

He laughed. "Some good points."

"Do you have any other positions lined up?"

"Yeah. Got another interview at 2 PM."

I smiled. "Well, it won't be stranger than this one. I strongly urge you to take anything before this one, even if Rick offers you more money. If you doubt me about all of this and take this job, before long, you are going to realize the huge favor this conversation is and that you should've listened to me."

He laughed again. By now, I could hear the next train arriving, and he shook my hand and thanked me, seeming caught between meaning it and thinking I was nuts. But I could tell he believed me. Being honest and proud of it has its advantages for how it aides sincerity. We parted ways, and I went back inside toward the AOC, grinning and reveling in the fun of what I had just done. Just as Rick had ruined my job, I had hopefully ruined something for him.

Sure, another candidate would eventually take the job if this guy didn't, but I had enjoyed it. Was it petty? Yes. Satisfying? Also yes.

I felt jubilant, but as I walked down a long, wide ramp back toward the AOC, none other than Matt came toward me, leaving early for the day, as always. It was Thursday, and he was on vacation the next day, so we would never see each other again. It had now been four days since I had been fired and he had not acknowledged I was leaving at all, not to mention under the circumstances. What manager does that? A dishonest, backstabbing one. The sin of omission was proof of duplicity, but he seemed to think it covered for him. I suddenly felt determined to rip that illusion from him, especially after he did what came next.

He gave me a big, thrilled grin and made the same hugely exaggerated motion with his arm as he went to shake my hand for the second day in a row. It was the sort of motion pro athletes do when they just made a big play and are slapping the hands of their teammates in celebration. But the words coming from his lying little mouth also irritated me. The grin was the biggest ever directed at me to this day. Because he got me fired and saved himself at my expense. Because he outmaneuvered me in a game of chess that I hadn't even known was being played until I lost it. Because he thought I didn't know it was him. And that was something I could take away from him.

He cheerfully said, "Well, if I never see you again, have a good weekend."

This isn't something you say if you'll see each other next week, so this was the closest to an admission that he knew I was leaving. And so it revealed that he knew (of course he did) but wouldn't admit it (of course he wouldn't). It symbolized his relentless deceit. And it pissed me off.

Shaking his hand only so I could squeeze hard enough to hurt him, I asked, "Are you ever gonna be straight with me, or are you just gonna fuck with me right till the end?"

His smile turned awkward as he pulled his hand from mine with an effort, but he quickly recovered and tried pouring on that fucking charm of his. "Sorry I didn't hear you in the echoing hallway."

"Bullshit. You heard me." I always hated it when people acted like I wouldn't repeat something, so I would always say it verbatim. "Are you ever gonna be straight with me, or are you just gonna fuck with me right till the end?"

Grin broadening, he said, "Sorry, I didn't quite catch that."

That he was once again trying to fuck with me, while acting like he was innocent, could not have been more obvious. I took a menacing step toward him and loudly repeated it. "Are you ever gonna be straight with me, or are you just gonna fuck with me right till the end?"

This time he at least didn't pretend he didn't hear it, only that he didn't know what I meant. God, he was a slippery snake of an asshole. Grinning like I was silly and incomprehensible, he asked, "What are you talking about?"

"So you don't know that Rick fired me on Monday?"

He poorly feigned surprise and sadness. "I knew Rick had talked about it," he said, dodging the question, "but he's threatened to fire me twenty times, so I never really believed it."

"So you don't know that Rick fired me on Monday?" I repeated.

"I hadn't heard."

"You're my manager. How would you not have heard?"

"I'm not really your manager. On paper, yeah, but Rick is."

"Bullshit. And he would've told you he fired me either way. Or are you admitting that you are this clueless of a manager, and that bad at your job that you wouldn't know something this important? I saw Rick interviewing someone instead of you doing it, so it certainly suggests you aren't considered good enough anymore."

He looked a little irritated. "I was surprised he actually did it."

I cocked an eyebrow. "You *were* surprised, not *are* surprised. You knew, and of course did. You're a lying little shit. Caught you, asshole."

A startled look wiped the grin from his face. He opened his mouth to say something and my glare hardened. He closed it and then skirted me in the wide hallway as others went by us. I turned as if to follow as he went, secretly amused by the concerned look on his face as he looked back. Then I turned back toward the AOC. Sometimes we have to take victory where we can get one, and defeating Matt by catching him lying to my face after five months of him lying to me and about me made me laugh. So did putting him in his place.

Not so easy when my back isn't turned, is it? I thought.

Was it petty? Yes. Satisfying? Also yes.

I was having an epic Thursday.

The next day, neither Matt nor Rick were there as I did some paperwork to close out my time at the Pentagon, turned in my badge, and left by 11 AM. I headed to USAIS, where Jack revealed I would come on as an independent contractor until they got the paperwork for full employment worked out. This was better than nothing and it was supposed to be a week, but I wasn't thrilled. I felt pleased with the way I'd handled the job transition with a smidge of deceit about the timing of my termination. With Monday the Labor Day holiday, I started on Tuesday, missing only that day of pay, but RCS paid out my vacation balance and I lost no money. I was satisfied. But it had been an awful summer working for them.

Since I wasn't an employee of USAIS, I didn't get an orientation, but Jack introduced me to a slew of people I would seldom see. My project was for a USAIS client, not someone internal. And virtually the entire company worked in one tower while the IT guys worked in the other. Unless I went over for Bagel Friday, when HR bought bagels and spreads, I never went over there. The only reason most people knew I existed was that Jack was a social butterfly who wanted to mostly give up programming. By turning work over to me, he could socialize far more and complete his transition to managing the IT staff. If anyone knew I had facilitated his schmoozing increased presence in the other tower, I doubt they remembered for long.

The IT department consisted of me, Jack, and two PC techs, only one of whom I'll mention. Billy was short, spunky, blond, and seemed friendly and down-to-earth. Unlike Jack, who seemed to revel in bachelorhood and couldn't stop eyeballing female coworkers and commenting on their features to us, Billy was married in his mid-twenties. I seldom learned much about him because he kept a low profile, but he gave a sense of trustworthiness.

Like the rest of us, Billy appreciated Jack's irreverent sense of humor and wise-ass remarks, though the latter frequently veered into the sort of sexist commentary that gets people fired for harassment. Jack also liked to call people a "fag" or "gay" as an insult, and he exuded the stereotypical manliness of former military; in his case, the U.S. Navy. And yet he had no sex appeal, like he was imitating the behavior of guys who got the girl even though he couldn't.

Jack came across as a womanizing pig who nonetheless didn't have a woman, and the only reason he got away with the remarks is that the four of us sat largely isolated in the other tower. Though Jack was only a year older than me, he carried himself with an authority and cocky confidence that, along with his quickly receding hairline, suggested he was five years older. And yet he was really immature. Due perhaps to his military service straight out of high school, he hadn't attended college, but he was sharp, quick, and appeared to love reading people and situations. He seemed destined for management.

I initially had an office for the first time since SysCorp's first month. And just like then, it didn't last much longer, a cube being my next home. The tall building stood right beside the I-495 beltway and overlooked Tyson's Corner in Virginia. This meant the drive home was just about as good as it gets from NoVA back to Maryland across the bottleneck of the American Legion Bridge. The traffic is horrendous. After 3 PM, it gets exponentially worse with every 15 minutes later that you leave, so I worked 7 AM to 3 PM, a schedule I would subsequently keep for most of my career regardless of work location, though I am not a morning person.

USAIS performed more than half of the security clearance investigations for the U.S. government. They may have even investigated me for my interim top-secret clearance for RCS. I would eventually learn that they dropped this investigation before completion so that I did not get it. Matt had cost me this with his bullshit. Jack had brought me on to take over Mirage, a database driven web app. I never knew the federal client for whom we had developed it, despite repeatedly talking to them on the phone in the months to come. I suspected he kept me ignorant just to screw with me, and as a lame way to hold on to his own power, because that was the kind of guy he was.

As for what the app did, the client trained investigators, who could have been FBI agents for all I knew. The investigators needed to take classes in things like using a telephoto lens to spy on someone from a distance. The driving course was really how to tail someone without the target spotting investigator. Due to the secretive nature of the courses, they effectively had codenames like "Photography 101." Investigators used Mirage to sign up for the classes. Then the app's admins tracked who completed them and did invoicing, including bonuses.

The app used the same tech that I had been trying to master while at RCS—ASP .NET for the front end and SQL Server for the back, with related web technologies like HTML. No thanks to Matt, I knew more than before, but not nearly enough. Fortunately, where Matt had failed utterly, Jack succeeded admirably. The code he showed me looked nothing like the junk at RCS and more like what I'd read about. It made sense. Jack was a good teacher and walked me through how a screen worked. I was sometimes a little overwhelmed with the details and had to return to him for clarification, but I came along. Once I got a screen done, he said the app needed several more that were similar, and the repetition drove home my learning.

The great thing was that it allowed me to drill everything. I started by opening up a screen he'd done and duplicating the code line by line for another screen. I sometimes didn't understand what code was doing, but I figured out some things by thinking about it, by researching, asking him, or by running the code in debug mode. That allowed me to step through the code, which executes one line at a time. I could hover the mouse over a variable and see that it was set to "100," for example, and that if the next line multiplied that by two, I could now see the variable said "200." This let me see how the application ran and what certain lines were doing. Within two weeks, my knowledge and skills had soared. The degree to which Matt had been an incompetent ass was the only thing overwhelming me then; in my twenty-year career, he's still the worst programmer I have ever worked with.

I loved my job so much that I didn't mind being very busy. After years of bullshit work, I had a real coding project on more modern, advanced technologies. The app was also in use in "production," as opposed to the site only running in development mode or on a test server. This was the project I had been searching for, having only had near misses with others. Already a far stronger programmer, I felt great about my prospects after managers undercutting me for over three years. My work ethic, attitude, and professionalism all returned to levels they hadn't been at in a long time, the restoration of my "mojo" a welcome change. I was back. I was happy.

The first brief sign of trouble was that USAIS didn't pay me for a month when it was supposed to be every week. No intelligent answers explained it. They were also holding out on a real employment offer. This wasn't contract-to-hire with a drop dead date of six months. It was contracting until they got their act together, and they still weren't doing it. This had been going on since before they hired me. It was even the reason RCS had the opportunity to fire me. I tried to keep the faith that it would work out and a real employment offer would arrive.

For a while there, it was just me and Jack as coders, and everything was good. I took over sole ownership of Mirage because Jack didn't have time, which was why I'd been hired. I only asked Jack something about his system if I needed to make changes and wanted to verify that my approach took everything into consideration before I made them. That quickly earned his trust and before long, he jokingly started telling me to just fix it without listening to what I wanted to do. He never touched the system again. In the meantime, he was doing general IT management stuff he never told me about while also programming another site called WebDesk, but he needed to stop working on that, too.

"Randy," Jack loudly said, walking into my cube one morning in November, "this is the new guy, Andy." Then he and Andy, who was right on his heels like a well-trained dog, both laughed.

"Oh shit," said Andy, cursing in front of his manager, "you can't call me that. I'll go by Chuck."

"Come on," said Jack, grinning, "Randy and Andy is perfect!"

"Fuck that," said Chuck.

My eyebrows shot up. *He dropped an F-bomb?* I almost never heard that in the corporate world, and not in front of a manager. On Day 1.

All three of us were virtually the same height, but Jack had the growing potbelly and Chuck was just big-boned and a little beefy, like a football lineman. He had a pock-marked face, crew cut, and always wore an ingratiating grin that made him come across as insincere and immature. Maybe that was why Jack and he hit it off.

Jack said, "I'll let you two hang out a minute." Then he left, and Chuck sat on a spare chair. It seemed obvious that he was in our IT department, but Jack hadn't told me anything about this before now. I had no idea what this guy was doing here.

"So," I began, "what are you supposed to work on?"

He laughed. "WebDesk, some site he doesn't want to do anymore."

I had only heard of the app but not seen it. Apparently, he was another programmer. "How long have you been doing .NET?"

"Never seen it."

That surprised me. Jack had taken a chance on me, but I had experience, if not enough. Why would he hire Chuck if the guy had no experience at all? I had felt pleased with Jack giving me a chance, and that maybe I had convinced him. But if he would hire a guy with zero experience, maybe I should not feel that way. Chuck had to have something else going for him, so I asked, "What languages have you been doing instead?"

Grinning, he said, "None. I'm not a programmer, man."

I stifled a guffaw. "Really?"

He laughed. "Yeah. Just graduated college. This is my first job."

I probably failed to hide my amazement, not that I was really trying. "How did you convince Jack to hire you?"

Another chuckle. "Katie's my girlfriend."

"Who?"

"Katie. One of the tech recruiters here. She set me up with it. She's friends with Jack."

Are you kidding me? I thought. Jack handed Chuck the job in what almost amounted to nepotism. After all the bullshit I'd gone through, especially after college, this guy has the career handed to him. I'll admit to some jealousy and resentment. No one enjoys busting their ass for over five years and dealing with a bunch of crap, and to reach a certain positive point, only to have someone else be handed the same result with no effort at all.

Within days, Jack, Chuck, and I began sometimes eating lunch down in the cafeteria, where Katie and three of her equally young female recruiter friends joined us. I'd never met or seen them before. A "we've-been-friends-forever" vibe existed between all of them, Chuck, and Jack, though the latter two had just met. I sensed I was the odd man out, but they were all reasonably nice and it didn't matter. Yet.

Back in our own tower, as the weeks went by, I noticed the increasingly chummy relationship between Jack and Chuck, prompting me to ask when they were getting married. My teasing paled in frequency to Jack's and his horsing around. They had moved us again, this time to an enclosed group of three offices where we could shut the door and horse around, which Jack introduced at once. He brought in small nerf balls and started battles to see who could peg others with the balls the hardest. I have to admit, Jack could be a lot of fun, if wildly unprofessional.

After a week or two, I realized why he and Chuck became besties and began giving me a slightly cold shoulder—both were smokers and took smoke breaks together, bonding without me. I tried joining them a time or two, but they did not include me in what were already inside jokes. They shared a more juvenile sense of humor, not that I was above such things, but at nearly thirty, I didn't laugh uproariously the way they did at teenager-level comedy. They also viewed my presence as an intrusion, partly because they saw it for what it was—they were excluding me with a justifiable reason (they smoked), and I was trying to join them without such an excuse, purely for social reasons they did not respect. Maybe they saw this as desperate, though it didn't quite reach that level. I just felt my exclusion and wanted to end it, but it didn't work. That they didn't want me there became obvious, and I only joined them twice before accepting that Chuck had replaced me as Jack's go-to guy.

Making matters worse was Chuck's project. Jack had designed WebDesk, a suite of apps to help USAIS staff do their jobs better. It was this more than my project, Mirage, that had earned Jack promotion to a manager position. Mirage was for a federal client (I'm guessing the Office of Personnel Management, or OPM, which did most clearance investigations). But with WebDesk for in-house users, this meant that Jack, and now Chuck, went around to meet everyone in the other tower to learn what they needed the system to do. As the months passed, everyone recognized, knew, liked, and respected Chuck. No one ever saw me except on bagel day. They had little idea who I was. Chuck's girlfriend Katie sat in the other tower and was well known, along with her cadre of friends, and this also raised Chuck's profile while I had no such advantage. I didn't think any of this really mattered but I was wrong. Like my former manager Hank at United Systems, Jack had his favorite in Chuck and wasn't subtle about it.

Despite this, I got along fine with Chuck and ended up teaching him more than Jack did about how to program in ASP .NET. Partly for this reason, I didn't resent him much; having someone come to you for help all the time is like a show of respect, even if there is no actual respect. I saw us as a team even if, on a social level, I had little standing, but I conceded that neither Jack nor Chuck were really my kind of people, in the end; were it not for work, we would not have known each other even if we got along well. Throughout my time there, I never had an issue with Chuck, partly because he wouldn't take anything seriously, so he never got upset about anything. Jack, by contrast, could be really snide, but always with plausible deniability that he meant anything by the attitude, which he delivered with a smirk.

One day, Jack rushed into my office. "Oh my God!"

"What?" I asked, alarmed.

"What's wrong with Mirage?"

I frowned, wondering if something I didn't know about had happened to the website. "What are you talking about?"

"You're still here."

I arched an eyebrow. "Am I supposed to be somewhere else?"

"You normally bolt for the door at 3, so since it's 3:01, I assume there's a catastrophe."

He was mocking me. I rolled my eyes. "Funny."

But I took some of this as a compliment because I knew Jack appreciated my abilities. My work had completely freed him from having to deal with Mirage. I had likely earned his trust by running changes by him so that he knew I was no rogue coder wreaking havoc. I also seldom caused bugs because I thoroughly tested. During my career, I was often surprised at how many bugs others introduced to software, with me often being a standout for not doing so. While I wasn't the greatest programmer, if I did stupid shit at work, it wasn't with programming.

I also freed Jack from dealing with the client, who could be problematic. I never met or saw Jade, but Jack said she was middle-aged. Her voice was gravelly, and while she seemed mostly pleasant, she had a flair for the dramatic. One day, she called me in a panic.

"All the data has been wiped!" she yelled.

My eyes widened. If the entire database had been erased, that was beyond catastrophic. Any system has two basic types of data—user-supplied and system-supplied. Mirage had titles of courses, which Jack had once entered into the database so that those signing up for a course could select which one they wanted. This is system-supplied data, which the user could not change. Such data is also known as "lookups" because users choose them from a drop list, just like we might select our state from a list of U.S. States. If we type them in, one person will enter "Maryland," another will do, "MD," or "Md," or make a typo and result in "Marland." If someone goes to run a report on all the "Maryland" data, they don't get the other versions of the data because they don't match. Programmers solve this by supplying a drop list to choose values from. And instead "Maryland" being stored, StateID = 4 (or whatever number it is) is stored. The other kind of data, user-supplied, is stuff the users type in and then hit "Save" or "Submit."

"Jade," I began, projecting calm, "what data?"

"All of it!"

I quickly pulled up the production version of the website she used and felt relief that, on logging in, everything looked fine. If "all" of the data had been erased, screens that depended on the system-supplied data would have crashed. They didn't. I also saw copious user-supplied data.

"Well," I said, "I see nothing missing, so the system appears intact. What exactly is missing?"

"All the invoice data!"

I rolled my eyes that she had now changed "all" to something less. I went to the invoicing part of the app. When students took Mirage courses, they were paid for having done so. Once Jade marked the class complete, the system auto-generated the invoices. She could also give students a bonus, which Jade manually added after. And as it turns out, this was what was missing. She had added that data and then discovered that the bonuses were missing. She swore she hadn't removed them. But what she *had* done was re-entered the data only to then call me and tell me it was missing. She had erased the evidence of it being missing. This was like creating a bloody murder scene, disposing of the body and cleaning up the blood, and then calling the police to get them to see the evidence that no longer existed.

"Can you tell me the next time this happens?"

"Yes, absolutely."

"I mean, don't touch the app at all. Don't re-enter the data. I can't see what's happening if you do that."

"Okay."

And so she did the next day. And I confirmed that the bonus data she claimed to have entered was missing from the website and underlying database; it could have been in the database but not showing up on screen. "When did you create the invoices?"

"At ten this morning. I did the bonuses right after."

166 | RANDY ZINN

It was now an hour later, and the timestamp on the invoice records said fifteen minutes ago, not sixty. I told her this. "You sure it was earlier?"

"Positive. I did that and went to get donuts for the students."

I got off the phone and told Jack what she claimed was happening. He told me there was another area of the app that would recreate the invoices, erasing the manually entered bonus data. I hadn't known that, having not worked on it before. I called Jade and asked if she had hit the button that would do it. She swore on all things holy that she hadn't. But it happened again. And again. And I finally decided to lay a trap. I altered the code that re-created invoices to also write into the database the username of the person responsible for clicking that button. The next time she called to say it happened again, I looked in the database.

"Are you sure you didn't click the reset button?" I asked, knowing the answer.

"Absolutely!"

"Okay. Well, I'm pulling up the data now. Hold on." I already had it on screen and just held the phone away from my head, sighing and trying to be polite before putting it against my ear again. "It says you pressed that button ten minutes ago."

"I did?"

"That's what it says."

"Oh. Well, I didn't *think* I pressed it."

So I busted her. I knew I would. I was pleasant about it and had already heard that Jade really liked me. Despite her being a little maddening, I liked her, too. This was the last time the issue happened. Jack couldn't stop laughing when I told him, saying he was glad I was dealing with her now and that he fucking hated her. I thought she was nice.

"When are you gonna buy me lunch for sparing you?" I joked.

"In your fucking dreams."

In December, they moved us once again within the same tower as remodeling continued. This time, Jack had an office with a window, but he arranged something else for Billy, Chuck, and I—a huge executive suite on the 11th floor, overlooking I-495, trees, and then Tyson's Corner in the distance. Each of us had a cube, but it was cool and we knew it wouldn't last.

My frustrations with not being an employee finally ended in January when both Chuck and I came on in that capacity. My relief ended on the very first day, when Jack swaggered over to my desk when the others weren't there.

"So how does it feel to be an employee?" he asked, grinning. He was seldom not grinning. But usually the grin seemed insincere. I got the impression he had a chip on his shoulder and tried to hide it with that expression. But this time the grin seemed particularly delighted. And I felt suspicious on seeing it.

"Lovely."

"By the way," he drawled, almost laughing, "you now have to work nine-hour days, starting today."

That brought me up short, as I had always done only eight hours throughout my career and this change was not part of the plan. Or not part of *mine* anyway. "What?"

"You heard me." The grin grew. He'd been looking forward to this moment, I could tell.

"Forget it. That wasn't part of the deal."

"I'm changing the deal. Pray I don't alter it further."

I ignored the *Star Wars* Darth Vader line. "I assume you're kidding."

"Why would I be kidding?"

Because only an asshole would do that, I thought. "You can't do that."

"Of course, I can. I'm your boss."

"What's the reason for it?" I expected to hear that some deadline loomed.

He started walking out the door. "Because you're my bitch now," he said over one shoulder, laughing as he disappeared.

I swore under my breath. I knew I had no choice and resented it.

I jealously guarded my personal time because there was so much I struggled to find time for. The 1996 tendonitis injury had taken my guitar playing away, but I had it back by 2001, with limits on playing time, like 90 minutes every other day. But it was enough to record and release my first instrumental guitar album the previous summer. I had just put together a live band, and we were sometimes performing; gigs were hard to get, and I was the band manager dealing with all of it. It was now early 2005 and a second album was underway, with me writing articles for guitar-related sites and doing other promotional work. Meanwhile, I had no time for my other passion, writing fantasy novels, but I always wanted to do both music and fiction.

Jack's unwarranted decision would cost me over five hours a week and soured me on the job. I decided that, while he could make me sit there an extra hour a day, he couldn't make me actually *work* that hour. And so I reclaimed that time by doing research or other personal tasks from my work computer. I felt no guilt at all about it. I was no one's "bitch."

But Jack ramped up the blatant negativity, often making snide remarks about me leaving right at 4 PM, as if he resented it. Did he expect me to stay longer? I had been an hourly contractor before and not approved for over eight hours a day, so all the snide comments before made no sense. Now they made no sense because he had made a point of making me work longer for no reason, so what excuse did *he* have for resenting anything?

My first clue came when I invited him and the others to one of my band's shows and he snottily asked me why he would want to do that, inspiring laughter from the group. I did not appreciate the reaction. Within days, as I left on cue at 4 PM, he snidely told me to have fun playing guitar when I got home. Was that it? Was he jealous? By then, I had earned endorsements from Peavey, Alvarez Guitars, and Morley Pedals, and the good press I received, while rare and not exactly front page news, had usually referred to me as a virtuoso. If envy caused Jack's attitude, it wouldn't have been the first time my guitar playing caused it. When younger, I have naively believed the results of my dedication would earn respect and admiration. And they did. But they also caused nasty attitudes in insecure people like Jack.

I was starting to think he was a jerk.

And that worsened the next time I asked for time off to go skiing with my wife. Before, if I missed a whole work-day to drive three hours to Seven Springs in PA, so we could enjoy the smaller crowds, he let me work four 10-hour days that week to compensate. Now? He would even let me use my vacation hours for it. I didn't understand the change, and he only responded with "Because you're my bitch" when I asked. My wife thought less of him, too, having not met him.

But that changed on Superbowl Sunday in early February. Chuck and Katie threw a party that my wife and I attended, along with our small IT department and the recruiting girls, a few of whom brought a boyfriend. Jack was the only single one. He was on his better behavior. My wife assessed him as fun but insecure and hiding it behind bravado.

Not long after, the CEO resigned. He had been against programming or automating business processes, so we hoped our lot in life would improve with a new CEO, who arrived in March. He brought new executives from an old job, and Jack's immediate supervisor was canned, Jack laughing about it despite having always said he liked the guy. The evidence that Jack was two-faced was easy to notice. I was thinking this was required behavior from managers.

I had been dimly aware that USAIS had three locations—in the Midwest somewhere, in Fairfax VA where I worked, and in a small town north of Pittsburgh, PA. The latter was headquarters. But the new CEO, who came from densely populated Irvine CA, decided to move HQ to the similarly densely populated Fairfax because a semi-rural town didn't cut it. He didn't want to be there, basically. I would eventually see it twice and don't blame him.

A handful of programmers and other IT staff existed at HQ and considered themselves the real deal, as if those of us in Fairfax were interlopers. The PC techs like Billy were needed here, but first Jack, then me, and now Chuck existed as coders who were proving our worth. I didn't care for the idea that we were beneath the PA tech staff in skill or importance. I had seen that attitude at SysCorp when Ted tried to get me jobs at HQ and they had looked down their nose at me. A turf war brewed once the USAIS CEO said our Fairfax location was now HQ, and not theirs. Jack laughingly told us about the fear circulating up there, about them losing their jobs to us. I guess we weren't so unimportant after all, huh? But then we heard a rumor that they might force us up north. I wasn't going if so.

Jack told us all to put our resumes up on the job boards just in case it all "went south" and we were out of a job, so I did. Within days, I had a job interview lined up, and I told the guys about it because I had no intention of leaving, and we had all laughed.

"Steve called me the other day to rat you out," a grinning Jack revealed, referring to one of the IT guys in PA.

I cocked an eyebrow. "What are you talking about?"

"He saw your resume on Monster.com, so I told him I was the one who told you to put it up."

He, Billy, and Chuck laughed, but the revelation bothered me. What business was it of anyone in this company to contact my manager and tell him this? People get fired for looking for a job. I have never understood why companies do it. Steve had essentially tried to get me fired. I wasn't even sure how Steve knew who I was, but Jack must have told him my name. Steve was apparently an IT manager who had enough access to Monster.com to see my resume; only employers could see them.

I felt unnerved.

And my peers laughed. Didn't they realize it could be done to them?

My fortunes subtly changed one day after the gang at work convinced Billy to throw a party with his wife for all of us. My wife and I went—and every other person from work skipped it. Fortunately, Billy's wife had also invited work friends so that it wasn't just the four of us with a ton of food and drinks, but Billy was visibly dejected, wondering if his coworkers didn't like him. I felt bad for him, so much so that, the next day, I emailed everyone and asked where they had been, pointing out the effect on Billy. I hadn't meant to be accusatory, but I was, which I only realized on getting the very defensive responses. One had been tired, another wanted to reconnect with her boyfriend, and Chuck and Katie ditched Billy for Atlantic City. Jack didn't answer.

After this, the cold shoulder toward me began. Part of me wasn't surprised, but Billy did it, too, and that *did* surprise me. I had inadvertently guilt-tripped them on his behalf and could surmise he didn't like it. Guys typically try to pretend that their feelings aren't hurt, and I had admitted their effect on him emotionally, a kind of betrayal of some sort of dude code to never admit we have feelings. One thing I've learned in life is how willing some people are to hold a grudge, and my job began morphing into such a place.

Since I had become an employee, Jack had gained a tendency to ignore me when I entered his office, making me repeat what I had just said, sometimes more than once. I knew he was doing it on purpose. He thought the passive aggressiveness was funny, but now it kicked up a notch. That week, the group walked to the hotel next door because USAIS was holding a town hall meeting there not long after a buffet breakfast we did. When Jack put his jacket on a seat, I put mine next to it. Chuck returned from the buffet and sat elsewhere, and I sat. Jack arrived with his plate of food, saw that I was sitting next to his seat, grabbed his jacket, and moved to the far side of Chuck. This created a gap between me and the group. I tried to talk to Jack several times at breakfast but he ignored me.

At the town hall shortly after, each manager introduced their staff to the company. With a smirk, Jack only said about me, "Randy does some Mirage programming."

I cocked an eyebrow. I did *all* of it. He made me sound unimportant, but without me, he wouldn't have gotten his promotion to only managerial work. I tried to let it pass, but then he introduced Chuck.

"Chuck has been instrumental in the design and development of WebDesk, which many of you are depending on, and which he and I will expand further in the coming months to help you with all your business needs. He's proving to be a huge asset to me and the company."

The glowing remarks startled me and I tried to wipe the shock off my face, expecting Jack to look at me and grin, but he didn't. He was grinning all right, but not confirming the reaction he had caused by looking at me. I felt certain he was making a point I heard loud and clear. Chuck was the greatest thing in the world and I was nothing. In front of the CEO and everyone at our new HQ. Making it worse was all the time I had helped Chuck with his work, being one of the two people teaching him programming.

I left without waiting for the others. Hours later, I was struggling with Crystal Reports, a tool that we all hated. I had repeatedly talked with Jack about finding a replacement, and he agreed, so when I ran into big problems with it once more, I yelled from my office that we needed a new reporting tool ASAP. Jack yelled back to shut up. Billy and Chuck were in his office with him and they all laughed loud and long, sort of behind my back and to my face all at once. It struck a nerve. After that day, I began seriously thinking to leave USAIS just two months after becoming an employee. As it turns out, I had that interview lined up.

Jack stuck his head into my cube the next day, face dead serious for once. "Do you really have a job interview tomorrow?"

I smiled and acted like it was no big deal. "Yep! Wish me luck."

He disappeared without further comment. Was this why he was acting like a jerk more than usual? If I left, he had to return to Mirage because Chuck didn't know shit about it and wasn't good enough to handle it. Everything he did on WebDesk, he did with Jack's help or mine, not that I was going to help him anymore. I could find a job elsewhere. Chuck couldn't, having only six months experience. I didn't need Jack. He needed me.

The next morning, I arrived before everyone like usual and went into Jack's office to put something on his desk. To my surprise, he had left his IRS W-2 forms showing his previous year taxes in plain view. I should not have looked, but I didn't care. It showed he made $6k more than me the previous year, and yet he had been promoted to manager in October shortly after I started and backfilled much of his work. With three months extra money from his promotion, I could assume we were making nearly the same in September when I started.

Did Jack feel like I was breathing down his neck? Was he threatened by my ability to take over, even though that's what he hired me for, or by the possibility of me leaving? Both? He needed to make his mind what he wanted, but I think he already knew—he wanted Chuck, a dependent lackey who would follow him around like a puppy wanting approval. Some of this may have explained why Jack continued to refuse telling me how to push the development code to production so that it was live; there are different ways to do it and I didn't know which one he was employing. He insisted on doing it personally, refusing to even tell me which way he did it, not to mention give me access rights to try. I sensed this was a bid to keep power over me and make himself less replaceable. I didn't blame him but also thought he was petty.

It wasn't a coincidence that Jack began repeatedly saying, without prompting, that he would never have a job where he couldn't do the design and architecture of a new system while acknowledging that, as a manager, he shouldn't be doing so anymore. This was an implied threat to keep me from doing such work. This would limit my prospects at that job and even after.

My relationship with Jack had changed. He had openly taught me how to do things and now openly prevented me from learning anything more. I had liked and respected him. Now I disliked and resented him. It started a little when Chuck arrived, but it wasn't until I became an employee that he changed literally overnight when this should not have affected our relationship. I saw no forward progress for me, the Mirage app needed less work, and Jack refused to let me work on the ever-expanding WebDesk. I saw the signs that I would not have a project soon (I paid more attention to this after the United Systems fiasco) and that my job sucked now, so it was time to leave.

But then Jack announced that a new Chief Technology Officer (CTO) was starting and might change everything.

CHAPTER TEN

The New Management

By now, Billy, Chuck, and I had been removed from that 11th floor penthouse, which was to be the new CTO's office, and we were now scrunched into a windowless room just big enough for four cubes arranged in a square, a wall dividing each so none of us could see the others. Billy and Chuck took the two on one side, while me and the other PC tech took the other pair. The result was that Billy and Chuck started bonding. You wouldn't think this would happen, given that all of us could hear any conversation in that room, and we were equidistant from each other and could chime in, but somehow it did. That they were slowly excluding me was part of it, and the remaining PC tech who sat by me had always been anti social.

A tall, thin Asian man with a flat face, Kaede arrived to meet the Fairfax IT staff on a Monday. As our new CTO, he held our fate in his hands. His arrival would affect all of us. At the least, he was Jack's immediate supervisor. Jack had told us he would meet with Kaede privately first, which made me wonder what he was going to say about me; I didn't trust him now. Then we'd all meet Kaede in a group gathering. On Tuesday, we'd each have a one-on-one private interview with Kaede for thirty minutes; Jack referred to this as "keep your job" interviews, with him sitting in. Then Wednesday we would all have lunch with Kaede, and then he and Jack would meet one last time, and any terminations were likely to follow. The mood was tense, with Jack repeatedly joking that he was going to "sell us all out" on Monday.

That morning, I arrived before everyone else like usual, and saw a stack of manilla envelopes on Jack's desk. I suspected they were performance reviews he told us he had been doing at Kaede's request. Between his recent behavior toward me and the way I had been treated at my last two jobs, I couldn't help opening one to see that I was right. Normally not a snooper, I found mine.

With five as the best and one the worst, Jack rated me three for everything. I didn't really have a problem with that. But there was an exception—for teamwork, he rated me a two. "Teamwork" is often code for how well you are liked at a job and that's exactly how I saw it. At Jack's direction, no one, including him, worked with me on Mirage, and he would not let me work on WebDesk. I was an island. He was right that I did almost no team-oriented stuff. Never mind all the help I had given Chuck. But rating me that way suggested there was an actual problem with my teamwork, not that no opportunity for it existed. Going into the week with Kaede, my concern for termination rose.

Snooping at my performance review was one thing, but Chuck's was off limits. But after the way Jack introduced us at the town hall, curiosity and anger drove me to it. I had to know, given all the blatant favoritism for him and equally blatant scorn for me, and the possibility of being terminated for both within days. This is one of those things where someone could certainly disapprove of me for peeking, but in my shoes, they likely would have done the same, or at least bumped their halo on the door frame on the way out of Jack's office. I don't regret it despite still feeling guilty about it fifteen years later.

Jack had rated Chuck a two for everything and a three for teamwork, the exact opposite of me. Both surprised me. I had half expected five for teamwork and everything else a three or even higher, even though that would have been bullshit. I had seen Chuck's work and fixed enough of his bugs when he asked me to—because my teamwork sucked, of course. How often he admitted to Jack that the screen worked because of me or if he told Jack he'd gotten it right without issues—or that I had refused to help him? Being suspicious wasn't my nature, and I didn't like my mindset or mood when given cause to feel that way. Regardless, Chuck's ratings were accurate and I relaxed a little. Being a dick to me seemed to be Jack's way of complimenting me. He would not be happy when I took it the wrong way and resigned, but then maybe he should grow up.

I felt better as I went to my desk to login, but then I found an email from Jack, with two nasty statements. One chastised me for not telling him what I was working on at the end of a day. It was now May, and I had worked there since September. He had never asked for this, so how could he give me shit about not doing it? If he wanted a status update, he could have asked for one in many ways that had no attitude.

The worst line was, "Every time I step out of my office for a minute with a question for you, 9 times out of 10, you've disappeared." This was a lie on multiple levels. Jack seldom, if ever, had a question for me. He wanted nothing to do with Mirage or the client and got his wish thanks to my work. He wouldn't even listen to me when I went into his office to talk to him about it. I resented that and here he was expressing resentment about something made up. How ironic.

But the 90% missing part was the most loaded remark. This is grounds for termination if true. And it was utter bullshit. There was nowhere else for me to be. No one in our company worked in our tower, and I had no reason to visit the other one. I did work for a client I had never met, and I didn't even know which federal agency they were. If I went to the food court, I went with our team. I don't smoke or drink coffee, so there were no absences to do either. Our building was so far from strip malls or shopping centers that driving was the only option, and there was no reason for me to go to one. Jack had been joking since I had started that "we never let Rand out of his office." The joke had worn thin but bore far more resemblance to the truth than this bullshit that could get me fired if repeated to Kaede, and I wondered if he had been BCC'd on it; that's getting a copy without me being able to tell.

I wanted out.

Later that morning, Kaede and Jack entered the conference room where Chuck, Billy, myself, and the other PC tech waited. Nothing of great interest occurred until the end, when Kaede complimented us on our energy and how well we all seemed to work together. I had long thought we were a good group until the recent sniping at me. The big revelation from Kaede was that he had already met the PA tech team and had found them listless and indifferent, very fearful of their jobs going away, and just generally uninspiring. He asked us what our secret was, and I knew the answer was Jack's casual, joking demeanor, which had a dark side that had been targeting me for months. Kaede said he wanted to replicate our team's disposition in PA, a desire that would soon destroy our team rather than duplicate its spirit.

Rather than on Tuesday, we did our one-one-one interviews with Kaede on Wednesday as Jack silently listened, arms folded during mine. I ignored him unless he called attention to himself. If he was trying to intimidate me, it failed for several reasons. I had seen the review he gave Kaede, unbeknownst to him. I was quitting soon. And I had overcome so much bullshit in my life—so much so that there is a trilogy of memoirs about them—that Jack would have shit himself if any of it had happened to him. Neither he nor Kaede fazed me, and my interviewing experience paid off. Despite having had speech problems for nearly twenty years, with those now gone for nearly a decade, I was smooth, fluent, informative, to the point, and did not wander off subjects or go into too much detail. When I was done answering something, I shut up and let Kaede think of his next question. After the interview, I sent him an email offering to demo Mirage to him.

Then the group piled into Kaede's rented SUV for lunch, during which Kaede mocked another executive as a bad used car salesman and made disparaging remarks about how ugly the female HR director was. Everyone laughed but me, though I feigned a smile of agreement. I was no stranger to people talking dirt about me behind my back and it just wasn't something I found funny when hearing it done to others. In my teens and twenties, I had also been teased relentlessly about having a large nose, and this had ultimately resulted in me getting a nose job while working at SysCorp to not only adjust my appearance, but to remove the psychological weight of people trying to make me ashamed of my face. Kaede was supposed to set an example for us, and I suppose he was doing so. He and Jack probably hit it off. I didn't like him.

During lunch, Kaede admitted that he and Jack were demoing Mirage for someone at the end of the day, so having seen my email, he asked me to lead it. Jack shot me a look of irritation and I inwardly smiled that I could steal his thunder. With Chuck sitting in, the demo went well and Kaede was very impressed with the program, which

Jack said surprised him after Kaede left. But even me making both of us look good to Kaede was not enough for Jack. He and Chuck stayed behind as I walked out, but they caught up to me at the elevator as I waited to descend. It was the end of my workday at 4 PM.

"Oh my God," said Jack, voice heavy with sarcasm, "it's four o'clock and you're still here. What are you going to do? Just what are you going to do?"

Chuck snickered, and I pretended to laugh until they walked past, me giving his back the finger. Why is my manager consistently giving me shit for leaving at the end of my *nine-hour* workday? I'd had enough and walked straight into his office the next morning.

"You have a minute?" I asked.

"Yes."

I closed the door behind me—a sign that someone is quitting and doesn't want others to overhear.

"Oh shit!" said Jack. He never seemed to take anything seriously. The grin almost never left his face, but sometimes it competed with the closest thing to a serious expression he could muster. Now was one such time. I had him worried. Good.

"Relax," I said, offering no smiles. I had thought a lot about how to say what I was thinking, and with my wife's help, had come up with a decidedly understated way of bringing up my displeasure. I tend toward wanting to just say it, so this was exquisitely polite, at least for me. "I've been getting the impression that you may not be happy with my work performance and wanted to learn the details."

"Not at all," he blurted out, almost interrupting. "Pull up a chair. I was only kidding yesterday."

I had expected that, having known many people who hide behind such an excuse. "Yeah, but the thing is that I've had supervisors who joke about things they actually

CORPORATE HELL: A MEMOIR | 183

mean but won't come right out and say, and it only created poor attitudes. I don't think you're the sort to do that, but my radar goes up when some jokes get repeated."

Jack nodded vigorously, and he wasn't smiling anymore. Sometimes wiping a grin off someone's face is its own reward. I had done it to Matt the last time I saw him at the Pentagon. Now it was Jack's turn.

"I totally understand," he said. "I've had the same thing happen. Kaede was really impressed with you and with the system. You're in."

I cocked an eyebrow. "No pink slip, huh?" I asked, referring to the old idea, which I had never seen play out, of being fired via some slip of paper that, for unknown reasons, was stereotypically pink.

He laughed. "No."

"All right." I still hadn't smiled and wasn't planning to. I was done playing along with fucked up jokes. I just got up and left.

As the week continued, Jack's behavior toward me changed. Gone were the snotty comments and emails complaining about invented crap. He also told me the fate of others, including himself. We had a budding IT guy in the other tower, and who had been on the verge of joining our team as another PC tech, but Kaede laid him off as too expensive and unnecessary. Aside from Billy, that left the other guy we'd had all along, but he specialized in network stuff and that work was now to be consolidated with the PA team, and he therefore had no future at USAIS; he would resign months later with one week's notice, which he cut to three days by taking vacation for the other two, burning bridges on the way out.

Jack was being permanently moved to the PA location to oversee the IT group there, mostly because Kaede thought they were timid, bored, and not excited to be part of anything, and Jack could change that. They also made a lot of mistakes, one of which happened that week. He asked them to estimate the cost of establishing a virtual private network (VPN) for a bunch of regional offices and didn't include hardware in their estimate because the regional offices did that work. This infuriated Kaede because we were supposed to be one company and yet different sections acted like they had nothing to do with each other. He also had to go back to the CEO with a new, higher number and explain the failure. He was livid. Jack was amused. Some in PA were being terminated, while a few would soon quit.

One result of Jack's relocation was that I would report directly to Kaede. With me having seven years of experience to Chuck's six months, and being more senior than PC tech Billy, I would also be the most technical person at HQ aside from Kaede himself. My job should have been more than secure. I saw opportunity and had already mentioned to him my interest in management. With Jack the official lead on Mirage even though he never touched it, it should have been me already, and WebDesk would need me in the position as well. Within a week, I emailed Kaede to say I was willing to help with the transition however he needed, even if only temporarily. I hedged because, at both SysCorp and United Systems, I had been subtly accused of not knowing my place for wanting to be a project lead. Kaede got me on the phone and was having none of my hedging.

"Where do you see yourself in the organization?" he flat-out asked me.

That surprised me and I still tried to hedge. "Well, with Jack moving to PA, I thought you might need more from us here, but I didn't want to presume."

"It's okay. You can be honest."

I doubted that. My honesty had never paid off for me that I could remember, and yet I couldn't help it. I reluctantly said, "I was hoping to be project lead on Mirage, where only I do the work anyway, and on possibly other systems we might need. I've built systems before and done all the requirements and other documentation."

"Right."

I knew he had seen my resume. "We also don't have coding standards and I've developed those before."

"Right."

"So I'd like to at least be involved if not lead it like I did at United Systems."

"Right."

Nice to get so much agreement. "I don't know what your organizational structure might look like or where I would fit into it."

"Where I see you fitting in is as business liaison for software development in this division. I'm glad you're stepping up because I was looking for you to do that, anyway."

I breathed a sigh of relief. "Great."

"Let's meet with Jack on Tuesday to talk about a transition plan because I want to remove all of those responsibilities from Jack as soon as possible."

"Great. Thank you."

I got off the phone feeling pretty good, but I regretted that Jack had to be involved because I didn't trust him and knew that Kaede did, but obviously he had to be there. I would effectively take over Jack's role regarding the software development (not the PC tech stuff), just as I wanted. But the meeting never happened. Did Jack kill my ability to take over his work? It seemed like it when I soon learned that he had taught Chuck how he pushed WebDesk updates to production and given him access to do so while denying me both for Mirage. This favoritism rankled.

Nothing really changed as the summer continued except pettiness from Jack continuing. On learning I was going on vacation, he snidely emailed me about who my backup was while I was gone, when that had always been him. When I pointed that out, he irritably said he wasn't anymore, the first I had been told of this. Did he resent being pulled off? He angrily asked me how long my plans had been made without arranging for a backup when he had prevented me from knowing a backup didn't exist anymore.

He wasn't my manager anymore either, and I purposely cut him out of all communication afterward. This included altering Mirage, which sent error messages to both of us, so that he would no longer receive them. This had often caused a snotty email from him about the errors, and it was ironic—the code causing errors was *his* JavaScript, which had stopped working. That Jack was an asshole could not be denied. I wanted nothing more to do with him and increasingly got my wish, not hearing from the prick for several weeks.

Sometime that summer, Kaede announced Mirage would not be developed any further. Only bug fixes were allowed. I felt some concern that my 40-hour per week project was dying and another was not being given to me. But then an opportunity appeared.

We had an application that tracked the status of our software projects, but it wasn't designed to do that originally and was thrown together in this way by Jack and Chuck. It had its problems. It assumed a project died when launched and had no maintenance phase or subsequent requests for changes. I don't recall other issues, but the half-assed nature of it made me think less of Jack in particular. I initially did not know it existed because it was part of WebDesk and Jack and Chuck kept me from seeing any of it except as an end user, not someone developing it. And my access as a user was tightly controlled so that I didn't see most of the apps included inside WebDesk. Let's call this mini software project app Status Tracker.

At a meeting between the Virginia and Pennsylvania programmers, Kaede asked us all to state what activities we spent our time on. He wanted a system to track the answers, so Chuck tried to do it on his own, maybe trying to score points. It backfired. Metrics Tracker was poorly conceived because he had little idea how to design systems to track information. Rather than breaking down the metrics into categories and getting more granular in various ways for reports to provide useful data, he only added the list of items (like coding, debugging) to a drop list. An analogy would be asking for an org chart and someone handing you a paper with a single box that said "staff" and had everyone's name in it in alphabetical order. No hierarchy existed. When Chuck launched it and I saw it, I laughed and wondered if it was a joke.

Then I saw my opportunity. The two systems, Status Tracker and Metrics Tracker, were not only unworkable, but they should have been part of the same system. Both tracked work against software development projects. That they were separate revealed a lack of planning or architectural thinking. I increasingly realized that Jack was a hack. Did I have more experience as a programmer, just not in .NET and SQL Server until he brought me up to speed? I had long since stopped feeling the least bit grateful for the opportunity he had once given me.

With all of this in mind, I walked into Kaede's office one day and told him what I thought of both systems, how I could fix and merge them, and that I wanted to take both projects from Chuck and redesign them. He agreed and asked me to look into them more and present a plan for doing it. I walked out feeling pumped up. This would give me some prominence, which was on my mind now that Kaede was continuing his efforts to get the PA and VA coders to know each other. He forced me and Chuck to the now-former HQ in rural PA twice that summer, and by now one or two of them had quit. So had our other PC tech in VA. The team that Kaede had liked so much had shrunk from five to three, and I had little to do with either Chuck or Billy, who had become buddies.

While this was happening, Kaede announced he had hired a "technology architect," Cory. My heart sank. So much for me leading the design of systems? How would this person interfere with my project? I wondered if the screw ups of Jack and Chuck had contributed to this, but USAIS was a two-bit operation when it came to software development, almost all of it for internal use, so I can't say it surprised me. Kaede didn't owe me an explanation, I didn't ask for one, and I knew I would learn on the job how this affected my future. Hoping for the best, I was not prepared for what was about to happen.

CHAPTER ELEVEN

The Punk

In September, Chuck asked me for my personal email address. This came as a surprise, given me being out of the clique. With Jack gone, I never went to lunch with the others anymore because I knew I wasn't welcome. They didn't ask me to either. There had to be some reason beyond actual friendship for Chuck asking, didn't there?

I asked, "Why? Sending me porn?"

He laughed. "No, I need it to test my HR system."

Kaede had him designing a website for potential new employees to submit their info to the HR department, as if Chuck hadn't screwed up enough apps. "Why don't you use your own?"

"I already did."

"What's wrong with a work email?"

"The system rejects those."

"What's going to happen when I give you my email address?"

"The app will send you a test email. I need you to forward it to me so I can make sure it's formatted right."

I knew from experience that it isn't easy to write code that generates a well-formatted email. There are placeholders for values like someone's name, and each time one of these appears, the string of text must be broken. To make it say "Hello John Doe. How are you?" the pseudocode would look like: "Hello " + @FirstName + @LastName + ". How are you?" But it gets more complicated with line and paragraph breaks, date formatting, and clickable email addresses. Getting it right is easier if you make the system send a test email to you and you see how it looks.

His request sounded harmless enough, so I gave him my Yahoo email address. Within minutes, he had created an account in his system using my info, so I got the email and forwarded it to him. Days later, I received an email from the HR Department, thanking me for my interest in joining the company and asking me to fill out some online form to complete my application. I sent it to Chuck, who had indicated I had an interest in some other profession than software development when creating the test data.

"Is this another automated email?" I asked from my cube, over the wall.

He laughed that I was getting this. "No."

"Is this system live? I thought you were still testing it."

"I was testing the live version."

Sighing, I said, "Great. Well, take my name out of there."

"I can't."

"Why not?"

"It doesn't have a delete function."

I rolled my eyes. He was a really shitty developer. "Go into the database and delete it."

"It's too complicated. It adds records into all sorts of tables."

I stifled a laugh. There is something known as referential integrity in databases, and smart programmers set it up. Using customers and orders as an example, you can't delete a customer until you delete all of their orders because if you did, the orders would all be "orphaned." Customers are the parents of orders, so you would kill the parents and have orders that don't belong to anyone. The orders don't reference customers anymore and we have compromised the integrity of the system. The orders had to be deleted first, then the customers. It was possible to program a delete operation that would delete all the records out of each affected table in the right order, but it can be a pain if records are in a lot of tables.

"Maybe if you weren't a hack, you could program the right delete function," I said.

Laughing, he said, "Fuck you, Randy."

"At least change the email address."

"Just tell them you're already an employee."

Knowing he wouldn't give me the login information to the database so I could do it myself, I ignored the email from HR, but then another came, so I wrote back and explained that I was already on staff and Chuck had used my email to test the system. I received no response. The emails kept coming, one every two or three days. Chuck continued refusing to alter the test account, and HR continued refusing to stop trying to recruit me. Maybe I should have just ignored them, but I wondered if the HR department would somehow mark me as a difficult or otherwise undesirable candidate and this might affect my *real* file at work. I got an attitude, asking things like, "How many times do I have to ask before you stop?" I knew the guy doing it was friends with Chuck's girlfriend and suspected they were doing it on purpose.

The day when I presented my plan for App Center to Kaede, Chuck sat in on the meeting. And so did Cory, our new Director of Software Development, on his first day. Jack told me Cory was 25 and only had a few years' experience (both lies—he was a year older than me). And most of the experience had been working with Kaede at a previous company. Similarly, Kaede also brought a woman and made her a Director of Information Security and Business Systems despite her having only two years of working in anything tech related, but she had no part in this story and was seldom seen. Both were given offices with windows next to Kaede's. I sensed any room for advancement had suddenly vanished.

When I presented my plan for App Center to Kaede, he said I needed to make it part of WebDesk, the app that neither Jack nor Chuck had ever let me work on. I only knew it as an end user. He also wanted an estimate for how long I thought it would take, but I hadn't considered that part and had little experience estimating that. It also wasn't wise given that I had never seen the WebDesk code and had no idea what was in there and what I might have to alter. As a user, it seemed simple enough, but most apps have areas that only some people can access and I didn't know what I didn't know. But Kaede insisted over my objections, and I finally said "two weeks." He accepted that.

Kaede agreed with my plan except for one important part—he didn't want to track what the programmers actually did. This defeated the point of it, which was tracking all phases of software development and how much time everyone spent on each task. Software is designed according to certain traditional phases, like gathering and documenting requirements, a design phase where screen ideas might be realized, then coding where the app is actually created, then a testing phase, and finally launch and maintenance. I didn't see the point of doing it without this, but Kaede was adamant. Fortunately, he had to leave the meeting early, and I turned to Cory.

"I agree with you," he said, sitting at the table. Something about his short height and small stature made him seem as young as Jack had said. He had blond hair, was clean shaven like everyone but me (I still had my mustache and goatee), and had a weak handshake. I couldn't read him but didn't particularly like him already. His demeanor lacked any warmth or friendliness.

"I don't see a point to the App Center without it," I said.

"Right. I want you to include it. I'll talk it over with Kaede and convince him. It can be much more useful than he might be thinking. Sometimes he's focused on other things and I think that might be the case here."

I felt pleased he had taken my side, because we were right. "Great. Thank you."

I started working on the system that day, after finally getting access to the WebDesk code, nearly a year after I began there. I had already done the requirements documentation and design work that I had shown Kaede. But now I found a problem, because the system was far bigger than I had known. It acted similar to an intranet, an internal company website with many systems in it. I had only been a user with access to one part of the app, but it had over a half dozen that were hidden to me when I logged in. My alterations would affect much of it and the scope had grown exponentially. I tried to figure out how long this might take. He was not pleased, but that paled compared to his reaction two weeks later when I showed some initial screens. I connected my computer to a projector, and Chuck and Cory attended the meeting.

Bringing up a screen, I said, "This is the all-important master list of applications the Virginia and Pennsylvania teams have developed, and which we still care about because they're still in use or will be. This is the central piece. Any time we're tracking metrics or status, we are doing so against items in this list."

"Wait a minute," said Kaede, leaning forward, "why do you have a duplicate list of apps?"

I cocked an eyebrow. "I don't. This is the only one."

"No, it's not," said Cory. "Chuck and I have been developing a similar app to register all web pages against."

"Since when?" I asked, frowning. They had been in all of my meetings about this, and my project had started on Cory's first day. If they started another app that duplicated what I was doing, by definition, it started after mine.

"Doesn't matter."

"Randy," Kaede started, "it's unacceptable for you to be duplicating their effort. It's bad enough that your estimate for this project was off, but now you're wasting time."

Chuck snickered, adding to my irritation.

"I'm not the one duplicating effort," I said.

"Yes, you are," said Cory.

"Oh really? On your very first day at this job, I presented this project to Kaede in front of you. It included a requirements document and designs of screens that included this one. You and Chuck both knew about it, and you are both in every meeting I've had about this. You have not invited me to any meeting for any of your projects, and this is the first I've heard about it. Even if you and Chuck dreamed up whatever you're doing after the meeting on your first day, it was still after I started this, and you're the one duplicating effort."

"Randy," started Kaede again, "it doesn't matter."

I looked him in the eye, rather coldly, I would imagine. "Well, it sure sounded like it mattered when you were blaming the situation on me a minute ago." I avoided pointing out that, now that I had proven this was Cory's and Chuck's fault, it supposedly didn't matter anymore. That really pissed me off.

He frowned. "The two of you will have to hash this out. I only want one list. Move on."

Not failing to notice Chuck grinning, I continued showing the other parts of the app that were in progress. The way development works, coders lay out the screen before writing the code that is triggered when a user interacts with it, so in some cases, the screens were visible but if I clicked on certain things, nothing happened because I hadn't written the code yet. But they could see how it should work, or if not, I explained it. When I got the metrics screen that tackled the items Cory and I had agreed should be included, Kaede irritably interrupted.

"I said I didn't want this to include tracking the details of what everyone is doing. Why is this in here?"

Aware of his unhappiness, I said, "After you left the meeting, Cory agreed with me about it being valuable and said I should include it."

"I did not," Cory stated, voice hard.

I blinked in surprise and turned with my mouth open. "What?"

"I think it should be included, but I certainly didn't tell you to do it when Kaede said not to."

My eyes narrowed. The little punk made me sound insubordinate when I had followed his direction. I knew what he was doing—bowing to Kaede on seeing the reaction. He was throwing me under the bus. "Chuck was there. He heard y–"

Chuck laughed. "I didn't hear shit."

I stiffened, then went cold, being no stranger to bullying and being ganged up on. I felt set up and was well aware that Chuck had been hanging out with Cory, mostly because Chuck was incompetent and needed Cory's help, just like with Jack before. He had a new person whose ass he needed to kiss. Other people were far better at playing these dishonest games than I was ever going to be. And I was sick of it.

Scowling at me, Kaede asked, "Is this part of the screen coded yet?"

Seeing his expression, which I returned, I changed my answer and lied. "Yes."

Kaede sighed. "Well, then you might as well leave it. But I don't want you showing any more initiative." He got up to leave.

I cocked an eyebrow, bothered by the reversal of opinion about me stepping up, which he had encouraged. "Should I delete the app? My initiative led to this project and was clearly a mistake we both regret."

He sighed and said over one shoulder as he disappeared, "Just finish it. And speed it up."

With Kaede gone, I glared at Chuck, who laughed and rose along with a smiling Cory. I wanted to punch both of them in the face. A new clique had formed, and I was once again outside of it. Being social increasingly seemed like the only way to get ahead, and screwing over someone before they screwed you over appeared to be the secret. Cory had established that if I ever complained to Kaede about him, it would just seem like retaliation and I wouldn't be taken seriously.

Within days, the little punk sat at my desk to go over App Center and its master list of applications. He brought his laptop to show his own master list, which was almost the only thing his app did, mine having other functions. The question now was who was going to change their work? My structure was more robust and advanced than his. I had one parent table with four children tables, and I had production data that needed to be migrated from the old, screwed up systems of Chuck and Jack into my system, with the code to do so written; Kaede had indicated he wanted this data migrated. Cory and Chuck had a parent table with a single child, and they were not migrating the data. I was finished with mine and they had hardly started. It seemed obvious that I won this contest before it started. Cory disagreed and went for cheap shots to get his way.

"We're just not going to migrate the data," he said, dismissing one of my strongest advantages. "Solves that problem."

It wasn't his place to make that unilateral decision and half a week of my work would vanish. "Kaede and Jack said they wanted that."

"I'll convince them otherwise. I made the decision."

God, he was an asshole. "I like how you have so little confidence in your opinion. I also have six fields you don't."

"I'll add them. And I don't agree with the order you have them there on screen."

I stifled a guffaw. "I can rearrange them in less than a minute. What order do you want them in?"

Not interested, he said, "It won't matter because we're not using any of this."

I could tell he had reached that conclusion before coming to my desk and didn't appreciate it. "You're not tracking nearly as much data as I am and your setup doesn't allow us to get detailed reports."

"They're not needed. No one has asked for reports."

I snorted. "So we're going to build a system to track metrics, but no one is ever going to look at the data? That makes a lot of sense."

"The reports haven't been defined, so there's no point worrying about what they want to see."

I looked at him in disbelief. "Any good developer plans ahead and creates a structured system so it has flexibility to report on whatever is needed. You practically have a flat file, not a relational database."

"Mine does what it's designed to do."

"Yeah, and mine can be used for the same purpose as yours, and is also does far more. If we go with yours, we lose functions. Mine is also finished and you only have the screens laid out, no code behind them. Obviously, mine should remain. If mine is gone, then I have to rewrite the rest of App Center to use yours and that's at least a week of work out the window."

Ignoring all of my good points as an easy out, he said, "Half of your App Center isn't happening, anyway."

"What are you talking about?"

He went on to say that he was taking over two parts of it that weren't done yet and absorbing them into his system, effectively stealing my design and ideas. Between this and my master app list, App Center would be gutted to two-fifths of its plan and with all the production data not included. The smirk he wore while announcing this made it worse. When I objected, he rubbed it in.

Cory said, "Well, I'm a director and you're not, so you have to do what I tell you to do."

"You're not my boss. Kaede is. And he wanted a decision based on merits, not something else." Like Cory's ego.

"I'm the technology architect and you don't get to make any decisions anymore."

That was a fucked up thing to say, not that it surprised me. He didn't seem able to understand technology architecture at all, or when another project was superior to his. I didn't appreciate the apparent confirmation that I was being slapped down. "Now you're just throwing your title around."

With a smirk and dismissive, backward wave of one hand, he said, "App Center is gone."

I flushed with anger at the contempt. This was no way to handle a coworker's project. App Center was conceived before this guy was working here, and we were supposed to discuss App Center's master list of apps, not the merits of the entire system, which he now unilaterally canceled with that backward wave. Besides solving problems Kaede had agreed with my solution for, I had wanted App Center to raise my profile. I didn't stick my neck out just to have

some new punk destroy it all. Cory had effectively disman-
tled both the app and my ambitions in one cold, insulting
conversation. And he wasn't done.

"How long will it take you to make the changes?" Cory
asked.

"I don't know. I would have to look at the code."

"You can do it right now."

I glared at him. "Yeah, I'm not doing it while you're
looking over my shoulder."

He smiled. "Afraid I won't like your code?"

"I couldn't care *less* what you think of my code."

"How long?"

"I just told you I need to look through it first."

"No, you're evading the answer."

"That *was* the answer."

"Give me a number."

I was still acutely aware of the scorn from Kaede when
he pressured me to give an estimate on App Center. I had
turned out to be wrong because integrating it with Web-
Desk, which I had never seen the inner workings of, was
far more involved than I had known. "You'll get a number
tomorrow. I already ran into a problem giving a number
without doing the research. I'm not doing it again."

He smiled. "That was a pretty big screw up."

Asshole. "Thanks for your assessment."

"I mean, how hard is it to know the code base and figure that out?"

I scowled. "I had never seen the code of WebDesk, or
of either of the two apps I am replacing because both Jack
and Chuck designed those."

"You should have gotten access and anticipated Kaede
asking."

I had zero interest in defending myself to the little shit,
but I couldn't help remarking, "Until the meeting where
Kaede approved the project and asked for an estimate, I

was not given permission to access either of them, so no. I'm not interested in you second-guessing what was going on before you even got here."

He rose and took his laptop, saying, "I expect an estimate by the end of today."

Then he left.

Barely able to contain my hatred, I began looking for another job, a decision aided by Kaede's announcement that he was hiring another director to oversee me, Chuck, and the other developers in PA; he seemed director happy, for there had been one before in Jack's boss, and there would now be four. While a new guy might have prevented me from working with Cory, I had to assume it might be another asshole. It also eliminated any possibility of advancement, which no longer came as a surprise. After the way Cory treated me, I had little doubt I had utterly fallen from grace, not that I'd had any. But it became increasingly clear over the next few weeks.

I completed what remained of App Center and walked away from it. Kaede gave me a series of short-term projects, asking me in front of Chuck and Cory for an estimate, and when I would give one, he would immediately turn to Cory and ask if it would really take that long, clearly showing no confidence in me in front of my coworkers. He was holding the App Center estimate mistake against me. Knowing his role and what he was being asked to do, Cory obliged each time, telling Kaede it should take me half as much time as I said, even though Cory had not seen my project and had no idea what he was talking about. When I couldn't make the unrealistic deadlines, Kaede made it clear he thought I was screwing around. My fury grew.

While this was happening, we learned that the PA developers were developing user controls. Any programming tool, like Microsoft ASP .NET, comes with controls like buttons that can be placed on screen. These have properties like the caption that allows you to decide what words are on the button, like "save" or "delete." But sometimes coders want to make their own controls, usually because they want additional properties or functions. To do this, we create a new one that is based on the built-in one. Not surprisingly, such a new control should be tested to ensure it works.

Well, none of the PA developers' user controls were ready, and yet Cory insisted over my objections that I use them on my projects. My screens would crash either on load or when I interacted with the unfinished control. As a result, I could not finish my projects. That the blame here lay entirely with Cory and whichever PA developer hadn't finished their user control should have been obvious. But Kaede blamed me for not getting my projects completed. Kaede and Cory repeatedly set me up to fail and I knew that an awful performance review and likely termination lay somewhere in my future.

Constant stress had me hating everyone, my thoughts black. I was having trouble sleeping and felt irritable throughout my life, not just at work. I had to get out of there and update my resume on the job boards every Sunday night because I had noticed that more recruiters contacted me each time I did so. Their search results for candidates were probably sorted by most recently updated, because that indicated who was actively looking rather than just fishing. With Monster.com, I could block my current employer, or any others, from seeing that my resume was active. I had little doubt that Chuck's girlfriend, or even the guy up in PA, would rat me out to management (again) if they learned I was looking. The fear of being caught and terminated heightened my anxiety.

I engaged in subterfuge to go on interviews. The simple approach was claiming I had a doctor's appointment and leaving early, but if I did several in a row, suspicion might rise. I could dress casually at that job but began wearing more button-up shirts and slacks, the latter part of a suit. I would leave my jacket and tie in the car on the back seat so it wouldn't be seen. Most interviews happened after work, with me changing once I reached the destination parking lot.

As usual, some recruiters contacted me about jobs that could be wrong for sometimes multiple reasons. They were too far away, including across the United States, when my profile said I would not relocate. The jobs were for technologies not on my resume and which held no interest. They were tools I formerly used (Access) and which I considered a step backward and a dead-end. The salary was too low. They couldn't hold my clearance. They were the wrong roles, like tester, technical writing, or administrator.

Even when a suitable position arose, the "technical interview" could be another issue. Sometimes this was included as part of the normal interview, while other times it was separate, coming before or after. It could be a computer test, verbal questions, handwritten coding, or even writing on a chalkboard while the tester watched. I could be told there was no test, an easy one, or a brutal one. They might tell me it focused on specific technologies, and sometimes those were ones not actually in use at the job or which they could see weren't on my resume!

The problem is that the recruiters were typically wrong. I might be told there's an easy verbal test that is on .NET when there's actually a brutally hard computer test that is on SQL Server and where no use of the internet is allowed to look things up, even though I would have that option if on the job. This last bit made the tests not a real-world scenario. In my career, every permutation of these combinations happened so that I never knew what was coming.

The person administering the test was always a programmer who had limited ideas on how to test a potential hire for their technical knowledge because that wasn't what they did for a living. What they thought was a good question varied greatly (I often disagreed, thinking the questions were stupid). In many cases, I was asked to verbally recite definitions of programming terms, as if I sat around doing that on the job. This was arguably the default testing scenario, the one most likely to happen regardless of what I had been told. As a result, I had an ever-growing file of programming terms that I re-memorized when job hunting just so I could give a quicker answer, instead of trying to remember a definition I hadn't looked at since the last time I'd been interviewing. I felt the whole thing was stupid and didn't see why references and years of experience weren't enough.

The tests were impossible to prepare for, inherently unfair, and often very difficult to pass as a direct result. And when I couldn't do well enough, a polite but dismissive assessment of my abilities awaited me, along with being rejected, of course. Along with awful managers, technical interviews were the bane of my career. I loathed all of it and my stress always rose considerably.

As my job search continued, one day Cory walked into my shared room with Chuck and Billy and up to my chair.

"Did someone pour water on my seat?" he asked. All of us had upholstered cloth seats on our chairs. Any water on one would be absorbed and invisible so that you would only realize the seat was drenched after you sat down and it soaked your butt. Any liquid on it might just roll off unless you took the time to press into the seat with your hand and ensure it became absorbed, though why anyone would want to do that remained a mystery.

I looked at him blankly. "Why would someone do that?"

He hesitated. "My seat was all wet."

"Maybe you peed yourself and forgot?"

Chuck and Billy laughed at Cory, and I wondered if I should have mocked people before. It was clearly the way to get ahead here. Cory went to talk to Chuck. Lifting my water bottle, I noted that, even though I had just filled it all the way up and had consumed none of it, it was still somehow only half full. I imagined Cory walking around with wet pants and underwear all day and smiled to myself. Petty? Yes. Enjoyable? Also yes.

In early October, my attempts to find another job landed me an interview with a company that had an excellent project with the FBI. My father had once contracted there as well, and I liked the idea of working somewhere he had. The salary and other negotiations were good. They were also located just blocks from my wife's job near Ballston, Virginia, far inside the Beltway. This raised concerns about the commute, but she said it wasn't bad and, if I got the job, we could commute together. I scheduled the interview.

Around 10 PM that night, I was studying for the inevitable tech exam and feeling agitated about it. It had now been a month since Chuck had used my personal account to test the HR System. I had received nearly two dozen emails from the same guy in HR at my current job, telling me to fill out my profile more or something similar. To every third or fourth one, I had responded and told him I was already an employee and asked him to stop it. I sometimes griped to Chuck, who always snickered, sometimes Billy, Cory, or both joining him in doing so. Were they egging on the guy doing it, as he worked with Chuck's girlfriend? I should have just ignored it once again, and often did, but in the moment's stress, I responded and wrote something like, "What's it going to take? Do I have to ask Billy to disable your computer so you can't send emails from it anymore?"

Two days later, I received an instant message from Kaede to see him in his office, so I went and found someone from security closing the door behind me. Kaede sat at a round table, doing his best to look stern but failing. Sudden suspicion that I was being fired soared and my adrenaline spiked. He handed me an unfolded piece of paper as I sat across from him.

"Did you send this email the other day?" he asked, as the security guy stood by, arms folded.

I looked at the printout, recognizing the email I had sent the HR guy. I shouldn't have made the remark about Billy disabling the guy's computer, of course, and felt embarrassed. But I was also angry, at myself, at Kaede blowing this out of proportion, and the asshole in HR, who was obviously getting my emails all along. And when he finally reacts to one, it is to show Kaede.

"Yes," I admitted.

"You're being fired, effective immediately, for violating company policies."

I flushed on hearing it said aloud, a torrent of pent-up frustration, disdain, and humiliation at their hands making me hot. But what caught my attention was the excuse. "Which policies are those?"

"Creating a hostile work environment and misuse of company systems."

I snorted, giving free rein to my reactions. There was nothing left to lose. "Oh, *I'm* creating a hostile work environment? That's a good one. What about all the crap from you, Jack, Cory, and Chuck towards me?"

Kaede added as if to explain the difference, "He filed a complaint with HR."

"*He* filed a complaint? Well, it sounds like you're telling me I should have filed a complaint against him and the rest of you. Is that the secret to getting away with harassment? No one writes you up in HR?"

"You also threatened the security of the company network."

"Oh, get real." I scowled at the exaggeration.

"You said you would make Billy screw up his computer."

My mouth fell open in disbelief. "First of all, that's a computer, not a network, genius. Some Chief Technology Officer *you* are. And second, I have no authority over Billy, who wouldn't do it even if I told him, which, by the way, I didn't. You know just as well as everyone involved in this that I was just frustrated with this guy, and with good reason."

"Look, I'm not interested in your opinion. You're not the kind of person I want working in my IT department."

I glared at him. "What did you just say to me? You have no business making comments about what sort of person you think I am. Especially *you*, after the way you treat people."

He shoved an envelope at me. "Here's your termination letter. Your computer has already been taken care of." He pointed at the security guy. "He'll escort you to clean out your desk and out of the building to the parking garage to get your badge. There are boxes at your desk."

If someone already seized my computer, that meant Billy knew before I did that I was being fired, like probably several people. I had just come from my desk, of course, meaning someone was placing boxes there while swiping my computer, making this a kind of ambush. I had heard of this sort of thing, when hostility was expected from the fired person, but they were taking all of this too far, not that I really cared anymore, though having "fired" as the reason a job ended wasn't great.

I noticed I was not being asked for my side of this. Sure, my email hadn't been smart, but they could have cut me some slack for me being at home, in a personal account, at 10 PM. Not being in a professional environment can influence whether you act professionally. This isn't an excuse, but reasonableness. But if I had learned anything about the corporate world by now, it's that reasonableness seldom shows up.

I felt certain that they were violating company policies as well. Once home, I looked it up in the employee handbook and saw that if I had been an employee for a year, they would not have been able to fire me, but enact some discipline and put me on probation. I had been there thirteen months, but half of it as a contractor, a technicality. They could have kept me onboard anyway, but chose not to. They had withheld an employment offer from the summer until January, screwing with me from the start and ultimately allowing this to take place.

This didn't feel like the real reason I was being let go. Kaede had held a grudge about that inaccurate App Center estimate. This might have passed were it not for Cory, who had destroyed the job so utterly that within weeks of his arrival, I was serious about quitting. I had never fit in since the moment Jack hired Chuck, his protégé in mockery, an unprofessional trait that had no place in the corporate world. Oddly, me not doing it had meant that I had no place in *that* corporate world. It rankled that having done Chuck a favor with that email address had ultimately come back to haunt me. I was potentially days from resigning after a year of working there but was now fired, something I would have to explain for years, whether to employers or during security clearance investigations. I was furious.

With an interview scheduled, the pressure to get that job rose. The potential new job had already asked my employment status and why I was leaving USAIS. I would not give them an update unless asked, of course. But I needed a reference and Jack was the only suitable manager one. I disliked him a little less now that I didn't work with him anymore, so I swallowed my pride and called him, telling him what happened. He hadn't heard yet, but I told him the truth. He laughed (of course) about the email I had sent, saying, "Oh shit." That made me flush with new humiliation; I am certain everyone thought my termination was funny and have been telling the story to this day. Only a need kept me from hanging up on Jack. He agreed to be a reference. While I didn't trust him and thought he was obnoxious, I still believed he wouldn't go so far as to destroy my opportunity. He wasn't *that* big of a jerk.

The day after being fired, I went to the interview at Katan Corp and did well enough to get a verbal offer on my way out the door, a written one coming in the next 48 hours. They asked no technical questions. The salary was $5,000 higher. I laughed about my timing and the money, feeling I had just dodged a bullet with a remarkable job switch. Within days, I spoke with Jack again and he confirmed talking with them and that my employment status did not come up. I never saw him or talked with him again and fell out of touch on purpose within a year, mostly because of his never-ending, condescending amusement. I don't need that in my life. He had never respected me, but then he respected no one.

While writing this memoir in 2021, I looked up USAIS and my former coworkers on LinkedIn. USAIS was the number one provider of background checks for the United States. The new CEO had come in 2006, the year I left, and from 2008 to 2012, USAIS management apparently deliberately circumvented requirements in their investigations.

They cleared a man who went on to murder a dozen people in a military facility. They also re-investigated the infamous Edward Snowden and cleared him. Snowden went on to release classified secrets. The U.S. Department of Justice revealed that they had launched a criminal investigation against the company, with fraud charges filed against them. To make matters worse, in 2014, a successful state-sponsored cyber-attack on the company led the Office of Personnel Management (OPM) to not renew any USAIS government contracts, effectively destroying the company. They settled the legal cases out of court. By early 2015, USAIS filed bankruptcy and ceased to exist.

Karma is sweet.

Jack still lives in rural PA, a place he said he hated ("Everyone has 80s hair!"), as a director of IT somewhere. Chuck got the promotions that almost certainly should have gone to me instead, soon becoming a software development manager and then director, a position he has maintained at various employers since; he also married the girlfriend who got him that job. Cory became VP of Technology at USAIS and is now the Chief Information Officer (CIO) somewhere. Kaede has been CTO and VP of Technology at various companies =. Based on their LinkedIn profiles, the pattern of Kaede handing people titles and jobs at another company when he moved there remained, some of those people like Cory following him around. The message was obvious—kissing ass and being an incompetent jerk will get you much farther than doing a good job, being fair-minded, and yet being disliked (for whatever reason). I'd be lying if I didn't say it bothered me. I couldn't be a manager if being an asshole to people was what it took.

A pattern existed—every time I was a contractor, my manager treated me with respect, but if I was an employee, mostly contempt came my way. Jack had made this especially easy to see with his blatant changes on the first day I switched over. The idea had been planted—maybe I should just remain a contractor for good. If my next job didn't pan out, I vowed to do this.

Would being certified gain me more respect or worth-while roles on projects? I wasn't sure but remembered the fiasco of trying to get my Microsoft Access certification at the start of my career. I had sworn off the idea, but I began looking into it again. Test preparation materials appeared to be better six years later. Passing one exam would make me a Microsoft Certified Professional or MCP, but that had limited value compared to passing two more and earning an MCAD (Application Developer). But what I really wanted was MCSD (Solution Developer) after five exams. This would raise my salary by five figures and hopefully get me more power over my fortunes in my career as a technical lead on projects. I soon bought a set of books and began studying.

When Katan Corp had asked for a start date, I told them two weeks later, not explicitly saying I had to give two weeks' notice but implying it. They made it three weeks, my vacation payout from USAIS paying for one of them. I needed some time off anyway, if for no other rea-son than to not walk into my new job with a chip on my shoulder from the last one. Timing wise, I lost one job at the start of October and started the new one by the end, so on my resume it showed no gap of employment because I only used months and years, as per industry standard. No one ever knew USAIS had fired me except my wife and the next FBI agent interviewing me for a clearance; I told him the truth and that I had made a mistake, and my clearance extension was granted because honesty matters and no one is perfect, so seeming like you learned something can get you off the hook. I didn't approach the unemployment office because I knew that being fired meant being denied benefits for five weeks, by which time it would be a moot point.

With the free time, I did errands around the house and audition a new bassist; the one from my live instrumental band had been copping bigger attitudes while not seeming to realize I was the artist whose name went on the bill and he couldn't push me around. I was also the front man, the manager, the songwriter, and the record label. We were not equals. Performing had been a disappointment because we were given awful spots, like 11:30 PM on a Sunday night. I don't know what I had been thinking, trying to do an instrumental metal band live, but pretty much all available advice for musicians with a CD was to perform to promote. Sometimes the advice just doesn't apply to your genre. This situation was another that caused me tension that came and went depending on circumstances.

My first day at Katan Corp finally began with my wife and I commuting together in my maroon Acura TL, the nicer of the two cars we owned. After going down I-270 in Maryland and over the American Legion bridge bottleneck, the ride down the George Washington Parkway in Virginia was usually pleasant; I had last done this while working at the Pentagon, though that was considerably farther. We reached her job first with her driving, because she would just go past hers and drop me off at mine a block away and go back to park in her building's garage (mine didn't have one).

Ballston was a small city sandwiched between other small cities so that, like much of the land within the capital beltway, it all seemed like one endless metropolis. Were it not for signs that read "Welcome to Ballston" or any other city, you couldn't actually tell when you left one for another. This particular area had a mall within walking distance and a multitude of high rises, most topping out around a dozen stories. Many such buildings had restaurants and shops on the first floor. I quite liked the area. Not far away were some homes of my wife's best friends, including the one I had finally made it to on 9/11.

Feeling much recovered from the evils of USAIS and hoping for the best, I arrived at the offices of Katan Corp halfway up a high rise, where the trouble had already started.

CHAPTER TWELVE

Certifiable

Before vacation, I had charged the GPS tracker, which normally lasted a week, but this time it had died.

"The FBI put the project on hold," said Dean, my new manager, who had interviewed me.

He had packed a few extra pounds on his stocky midsection and stood a half foot shorter than me, short blond hair sticking up from a round face. While both of us had a mustache and goatee, his was blond to my black one, even though I had dirty blond hair. I had liked Dean at my interview and continued to do so now that I had started. He was a couple years younger and had two fewer years' experience programming than me, and he seemed to appropriately see us as equals aside from the management role he had.

Dean alternated between a somewhat serious "I'm your manager and must look authoritative" demeanor and a sudden grin of what I took to be his real personality—being down to earth and finding many things funny, just not in a mocking sort of way like Jack. It was as if he knew better than to behave unprofessionally and he upheld the decorum of managers. While he did a great job of pretending this was who he was, I could make him stop it by making him laugh. I sometimes got the impression that he envied me because I could say things that, as a manager, he would not let himself say. The result was that he knew I "got it" about certain things and we sort of bonded over the mutual understanding of a situation between us and someone else.

I had joined a group of four guys, including him, who sat one floor down from the rest of the company in mostly empty space that was being renovated, like the main offices we would soon join. Of the other three, two of them were programmers. One of these was a tall, laid back Indian named Ishaan. The other was a former Navy man like Dean, who had brought him over from their last job. He had also brought the non-programmer, a retired Marine named Mack who worked as a project manager, almost always at the Marine Corps base in Quantico. Mack rode a Harley and looked the part with his leather chaps, stubble beard, cigar smoking, and "I'm a badass Marine and you're not" demeanor. Many Harley riders look down their noses at those who, like me, ride a sport bike, as if we're even more pathetic than those who don't ride a motorcycle at all. Mack did it with humor, as if he didn't really mean the contempt.

I came to think of the five of us as a unit, four of us bound by being technical, three bound by having worked together before, and all of us bound by being alone on our floor. I liked the group and felt welcomed, though I did notice that Dean and Mack seemed particularly close and excluded the rest of us from their relationship.

After a couple months, Katan Corp moved us upstairs to join maybe fifty staff. I don't recall the company's actual size, but I believe they were over one hundred, with many offsite all week at clients and not having a seat at HQ. The result was that I could see someone in the office and think they were new when they had been working there longer than me. But four of us received a pretty good set of cubes (by the windows) outside Dean's new office.

Companies always said I wasn't being hired for a specific project, but this was a lie. They always had a need for me on one, in this case for the FBI. But they always tried to reassure me that there was plenty of work after this. I increasingly grew suspicious of this claim. The way government contracting works, companies can win a contract for five years of work with the FBI, for example, but it comes as one year plus four "option years." This means the FBI has the option of booting the company for unacceptable performance at each anniversary. If the employer doesn't have suitable work for me, they might lay me off or give me unsuitable work. I found myself in that position on my first day with Katan Corp.

From late October when I started, through January, I had no "real" work to do and did whatever minor projects Dean or his manager, a VP, could find for me. One day, the VP called me into her office and I half expected to be fired, but she only wanted to tell me that the TSA clearance they'd had me do paperwork for had been granted and I could work on some documentation for a system for TSA if I wasn't busy. I wasn't, having spent my time studying for certification exams and once covering for a coworker on vacation. I was mostly bored, and while everyone was friendly, I felt frustrated with the lack of meaningful work, but was otherwise in good spirits. How long could I take it before wanting to leave?

By now I was learning that many federal agencies want staff to have a clearance granted by that agency. My DOD clearance worked for all branches of the military, but TSA wanted me to get one through them. This would happen at other times in my career so that I sometimes had multiple active clearances. The bad part was redoing the paperwork, but clearances came through pretty quick if I already had one, like someone was rubberstamping the new one.

That January 2006, the Vice President of Technology quit, and in doing so, he put Katan Corp at risk of losing its status as a Microsoft Certified Partner. The thing about both these certifications and others is that the federal government sometimes stipulates that companies can only bid on a contract if one of two conditions is met: there is an employee with a specific certification at the time the company submits a proposal, or the corporation has enough certified professionals that a place like Microsoft has allowed the company to become, in the case of Microsoft, a Certified Partner. This comes with some benefits, like esteem, the use of a specific logo on websites, etc., and deals on software. Microsoft maintains a verifiable list of "certified partners" so that the government can check that a company isn't lying. With the VP quitting, his certifications would no longer be associated with Katan Corp by the time the annual review happened... in February.

On the verge of losing its Microsoft Certified Partner status, the company was scrambling. They needed two people to have passed at least three exams for one certification or another. Dean was the other guy who had already done so. No one else had passed even one. And that's when Leo entered the picture. A relatively new PC technician, he knew about "brain dumps" and, in three weeks, used them to pass three exams.

The way the exams worked at the time, each test had about 45 questions on it. Those 45 were taken from a larger pool of questions, usually between 125-175. Out of that many, only 45 were on the computerized exam, selected at random. A brain dump was the entire pool of questions and their answers, usually in PDF form. Many websites listed the brain dumps by the exam number and, for free, we could download one, memorize the answers, and pass an exam.

The only catch was that the answers were also randomized. It wasn't enough to know that the answer to question one was B. For starters, it would not be question 1 on the exam, as it could not appear at all or be anywhere from 1 to 45. But even if I memorized the question, the answer might be B on the brain dump, but randomized to be A, C, or D on the exam. I had to memorize the content of the answer (and the question). The case could be made that this meant I honestly knew all the answers, not via understanding per se, but via rote memorization of which was correct, and this could be considered a valid way of learning. But of course, it was still cheating, and none of us believed Leo, that any of this actually worked.

Until he sauntered across the street at lunch time to a testing center that happened to be there, passed his third test, and came back with the printout showing his score of over 90%, when 70% was passing. Even then, we still didn't quite believe that was how he'd done it, but then Ishaan got a brain dump and repeated the feat days later. Then the other programmer did it. Feeling left out, I did the same, memorizing 187 questions and answers on the brain dump, then scoring 981 out of 1000 on the 43 exam questions in 15 minutes. Now at least four of us were Microsoft Certified Professionals, meaning we had passed at least one exam. Katan Corp covered the $150 exam course if we passed.

It was now 2006 and, if I thought about it, I still simmered about trying to pass that Microsoft Access certification back in 1999. I had been a good boy then. I listened and believed what Microsoft said about preparing for the test. I studied my ass off. And then had my ass handed to me, at a cost of over $125, when the materials they recommended I study did not prepare me for the exam. I was still mad. And I had just found a more reliable way to pass the tests and raise my salary for many years. I had been studying for a test for months and found a way to pass one within a week. I still intended to study the materials, but when it came to the test, I had solved a problem.

And now I had my first certification. And I wasn't done. The programming certification from Microsoft was called MCSD (Microsoft Certified Solutions Developer). Earning it meant passing five exams. Within days, I had memorized 107 questions for my second test and passed the 44 exam questions. To quote my diary about this:

I was done with the second exam, the SQL Server one, in nine minutes. When I say nine minutes, I mean that was the interval in between me signing in and signing out. During that time, I took off my coat, was escorted into the room, the guy logged into the computer, I answered the questions, reviewed them, submitted the exam, walked back to the other room, told him I was done, got my coat, and then signed out. It probably took me three minutes to take the test itself. I only got a 931 that time, but you need 700 to pass.

Within another week, I had passed the third exam to earn the Microsoft Certified Application Developer (MCAD) certification on the way to the MCSD.

I had long thought the whole thing with certifications was bullshit. In theory, someone who legitimately passes exams is better at their job than someone who hasn't even tried, but this is not true. Plenty of highly skilled technical people couldn't care less about them and don't bother, especially given that the certifications come with expiration dates. The work to pass just one exam can be significant, and many certifications require four or more exams. This can be a massive amount of time out of a personal life, and they won't necessarily make you better at your job. Or not for long. Technology keeps changing, which is one reason the damn certifications expire. Want to do it all over again? Neither do I.

Microsoft, and similar companies, have done a good marketing job convincing companies, and governments, of the merits of certified staff. And the government buys into it, sometimes stipulating the requirement that companies must have certified staff to compete for a contract. And so corporations try to hire and retain staff just so they can bid on the contracts, if for no other reason. I can only speculate that Microsoft couldn't care less that brain dump sites existed at least back then, because they were all over the place, and Microsoft *had* to know about them and did not appear to be trying to get them taken down.

Did they care? Why would they? Governments still stipulated the requirements. Corporations still sought certified staff. And technical people still paid for the exams and testing materials. And all of this played into Microsoft's hands—raising the clout of Microsoft technologies in the corporate and government contracting worlds, and increasing their market share. Imagine all those Microsoft technologies infusing ever more corporations.

Not stopping the brain dumps is the same rationale behind half-hearted attempts to stop pirating—people get used to using the stolen software and eventually become paying customers, or increase the market share of users at the very least. It's better for Microsoft for people to become lifelong users of stolen Microsoft software than a lifetime user of a competitor's. I believe Microsoft has played the "long game" for decades with all of it. For the certifications, who cares how they are earned, as long as they are earned and the game is played? That's my theory, anyway.

I was already studying for my fourth exam when Dean walked up to my cube on a Wednesday morning.

"Hey man," he started, "you busy?"

I smirked at him. "For you? Always. What's up?"

He grinned. "Do you think you could pass two exams by next Tuesday? It's for a different certification."

"Not the MCSD?"

"Yeah, it's MCDBA, database administrator."

"It's only two tests?" I didn't think any of them were that short. The Microsoft Certified Professional (MCP) one given after passing one test wasn't a "real" certification so much as a sign you had passed at least *something* so far.

"No, it's four, but you already passed two of them. So have I. Same two. They count toward either MCSD or MCDBA. But I don't have time to do this by then. You're the only other one who could."

I wasn't sure if that was just the truth or a little flattery. "I'm curious why this is coming up."

"We're trying to bid on a contract with the TSA and we need a staff member with an MCDBA certification, or we can't even submit a proposal. And you already have their clearance, too. This is a big deal if you can do it. There would probably be a big bonus in it for you, especially if we end up winning the contract."

I had seldom been shown any appreciation at a job. Quite the contrary. But Katan Corp seemed different, and I liked Dean, trusting him. He was a good manager and a good guy. Before now, I had memorized about 30 questions a day for the other tests, giving myself a week to learn them all. Succeeding at doing two in a week would depend on how many questions were on the two tests, and if brain dumps for them were even available. I asked him to give me a few minutes to check, so he nodded and came back five minutes later. I purposely adopted an unfazed demeanor because that was my sense of humor when delivering info that would faze any rational person.

"How's it look?" he asked.

"Well," I drawled, leaning back in my chair, "one test isn't too bad. Only 140 questions."

"And the other one?"

I paused for effect. "Three hundred and twenty-four."

A look of mild shock appeared in his eyes before he grinned with his lips tightly closed, as if refusing to admit it was insane and hilariously bad. Something about his expression suggested he thought the answer might actually be yes as he asked, "Can you do it?" I started to think, and he added, "Whatever you need. You can have my office."

For some reason, that idea made me feel guilty and self-conscious. "I don't want to put you out. How about that empty one next to you?"

"Yeah, we can do that. I guess you could do the small test first, get it over to concentrate on the bigger one."

Shaking my head, I said, "I might agree, but I think if I can't do the big one, there's no point."

"Whatever you want." He hesitated. "Are you sure? If you say yes, they'll work on this proposal all week and at night, and through the weekend to get ready, but it all depends on you. Not to pressure you."

"No, it's okay. I get it. I can do it." I had been looking away from him, thinking about how to pull it off while we were talking, but now I looked him in the eye. "I can do it."

"Great."

He walked away, and Ishaan and the other programmer, who had overheard this talk, called me crazy. To my surprise, neither had taken a second exam. Over the next hour, Dean and I worked to clear my schedule of as many tasks as possible, and the company owners, who were a married couple, stopped by to wish me luck and thank me for trying. Before long, many staff knew about it, including multiple managers, because other people had to be given some of my work. In a show of respect, everyone mostly left me alone and kept quiet around me. Quoting my diary:

My method was to memorize 25 questions, and then review all of them. Then I'd move onto the next block of 25. On Wednesday, I learned 75 at work, reviewed them, and learned another 50 at home and reviewed them. Thursday morning, I reviewed those 125 and learned another 50. I was on a roll, and it's a good thing because one of the proposal people came by and said that I needed to help her massage my résumé for the proposal. They wanted to make it look more like a database administrator's résumé, which meant not lying but pointing out different things in my history than I normally do on a résumé, which means I had to do it according to some flimsy guidelines they gave me. That took a long time, and I had to go to TSA for the rest of the afternoon, which also didn't help. Dean was unable to get me out of that, though he tried. This meant I had only studied until about 10 AM that day instead of getting most of the day like I really needed. I was not pleased.

Thursday night, I learned another 75 and reviewed all 250 at the end of the night. I was really starting to burn out by that point. Dean let me work from home on Friday, which was a good idea. I finished learning everything, but it wasn't that simple. I should mention that there are a lot of pictures that are supposed to be in the exam and none of them were in the brain dump! This means no visual references at all. Worse, 37 of the questions had no answer because the answer was also a missing image. I had to read the questions and the explanation of which was the right answer and figure it out. That was one of the last things I did. I just had to hope that none of those questions were on the exam. While I was doing my reviews, if I missed something, I would mark it and later go through all the missed ones to drill them.

So Saturday I get to the exam in Silver Spring and start taking it. The first question was one I'd never seen and had a simulation, meaning you're supposed to click a button that *will bring up something simulating the actual environment of the subject. In this case, the exam was called Managing and Maintaining Microsoft Windows Server 2003. Well, the simulation would not even launch. This was a problem because you can't even choose an answer without the simulation, so you have no choice but to not answer the question.*

My strategy for passing the exam was simple.

First, I would skip all questions that have the simulation because I knew I hadn't seen them. I just marked them for review and I would return to them later. When I did this, that's when I discovered that all four of the questions for the simulation were not working. I went to get the administrator of the exam, and after 10 minutes of screwing around and calling someone for help, he was unable to do anything. He just said that if I failed the exam, they'd let me retake it for free. While that was nice, it was still obnoxious. This meant I had no choice but to fail four questions right off the start! I knew this meant I could only miss at most six questions and I had marked another seven of them as me not being sure of the answer. I spent a lot of time reviewing everything really carefully before finishing the exam.

I was so relieved when I saw I had passed, and then amazed when I saw the score was 976 out of 1000. That meant I had only missed one question, and I'm not sure how that score is possible considering I automatically missed four questions by not answering them.

I sent Dean a text telling him I passed (he was waiting for it) and received something like "Awesome dude!" I took the rest of Saturday off for a much-needed mental break. Then, on Sunday and Monday, I more easily memorized the other exam questions in between trying not to get caught up in praise from amazed coworkers and the owners. On Tuesday, I passed the test by lunch, bringing back the printout as proof. The deadline to submit the proposal was COB, and we made it. Both in person and in writing, the CEO and her husband Dave (the company President), and Dean's boss (a VP) all congratulated me. They gave me a $500 bonus, which I accepted but thought should have been more. It didn't even cover the extra hours I put in.

Given that I am Learning Disabled and have Inattentive ADHD, the feat was especially cool, but no one at work knew this about me. I am capable of wicked concentration when motivated, and I take nothing to help because I didn't know about the ADHD until my late twenties, and by then I had learned to control it by staying busy.

My learning disability is quite specific and boils down to an inability to remember sequential information that is verbally given to me. I had gone around that since being diagnosed in 7th grade, mostly by writing down everything in school as I heard it. But it didn't apply to the brain dumps. My confidence had been abysmal in grade school, but had rebounded once diagnosed and given coping strategies. Passing those tests the way I did was right up there with acquiring four years of classical guitar skill in only two years to earn my Bachelors of Music in classical guitar, Magna cum Laude. And I had gone through personal hell during that, but that's another story found in *A Blast of Light*.

Over the next two weeks after those exams, I memorized the other two brain dumps and passed the remaining tests to complete my MCSD certification. And then I learned that Katan Corp won the contract with TSA, the one my MCDBA certification allowed us to bid on. Normally they aren't awarded that fast, but we got it and they cited my cert as a major reason. Unfortunately, Katan Corp was assigning me to the project. That's when I learned it was for a Microsoft Access database, a major technological step backward. I wanted no part of this and saw it as akin to punishment. It also validated my attitude about certifi-cations—a software *developer* and a database administrator are not the same thing, and the "DBA" in MCDBA means database administrator. They did not need someone with an MCDBA for a lightweight database system, and all Ac-cess databases are light. Whoever added that requirement to the contract didn't know what they were talking about. Then again, they weren't getting a *real* MCDBA, but some-one who cheated on the exams.

It had now been five months, and I hadn't launched .NET or SQL Server to work with them unless backfilling someone on vacation. I was not happy. With my certifica-tions, I could easily get a much higher paying job. The FBI project was still on hold, with Dean saying it would finally start that summer, but it was too long to wait, and his boss had spent my entire time there trying to make me work at TSA HQ in Pentagon City, overlooking the Pentagon. This was an unacceptably long commute, and I decided I'd had enough and wanted to leave.

But then I learned more about the TSA project from Tess, the project manager for this at the National Screening Force (NSF) at TSA. The existing system was indeed an Access database, but rather than being a mess I had to fix, it was just too simple and slow for TSA's needs. Better yet, TSA wanted me to assess it and their network bottlenecks, then provide a proposal for a .NET and SQL Server-based system to replace the app. My eyes lit up. This was what I did for a living! Or tried to when my employer wasn't side-tracking me. I warmed up to the project.

Tess was five years younger than me and had almost as many years of project management as I did programming. She stood average height and was a brunette with straight hair past her shoulders in a long bob. With her hair done, tasteful makeup, nails polished but discreet, and with a modest amount of understated jewelry, she always presented herself well. She typically wore a tan or dark business suit with a jacket; I never saw her without one. Tess looked every bit the eventual executive. Her demeanor was friendly, sincere, and pleasant. I also found her to be smart, astute, and reasonable, all qualities often lacking in those I worked with. I liked her immediately and that only improved in time.

"So I wanted to say from the start," she began, as we sat in a meeting room to discuss the project, "that I know I'm technically your manager while you're on this project, but I see us as equals."

"Thanks." Her statement surprised me, not because it wasn't true, but just that she admitted it. Dean's boss had already told me that TSA considered me the more senior of us.

"We're like two halves of the same coin here. I know that between us, we can get this project moving. Everyone else on this is also so green that I'm actually really glad someone with your experience is joining me."

I smiled in commiseration, wanting to help her. "What are we dealing with?"

"About a dozen people. We're thinking of hiring three of them from the previous company that lost the contract to us. I need to talk with them and see how good a fit they are. I know everyone down there is pretty unhappy, so they are excited to see us start. That's a good thing!"

I nodded. "I imagine they want us to hit the ground running with improvements. What's the story on a handoff from the other company?"

"We're getting one. Or you are, anyway. The previous Access database guy is supposed to meet with you for the first day to show you how he does everything."

"That'll help."

"Yeah. I also wanted to say I will not be there much in the first month. I have to close out my involvement with the other TSA project and turn it over to someone else."

I knew what she meant because I had helped that project a few times, mostly when the current programmer there went on vacation and I backed her up. That mostly involved babysitting the app and making sure I was visible as support in case something went wrong, but nothing had.

"So I have real power for a month? Is what you're saying?" I joked.

She laughed. "Well, let's not get ahead of ourselves. I'll be there for the first couple days because I already met the client. This is in a different building from the other TSA project. I'll make sure you have everything you need and meet the important people. If you need anything over the next month, please don't hesitate to reach out to me or back here to Katan Corp. But I'm sure you'll be fine."

And I was. The staff knew their jobs. They operated the NSF office under the direction of government people.

TSA had emergency and seasonal airport screeners who needed to request or be assigned to airports on an as-needed basis. This was what the NSF system tracked, with the staff taking calls and emails from screeners about their preferences, meeting with TSA managers to determine what screeners were assigned based on various criteria, and then scheduling them. There was also an offsite travel agent who made all arrangements (planes, cars, hotels) for the screeners, whose information she needed, the itinerary then returned to the NSF staff, who had to forward it to the screeners. The process was cumbersome.

As a result, none of this worked very well partly because that NSF database wasn't well designed and produced inaccurate reports, none of which were automated. This meant my predecessor, and now me, had to manually produce reports every week; as a skilled programmer, I was having none of that and would set about fixing and automating this stuff, then giving staff a button they could press to access every report whenever they wanted.

My first day was spent learning how it worked from the guy who designed it and who would leave because his employer (and him) had performed so poorly that TSA had put out the contract for "recompete," and Katan Corp bid on it and won because of my certifications. I was replacing him, but he was cool about it partly because TSA would notice if he and his employer didn't cooperate with a smooth transition, and TSA might never grant them another contract. With any luck, his employer had other projects for him.

I didn't even mind the commute because Katan Corp said the location wasn't my normal one and therefore time to travel there from our building counted as work time. This meant no change to my schedule. I sometimes dropped in at Katan on the way to TSA because my wife still dropped me off at Katan, which was right next to the metro. I even had a window cube at TSA; being senior staff has its perks. Katan paid for the metro, though Dean's boss killed that months into it. Overall, it was a good deal, and I came to love the project.

Tess and I made a great team and hit it off partly because we were both senior and rolled our eyes at each other about stupid things the junior people did. At times, she would pull me into a room and close the door so she could vent about something, knowing I would "get it" about her exasperation. We would laugh, she would thank me for indulging her, and we'd go about our business. She often asked my opinion on even non-technical stuff because the project was the two of us and she had no other sounding board. Everyone else answered to her. Well, I technically did, too, but I saw why she didn't want to look at it that way—she would be on her own, though I figured she could handle it.

An example of this teamwork about junior staff came after I was helping one of the very young women with a problem at her computer. She sat on the desk behind me and put her feet up at her butt, soles down, knees under her chin. This is not a professional position to take and was made worse by her thin skirt sliding down from her sharply bent knees to her waist, exposing her panties at the crotch to any passerby. If she had been wearing a Maxi pad, I would have been able to tell. That we were facing a hallway and the cube walls were short and easily seen over exacerbated the inappropriateness. I saw her doing it from the corner of my eye.

"Put your feet down, please," I said.

"Why?"

"Because that's not appropriate."

"Why?"

Did I really have to explain? I reluctantly turned to her, averted my eyes, and whispered, "Because I can see your panties and so can anyone else." As if to prove the point, a man walked by and ogled her. She didn't seem to mind.

"It's just underwear."

Seriously? I hardened my tone. "Put your feet down, now."

She sighed and did it as I continued working on her computer. But a minute later, she put them back. This exchange happened repeatedly and when I was done, I went straight for Tess and asked to talk with her by the elevators, telling her what the girl was doing. She rolled her eyes, stifled a smile, and looked suitably disbelieving.

"*Thank* you," she said. "I'll go talk to her."

I grinned. "I knew you would."

We had about a dozen NSF staff, three of whom we hired as Katan Corp employees from the previous contracting company. Most of them were in their early to mid-twenties and a little green, meaning they did or said unprofessional or unwise things that the client noticed. The client had a "good cop, bad cop" pair of guys, the stern one, Diego, being the other's boss and the one whose attention we did not want because that was seldom positive. Diego was mostly Tess's problem, and she managed him well. The other guy was great, and I probably dealt with him the most; we hit it off so much that he later became a reference for me.

Most of my work on NSF took place between April and June. To some extent, we had a low approval bar to get over after the last company got themselves booted, and Tess and I quickly impressed the client with our handling of matters. I fixed all the problems with the database and automated reports to where I could get myself increasingly removed from meetings. My presence had been needed so I could understand and then manually create a report, but after several iterations, I realized they always wanted the same ones, so I automated them and no longer needed to be there.

Tess liked to tell me I was the most popular person over there for having made everyone's job easier. It showed, too, as people gave me genuinely heartfelt greetings, and even the "bad cop" client Diego sometimes dropped by to shake my hand. Being respected (and treated fairly) was a welcome change and long overdue.

When I started, Dean was a .NET developer like me, except that he managed me and two others. They then promoted him to Director. When the VP of Technology resigned in January, Dean became "acting" VP and then assumed the role for real. Within months, the CTO resigned, and Dean became acting CTO before officially getting the role. It was a stunning streak of promotions based largely on being in the right place at the right time.

I was a little jealous. I was two years older and had two years more experience. He wasn't qualified to be either VP or CTO any more than the rest of us. He admitted more than once to being in over his head, being overworked, and having to deal with many things he didn't want to do. It could have been any of us, but at the start of that promotion run, he had been the only IT manager. While he had superb timing, I seemed to specialize in bad timing. But I was at least work friends with the most important technical person in the company, and had impressed him with that certifications stunt.

That May, Dean gave me a promotion and a $7000 raise for that. Katan Corp was weird in that they had invented a bunch of titles that meant nothing to anyone, including those who worked there. I had been a Technical Advisor and was now promoted to Technical Associate. The next promotion after the latter would simply add "Senior" to the title, and above that were director roles; we had no IT directors so that the organization was flat. This was caused by everyone above Dean quitting and him shooting up the ranks and not pulling anyone up behind him, nor hiring anyone to fill them.

None of these titles had existed before that year, and I wondered if Dean had invented them. We now had several promotions we had to advance through to reach even the director level. Dean hadn't gone through any of them. It was almost like obstacles had been put in the path of IT staff to prevent us from ever reaching management positions, but I heard rumors that the owners were trying to give people chances for more frequent promotions. The result was unnecessarily granular ones.

Probably due to passing so many certification exams in a row (seven!), Microsoft contacted me about becoming part of their Microsoft Consulting Services group. This meant I would work out of their Reston, VA offices 30% of the time and be sent to whatever client needed my help the rest of a week, never knowing where I would end up. I didn't like that idea at all because the traffic was notoriously bad, but the potential prestige of working for Microsoft had me curious. I did a tech screen over the phone and did well enough to earn an in-person interview that was supposed to last for hours and include lunch.

The first portion of it was the non-technical part. I typically did well on those because I was articulate, but I was about to have the worst technical exam of my life. What I did for a living was to take data from a database, put it on screen on a website, and allow the user to manipulate it before saving it back to the database. It's an oversimplification, but that's basically the job. What I didn't do was manipulate the Windows operating system.

And yet virtually all the questions they asked me pertained to the latter. And I knew that my certifications, especially that MCDBA one I never wanted but did for the TSA contract, were the reason, due to the exam subjects. I bombed the verbal test, a kind of karma for having cheated, though I had read the books for the MCSD cert, just not the MCDBA ones that Microsoft seemed focused on. I didn't really care, but came away feeling deflated by the experience. Over the years, they contacted me several more times about working there, but the memory, and their desire to send me to client sites all the time, made me decline an interview.

Sometime that summer, Katan Corp rented out a big conference room on the building's first floor, to make various presentations about contracts awarded, promotions, and similar accolades or remarks on company expansion efforts. I had already met Kate, a .NET and SQL Server programmer working at another TSA building. I had back-filled her position when she went on vacation earlier that year, and this was what had first caused me to interact with

Tess, the project manager. Kate was a thin, tall white woman with shoulder-length, straight brown hair. And she was a talker, strong willed, and opinionated. But she was pleasant, if lacking in a little self-awareness that maybe she shouldn't share some things with others. The openness was charming in a "what you see is what you get" way. I liked her even though a little Kate went a long way.

As I descended in the elevator to reach the first floor conference room, Kate stood in front of me. The only other people in it with us were the original group of IT guys when I started: the retired Marine Mack, Dean, Ishaan, and the other programmer. We still sat together and had a joking bond that reappeared as the elevator doors closed, all the guys standing behind Kate.

"I'm so excited to be presenting!" said Kate, clutching the laptop she would use.

Teasing a little about her excitement, because I had never seen anyone express so much enthusiasm about that, I said, "And I'm sure I speak on behalf of all the guys when I say that we're looking forward to it." The boys snickered more than I would have expected, and I cocked an eyebrow at them.

"Thank you!"

"Do you have a lot of experience?" I asked. "You seem nervous."

"Not as much as I want," she admitted.

"Well, if it goes well, maybe you'll get more chances to do it."

"I would *love* that."

At this, the guys muffled more laughter, and I glanced at them again, seeing wide, disbelieving, mirth-filled eyes. And suddenly I realized what they were thinking. The word "presenting" means giving presentations, of course, but it also refers to a female animal in heat, raising her backside for one male after another to mount and impregnate her. I hadn't realized the unintended double entendre until now. As the combination of my questions and Kate's enthusiastic answers registered, I blushed and shot a "stop that" look at the guys. Trying to take my mind off it, I thought of the big crowd awaiting us and her apparent inexperience.

I asked, "Does doing in front of many people seem awesome or awful?" On hearing the guys chuckle, I realized it could mean something different from what I intended.

"The more the better."

More snickers.

"Have you been practicing?" Geez, now it seemed like everything I said meant something else.

"God yes."

At her enthusiasm, the guys continued silently laughing. I asked, "A lot or a little?"

"A couple times a day."

That was a lot, and I remarked, "You sound really into this."

"I am!"

"Well, I hope it goes well."

"Thank you!"

The elevator stopped and the doors opened. She exited first as I said, "Good luck."

She smiled and walked away as the rest of us filed out, and within seconds, the guys doubled over in laughter.

A grinning Dean looked at me. "You need to be careful."

Smirking wryly, I said, "I wasn't doing it on purpose."

Mack clapped a hand on my shoulder. "That was the funniest conversation I've ever heard."

Now I was a little worried. With all the times I had gotten in trouble at work, I felt paranoid, but Kate never realized the unintended subtext of that talk and I escaped an uncomfortable conversation with HR. I went over it in my head repeatedly and talked about it with my wife, who thought it was funny and technically innocent, so I relaxed.

During the presentations (she did fine, by the way), I was called up before everyone and given a certificate of appreciation, my promotion announced. The CEO and her President husband Dave told everyone that I had passed two exams in a week without admitting the poorly kept secret of how I did it, and that the TSA contract was the direct result. The last time management had spoken of me to the company at a town hall, it had been Jack grinning while understating what I did and lathering Chuck in praise. I didn't miss them.

Back at TSA, Tess fired a woman for reasons I don't remember, replacing her. Two weeks later, she went on vacation for a week and left a junior project manager named Janet officially in charge, but they still considered me the most senior person. My role was the same except to help Janet as needed if she ran into trouble. And she did. Her demeanor was calm and yet a little anxious. It became clear that she had little experience doing this and was looking to me for how to handle situations. I didn't mind partly because she seemed nice and I always liked to help. They also admired me at TSA, making it like an island of respect in the stormy sea of contempt I normally sailed on in my career, before someone broadsided me and I went down with my ship.

Deondra, the woman hired to replace the fired one, sat across the cube wall from me. Before leaving for her trip, Tess told me Deondra was late almost every day since she started, going on two weeks, and to monitor her because another firing might be needed. It happened again on Monday and Tuesday, when Janet walked past Deondra's desk to reach me, looking timid and uncertain.

"Hey," she whispered, looking apologetic for bothering me, "do you have a minute?" She always wore black business suits that went well with her long, straight black hair.

With some humor, I asked, "Why are we whispering?"

She smiled sheepishly and leaned closer. "Diego just told me Deondra appears to be asleep at her desk."

CHAPTER THIRTEEN

Management Material

My eyes widened. Diego was the bad cop at the client, the one whose negative attention we never wanted. He was a good guy but former military and put up with no bullshit. If Diego was right that Deondra was asleep at her desk, this was horrendous. Even if he was wrong, the appearance was awful. This was bad.

I stood up slowly and peeked over the cube wall. There sat Deondra in an upright position, facing the computer and me. Somehow, her head was still vertical, maybe because it rested on her breasts. She was a large woman and the rolls of fat on her neck probably helped. Her breathing was steady and even, chest rising and falling with her quiet snoring. Silent, disbelieving laughter shook me as I sat again.

"What do I do?" Janet asked.

I wasn't sure. Somehow, no matter how many odd situations came up in my career, new ones I'd never seen before still arose. I gestured for her to follow me and we walked to the elevators, where we both gave into commiserating laughter.

"Okay," I started, "thinking out loud here. Let's pull her into a meeting. I guess I'll do the talking."

"*Thank* you."

"I think I know how to handle this. One thing we want to do is pretend we did not catch her sleeping, but that it just looked like it. Give her the benefit of the doubt. She'll be embarrassed, I assume, so let's not make it worse."

"That's good."

Janet followed me back and when I was several steps behind Deondra and closing in, I spoke loudly to wake her up while her back was still to us, providing her a chance for plausible deniability. "Deondra! Janet and I wanted to talk to you about something."

I saw Deondra jump in her seat and used my resulting smile to put her at ease as she turned around and followed us to a meeting room, where Janet closed the door and we all sat.

"How's the day going?" I asked casually.

"Good."

"Great. So listen, I wanted to give you a heads up. Diego came to Janet just now and said he thought you were asleep at your desk." The look of alarm on her face gave me pause. "I assume you weren't, of course, because that's just silly, but the important thing here is to not give the impression. I mean, don't even close your eyes for a minute while sitting still. He's tough on all of us and we can't let him jump to conclusions like that, okay?"

"Sure."

"Cool. That's all we wanted to mention."

We all filed out and Deondra went back to her desk as Janet turned to me, looking relieved. "That was awesome."

I felt like I had handled that well, unlike many other situations in my past. Maybe I was getting better at this. I was enjoying the increased responsibility and having a positive impact that wasn't resented, but nothing lasts forever.

Unfortunately, Deondra called in sick the next day, even though she didn't have enough vacation hours to cover a day off. This wasn't Janet's problem, but mine, because Tess had asked me to monitor exactly these kinds of issues with Deondra. I contacted someone back at Katan Corp and gave an update on Deondra, who was already under scrutiny. The result was a decision to have a manager speak with her as a last resort before firing her, but with Tess gone, we all agreed to have a "team lead" at TSA named Brianna talk to Deondra, report back to me, and I would tell Katan Corp how it went.

The next day, I was standing by my TSA desk and looking out the window to the ground far below. From our staff, Deondra, Brianna, another woman, and a guy were all leaving. I noted the time because they only had thirty minutes for lunch and Tess routinely emailed staff, CCing me as usual (partly to show I was also effectively management there), about time and attendance. An hour later, an alarmed Janet came to me, saying that Diego had irritably asked where everyone was and she didn't know, which made her and us look bad. I walked back to the area where they sat (we had all been together at first until they moved us to three areas), and all four were missing, but the guy returned just then.

I spent the next half hour standing at my window before finally seeing the women return. Then I told Janet to bring all four to a meeting room, where she and I sat across from them. This time I wasn't sure what to say, but Janet and Tess were both counting on me to help prevent exactly this kind of thing and I had to address it. I sensed they believed that, with Tess gone, they could get away with this.

"So," I began, "you guys know you have thirty minutes for lunch, but you were gone an hour, and the rest of you for ninety minutes. The worst part is that Diego noticed.

Knowing him, he's probably memorized everyone's hours and watches the clock. You need to be aware of that. He asked Janet where all of you were, and she didn't know." I shook my head, trying to moderate my tone and words, but my honesty always gets the better of me.

I continued, noticing that they were stone-faced. "You can't do that for several reasons, one of which is that it doesn't look good when we don't know why people are gone or when they will be back. This is not a position to put us in. If you need extra time, you need to get permission first and let us know so we can cover for you."

"This is my fault," began Brianna. "I wanted to talk to Deondra like you asked, so that's why we were gone so long. It was work related."

I nodded but observed, "You have to tell us."

"I know."

"I don't see why that talk had to happen out of the building. Leaving is very noticeable."

"I just thought it would be more casual."

More casual than this conversation, certainly, so maybe she had a point. "I also don't think it needed to be ninety minutes. You guys have so much work to do all the time and the client is always watching productivity."

"I understand. You're right."

I noticed her frowning as if stifling a glare. "That explains the two of you."

"I asked Ruby to drive us," she said, indicating the other woman.

I scowled, thinking this was another poor decision. "That just got her on Diego's radar, too." I looked at the lone guy. "You didn't go with them?"

He shook his head.

By now I had noticed that Brianna looked irritated more than apologetic. I belatedly realized I was giving the team lead shit in front of her team, and I should have excused the others first. Maybe I *wasn't* getting better at this. But I hadn't known she was the culprit for most of it until she confessed.

"All of you need to make up that time, preferably today, and be very visible to Diego in doing so. Trust me, he is watching. Let's re-earn his trust."

I excused them and they left. Janet and I later tried to talk to Brianna about how the talk with Deondra went, but she refused to tell us anything, an act of insubordination that didn't sit well with either of us. I was the one who asked her to do that talk on my behalf, and that of Janet, in the absence of Tess. She said something like preferring to talk with Tess about that, as if that was her choice. Katan Corp management looked to me for the result of that conversation and a defiant Brianna refused to give it. She also seemed to think I was out of line to talk with them about their lunch outing. All of this prompted me to send detailed emails to Tess and management about staff behavior that week, and Tess was none too pleased with them on her return, but thanked me profusely. Being appreciated was still something I was getting used to. In a meeting with them, she did me the courtesy of pointing out that I'm just as senior on the project as her and they are to take direction from me as needed. She was awesome. Brianna lost the attitude, Deondra shaped up, and life went back to normal.

Just before she came back, a company Vice President (who had been Dean's boss before he became CTO) resigned. They chose Tess to replace her, overseeing all Department of Homeland Security programs. This was a significant promotion, and I was happy for her, if a bit jealous. She had worked there only two months longer than me and, after two projects, one still underway, got this. Given how impactful I was at TSA, I hoped my work would be recognized, too; my recent promotion had been given for what I had done before actually starting on NSF. It seemed like Katan Corp handed out huge promotions with even a minor success. Maybe I could earn one if a chance arose.

Like Dean before her, Tess repeatedly admitted to me that she was overwhelmed and overworked, so I offered to help whenever she needed it. By now, Tess was my favorite person I had ever worked with. She had Janet replace her for good as project manager at TSA's NSF office.

By this point, I had fixed and automated the system to such a degree that, with approval, I reduced my hours on-site from 160 over four weeks a month to just one. Yes, one. This sort of thing would eventually lead me to joke that I was in the business of putting myself out of work. We assigned a new guy, Dexter, to be present in case database changes were needed. He technically answered to Janet, but in reality, he answered to me, as I was still responsible for the system. The most important direction I gave him was that he needed to run any changes or requests for additions past me rather than doing them without letting me know. It was the approach I had taken, when in his position, when I worked at USAIS with Jack.

I had also completed my assessment of the system and the TSA environment. Being skilled at documentation, requirements gathering, analysis, and system architecture helped. On seeing the report, the Katan Corp president, Dave, asked me to present to him and Dean my impression of the software development opportunities at TSA. This was not part of my job description, and I felt like I was stepping up into business development, something that I was keen to do, so I was excited. The meeting went great, and they decided to create a proposal to submit to TSA for the new NSF app.

I had never done a proposal before, but this was virtually Dave's job and he gave me document templates I could use for inspiration. In the past few months, Dean and Tess had gained some involvement in proposals and were to be involved, but much of the work fell on me because it was a "technical proposal" and an IT person had to write most of it. Dean was too busy and didn't know what I did about TSA, so we agreed he would just supervise my part of the documentation.

Tess did her section at some point, and while she was a skilled writer, the poor writing in it surprised me. I could tell she was just too busy to focus. When she admitted to not being happy with hers, I offered to rewrite it.

"Oh God, would you?" she asked, looking frazzled.

I laughed. "Sure."

"My part is like a draft. I know you can fix it."

"I'll have it back by tomorrow."

"Thank you!"

"Any time."

I edited it for her and returned it, getting another heartfelt thank you. Being appreciated was starting to feel normal, and I felt grateful for the quality of people around me at work.

And then I ran into some trouble with a Katan Corp executive named Bob. He made such significant and unhelpful changes to the proposal that a furious Dean walked away from any further involvement with it, an approach he had taken before with other issues, and which wasn't appropriate for a man in his position as CTO. His abdication left me even more responsible for the proposal. Bob also upset me. For reasons I don't recall, it took me two days to undo what he'd done to it. It was from me that Bob learned neither me nor Dean were happy, to put it mildly, and he backed away from it, too, to my relief. Only Tess and Dave were now touching it, but both of them had significant other activities to attend to. I didn't mind, really, stepping up and hoping to prove myself as more than just a coder.

Now that I was back at Katan Corp HQ virtually all the time, I learned how many things had changed. I had already known about several attempts to have my cube given to someone else, as if I would be at TSA permanently, Dean squashing this. When I had started the previous October, there had only been four programmers, including me and Dean. Now we had over a dozen and multiple projects, each of them using .NET and SQL Server. I assumed they would put me on one, but Dean refused because those projects were fully staffed and I would, in theory, be leading the development of a TSA replacement system. The result was that I had little to do except minor maintenance and tweaks to an existing system that was poorly designed and used much older technology. I had yet to work on anything I considered worthwhile for my career except paperwork. This was seeming familiar, and I was now hoping for the replacement TSA system.

When I first returned to Katan Corp, some of the new coders greeted me as if I had just been hired. This was the problem with being offsite virtually all the time. I smiled and corrected them that I had been there longer than them, usually getting a laugh. They seemed a nice enough bunch, but I also noticed they were a clique who sat together, away from me, Ishaan, Mack, and the other original coder. We were senior to them but effectively sequestered from them by location, and in my case, months of absence. I suddenly felt like a stranger and that I didn't fit in. I wasn't happy that they all got to work on a new project with the right tech and I was stuck with nothing or babysitting old shit. It's one thing for this to happen for a while, but I was around nine months into the job and this was all that there had been. The FBI project for which they had hired me still wasn't happening. My frustration grew. Only the possibility of the new TSA app, and otherwise being treated well, kept me from quitting. My technical skills were rusting. I was frustrated.

One day Tess came to my cube at Katan Corp, where we both usually were now, looking stone-faced. "I need you to go to TSA today."

That surprised me. "Why?"

"Dexter."

My face fell and her grim expression told me I had reason to worry. "What did he do?"

"I don't know, but Diego is demanding you return and fix the system. They apparently can't get any reports to work and there's some other issue. Can you please head over there now?"

I sighed, not about her, but Dexter, and her commiserating expression told me she understood but also knew I would fix the problem. Being trusted to get it done made me feel good.

I soon discovered that Dexter had been lying to me that he wasn't making changes. He screwed up the NSF database so badly with incremental mistakes that none of the reports were accurate anymore and critical data entry screens crashed because of data fields he had poorly added. He made Katan Corp, me, Janet, and Tess look bad, and none of us were amused. Diego was bristling when I got there, but the "good cop" guy smiled and joked that he knew I was glad to be back, especially under those circumstances. It took a couple days of fixing dumb design decisions Dexter had made and I was once again a hero (I'll admit to loving that). But they tried to get me reassigned there.

At some point, I pulled Dexter into a one-on-one meeting at TSA and asked him why he had done this, and he insisted he knew what he was doing and didn't need my approval, that it was his call. The attitude didn't sit well.

Did he somehow miss the part of screwing up the system by not following my directions, forcing me back to fix it?

"There's a difference between good initiative and bad initiative," I began. "The good kind is when the client wants something and you run it past the person who designed the system—that would be me—before doing anything, to make sure you don't screw something up because there's more to it than you might have realized. The bad kind is when you just do it, something goes wrong, and you hide that from me, too."

"I could have gotten it working," he insisted.

Was that the justification for hiding it? I wouldn't learn of what he'd done? "If that was true, I wouldn't be sitting here. This app is mission critical, too, so they don't have time for this. You obviously didn't test or double check any of this before putting it out there for them to use."

"They trusted me to do it."

I loved it when someone set themselves up for a rebuttal. "Well, they don't anymore. I'm the one they trust. I don't want this to happen again, you understand?" When he looked sullen, I added, "I'm just going to ask the client to CC me on all requests for changes. That way I don't have to worry about you hiding them from me."

He said little and was clearly unrepentant. When it was time for performance reviews later that year, they asked me to do his because I was the closest thing to a technical supervisor he had. I wrote that he needed to follow directions better and understand the consequences of his behavior, but that he didn't seem inclined to admit to a mistake or learn from one. Many years later, I would see on LinkedIn that he earned a doctorate degree in IT. God help us all.

In the aftermath, Tess agreed with the client's desire to get me reassigned to TSA full-time, a kind of backhanded compliment, but neither me, Dean, or other Katan Corp management agreed with that idea. I sent her an email detailing my reasons for not thinking it was necessary, though I don't recall what I told her—most likely it was about the death grip that I was putting on Dexter's autonomy.

Not long after, Dean called me into his office. I had once feared being fired on hearing these words, but I felt at ease with my job and didn't worry. But perhaps I should have.

"Is everything okay with you?"

The question surprised me. "Yeah. Why?"

"Well, don't make too much of this, but some people have said you've been a little testy lately."

That brought me up short. Someone had been bad-mouthing me? This was all too familiar, and my guard rose. "Who?"

"It doesn't matter."

I frowned and gave him a knowing look. "Of course it does." When he didn't specify, it forced me to speculate. "Both of us were upset with Bob's work on the proposal. No one was happy with the behavior of the TSA staff while Tess was gone. I'm certain she's not pleased that I don't want to return to TSA until this proposal for a new system is awarded. And Dexter screwed up big time. Are some of these the people complaining?" I didn't see how it could be anyone else.

He smiled a little. "I just wanted you to be aware."

"Thanks." Part of me appreciated the heads up and an assumption that I was still a decent guy, but who might be under some sort of stress. But I also felt I had good reasons to not like some of what had recently happened. After talking about it, I voluntarily forwarded emails I'd sent Bob or Tess about the recent issues and he agreed they were being too sensitive.

Katan Corp had a detailed process for finalizing a proposal. This included a team that ensured it met all the requirements. Since I was the one who wrote both the requirements and the proposal's technical section, I had made this easy, so much so that the meeting, which was me, Dave, and Tess, was normally scheduled for three hours. We were done in thirty minutes. Dave said this was a company record and he couldn't believe it.

"Great job, Tess!" Dave gushed. "I'm really impressed with your work on this."

"Thank you!" she beamed, accepting that.

I looked sideways at her, waiting for her to say I had been instrumental in it. Not only was most of the document mine, but I'd rewritten her part. She didn't say a word and as Dave prattled on, I sensed the moment to stop her from taking all the credit had passed. Disappointed in her, I didn't want to help Tess like that again.

After this, Katan Corp sent the proposal to TSA, who subsequently sat on it despite having asked us for an "unsolicited" proposal to replace the system. Yes, they solicited an unsolicited proposal. I wasn't really sure how that worked, but someone explained to me that this was a way that a company like Katan Corp could be awarded a contract that was never put out for bidding by other companies. In time, we learned TSA was thinking of doing that anyway, which I found obnoxious. It meant that they would use my/Katan Corp's requirements document and assessment to solicit additional proposals from other companies, instead of Katan Corp, to be granted the software development work I had defined. It just seemed rude.

Between then and November, nothing changed. The only moment of interest was when Kate resigned from her TSA position. I had long since learned that Dean hated her for insubordinate behavior. She frequently told the client she would do work that was outside our contract with them, with Dean telling her she couldn't do that. Kate would also show documentation to TSA before letting Dean see it, and the paperwork often amounted to another promise of work to be done. She acted like Katan Corp didn't exist and she was her own boss.

At one point, Dean even had me try to talk her into stopping this behavior when I once again backfilled for her vacation. People have long jumped to conclusions about my thoughts and character, and Kate somehow decided I agreed with her position that Dean was just a control freak. I found myself caught between them, but I used Kate's feeling of bonding with me to nudge her into understanding why she needed to show Katan Corp things before the client. She had reluctantly conceded.

Now, months later, she was resigning because her very cozy relationship with TSA had resulted in TSA offering her a position with them as a government employee, and she had accepted. When Dean told me this, he laughingly said Dave had asked if Katan Corp should make a counteroffer to keep her and he had said no. He was glad to be rid of her, though he didn't tell Dave that. What happened with the work I don't really know, but I assumed the contract was ending and TSA brought the work "in-house" by having their own person, Kate, do it.

Though I'd already had a mini-performance review earlier in the year, the annual reviews came around in November. I had done significant work that was not part of my job description. Dean recognized some of it, but he also wrote that I had acquired the ability to gather software requirements. For a moment, I wondered if he was just trying to make it sound like this was another area of advancement for me, but something told me he honestly didn't know I had been doing this since before *he* was a software developer. I wasn't quite expecting a second promotion in six months, but both he and Tess had leapt upward and I was doing some work at the same level as them, so I had hoped for more. I might have settled for high marks, but Dean only gave me threes and fours out of five. I felt a little unappreciated and still frustrated that I had no significant software development projects. On the plus side, they gave me a raise of several thousand on top of the earlier one. But any satisfaction was short lived.

Days later, when I came back from lunch with my wife, Dean was in the lobby and asked me to come with him to meet someone. Next to Dean's office, and standing as if he had exited the empty office I had once used for studying, a tall black man was chatting with other programmers. I figured he was a new hire and was right. Dean introduced him as the Director of Software Development. I felt only shock.

My gut, and that recent performance review, told me he hadn't even considered me for this role. It was entirely possible that I wasn't qualified for it, but my evaluation of potential software development at TSA qualified as that sort of work. So did me doing all technical parts of the proposal, and the system and network assessments upon which it was based. There was more to being a director of software development, but surely I had shown aptitude and deserved a shot.

Katan Corp also had a demonstrated history of promoting people into senior positions from within. I had done more to warrant a leap upward than either Dean or Tess. He was no CTO, and I didn't think Tess deserved her jump to Vice President either. Both had been stressed by their new roles, and yet here I was stressed by not getting one.

Dean had simply been lucky with his promotions. He had less experience than me and, due to timing and opportunity, had soared from developer to director, to VP of Technology, and finally CTO in less than a season. He was now one of only two "Senior Vice Presidents," which meant he was tied for third most prominent person in the company behind the President and CEO, who were married. For him, of all people, to not give me a chance after months of me stepping up felt like a slap in the face. He had snubbed me on appropriate software development work since hiring me, too.

Shortly after this, the company announced that, as part of their employee satisfaction push, they had put up an anonymous survey for feedback, encouraging all of us to be honest. I did my part and talked about problems with not being assigned meaningful or appropriate work, or being omitted from opportunities not due to qualifications but some other criteria, like already being assigned to meaningless work when the new opportunity came up. I wasn't thinking that if I gave too much detail, they might realize it was me, and I would ultimately suspect that they knew and that I wasn't as constructive in my feedback as I should have been. This is a guess based on what was about to happen and is my only explanation for it, because otherwise it makes no sense at all.

After this, I had another conversation with Tess that included her remark that she didn't think TSA was ever going to award the new project. With this seemingly dead, and Dean not assigning me anything but crap work while waiting for it, I asked him for a meeting to discuss my options. I had spent all of my time babysitting an Access database or doing .NET and SQL Server, my preferred technologies, which was good, but the project was quite old, cumbersome, and only need maintenance when I was the kind of coder who built things. I was bored and going nowhere, my less experienced peers getting the cool, new projects while I languished. Dean needed to fix this.

"I think there are one of two things for you," he said, wearing his manager demeanor.

"Okay," I said, glad at least something was on the table.

"One is to continue doing .NET and SQL Server, but the new project is in Quantico at the Marine Corps base, with Mack as the project manager."

I wore a dubious look. "That's ninety minutes from my house one way, on a good day." I had done a few weeks down there before with Mack, who I got along with fine, even though he seemed to think that only Dean, a former Navy guy, was man enough for him.

"The only other option is to stay local and do Cognos."

"Cognos? What's that?" Having never heard of the software suggested it wasn't likely to be part of my plans to solidify my career as a senior .NET and SQL Server developer.

"It's a reporting tool. We can send you to training for it and you'd be our Cognos expert. We can pay for you to get certified."

I didn't like the sound of that. It was akin to saying I'd be their Microsoft Access expert, repeatedly assigned to projects using technologies that weren't part of my career plans and which would keep me at a junior level. "Why can't I do .NET here? You've got all these guys you hired after me and all of them are doing it."

"My hands are tied."

So are mine, by you, I thought. I tried to look interested. "Can I think about it?"

"Yeah. Let me know soon."

I left and, after looking into Cognos and considering it a dead end technology for me, decided it was time to quit. My skills were dying and Dean was the hangman. He had become like Hank at United Systems, never giving me appropriate work, assigning me crap, and treating me like an afterthought. I suddenly realized I hated my job. I told Dean I would take the Cógnos assignment but not the reason for my decision—going to Quantico for the other one would make it almost impossible to do job interviews. That

Katan Corp would send me to Cognos training only to have me quit was unfortunate. I did attend it by month's end.

And on Monster.com, I activated and hid my resume like usual, this time to prevent Katan Corp from seeing it. The calls and emails came pouring in, probably courtesy of my certifications. I told companies I wanted to make up to $13k more and most didn't even blink. My upset with Dean grew after my first few technical interviews because I was asked things I should have known off the top of my head, and I couldn't remember due to hardly using my tech skills in a year. It solidified my desire to leave. Dean was destroying my career and by staying, I was letting him.

Unwisely, I told Tess and Ishaan of my impending departure before I had a job offer. They were only surprised that I hadn't already left, which seemed to validate my decision. Tess agreed to be a reference.

The interviews came so fast that I had three in one day (the fourth canceled). Two were for software development companies, which increased my interest. The problem with many companies in the D.C. area is that they don't do app development. They do something else and need coders. This is especially true of government contracting firms like Katan Corp, which did "business process re-engineering." That meant changing the way an agency did business. That re-engineering typically included coders to modify systems already designed in who-knows-what-technology, and companies like Katan Corp were technology agnostic—it didn't matter to them what programming language the software needed to be done in, with the exception that proposals typically included the resumes of qualified staff with that experience. This was how earning my certifications to win that TSA contract had come back to haunt me. If I hadn't done that, I would have been available a month or two later when Katan Corp hired more .NET developers to work on other contracts they had won since. My old nickname, "The Black Hole of All Luck," rang in my ears.

One of the software development companies I interviewed with specialized in the "Microsoft stack," as it's known—they only used Microsoft tools to do programming. They specifically competed for contracts that required that and not much else. And in theory, they would never run out of programming work because the company would fold. I was acutely aware of my project-based career path and that working at a place like Katan Corp meant doing whatever tech work they needed me to do, even if it didn't align with my career goals. When interviewing, I always confirmed this alignment was there, but after the initial project was over, that alignment often stopped. It increasingly seemed like a bad idea to stay with any employer, which was why I considered permanent contracting. But maybe a software development company would do the trick.

But I didn't like the people I interviewed with at DataSoft. I couldn't put my finger on why. They asked me no technical questions, which I found odd given what they did. But when they sent me a job offer via email for more money, I took it. The same day, Tess told me TSA had demanded I return full-time to fix another problem Dexter had created, so I told her I was resigning the next day, the implication being that I hoped to get out of it, but I ended up fixing it and having time to make my farewells at the place that had most valued me in my career. I became glad that I went, saving the day one last time and having people be so happy to see me.

Despite my frustration with Dean, now that I was leaving, my mood improved considerably, and I wanted to resign in person because email is cold. Little did I know the cold reaction awaiting me. I had noticed a cold shoulder from Dean and the President Dave, who was usually exceptionally cordial to everyone. In fact, that caught my attention, as he repeatedly said hello to people all around me with a big smile while acting like he didn't see me at all.

I was supposed to be home the next day and Dean was soon leaving on Christmas vacation for much of what would be my final two weeks, so I emailed and asked if he would be in the following day. He replied I could just call now to discuss whatever was on my mind, but I said I wanted to do it in person. He replied, "Do I need a tissue?" He had figured it out, basically, partly from this, my repeated absences for interviews, my reaction to the Cognos thing, and potentially someone telling him of my intentions or him figuring out my displeasure. I later learned that Ishaan was present with him at the time of this email exchange and he confirmed Dean knew I was resigning. Dean said there was nothing he could do to stop me from leaving because it was out of his hands, suggesting it was up to the owners to make me a counteroffer.

Thursday morning, I walked into Dean's office to resign, shutting the door. Then I sat before his desk, him behind it. I told him I was leaving.

Face blank, he said, "I assume this is because of the TSA project not coming through."

My demeanor casual, I said, "Partly that. But I haven't been able to do any real .NET work since I started and I'm getting rusty. I just don't think you have the work for me." I avoided pointing out once again that he'd given every last other programmer that kind of work, one of them (with less tenure) managing a bunch of others while I had nothing.

"So when is your last day?"

"Two weeks from today." I paused, but he said nothing else. "I assume you need the resignation in writing."

"Yeah, I'll need that."

We looked at each other silently for several awkward seconds, his face still blank and unfriendly. I suddenly grew as cold as his mask-like expression. I got up and left without another word and he said nothing else.

I hadn't expected this reaction. There was no asking where I was going next. No saying he was sorry to see me go, or that he understood. No suggesting another project for me. None of the friendliness and trust. Some of these I didn't expect. Others I absolutely did. The coldness made a huge impression on me, one that he compounded when he never spoke to me or acknowledged an email from me again. I abandoned the idea of ever asking him to be a reference. I was so disappointed that I couldn't help questioning what our relationship had been. Many years later, my upset from this scene having faded, I somewhat reluctantly hit the "connect" button on his LinkedIn profile and he accepted, the only acknowledgement since that day.

The owners never spoke to me again either, nor was a counteroffer made. I was the most certified staff member, with an MCP, MCAD, MCDBA, and an MCSD in ascending order of value (never mind how I got them). No one else had more than the first two. Certs were highly valuable, but there was no attempt to keep me onboard. Even after repeatedly saving the day at TSA. Even after the record-breaking review meeting over the proposal. Even after a bonus and two raises. After a promotion. After helping them win the TSA contract that led to Tess becoming a Vice President. What could cause such disinterest?

A month earlier, the company had sent out a survey for people to take about their experiences at work. They repeatedly touted that it was anonymous and we could therefore be honest. While I had expressed happiness with their handling of recognizing achievements, I had also expressed unhappiness about not assigning staff appropriate work, or something that fits their career goals. Had they figured out that the one objecting to these was me? It was the only thing that made sense. My "anonymous" survey answers had to be it. Had they only expected praise for their employee satisfaction work? Dave was certainly proud of it, with good reason, but had I shit on their "we're a great company to work for, always!" delusion? Yes. And not even talking to me seemed to validate that they weren't as great as they seemed to think. I had wanted to stay but Dean made it impossible, and they could have talked me into it, but they did nothing.

I remembered that when Kate resigned, Dave had asked Dean if they should counteroffer, and because Dean hated her, he said no. I received the same treatment—no counteroffer. Was the sentiment behind it the same? I felt disillusioned all over again, having little experience to show on my resume after a year working there.

By contrast, Tess was very remorseful about my departure, saying she knew I would be missed, especially at TSA. She was very disappointed in the company's response to my resignation and couldn't believe they weren't trying to stop me. Many others felt the same, and I focused on that, trying not to let a few people impact me too much. I emailed Dean, asking him for someone to turn over my TSA work to or get someone else up to speed on it besides Dexter, and he ignored it, so Tess asked and he refused to answer her either. This left me and Tess to take the initiative ourselves. All of this showed he wasn't as good of a manager as he seemed to think.

In my last days, I learned that another prominent programmer was quitting, too, and everyone was complaining about the work they were doing. Dean had an unhappy IT shop. One guy quit right before I did. Days after my departure, Ishaan emailed me at home, saying Dean had my hard drive erased the day after I left. This seemed unnecessarily hasty, like slamming a door... on his own foot. I was asked if I had put my work anywhere else because it was gone. I had not. I laughed.

In the years after, I sometimes wondered if leaving Katan Corp was a mistake. Which was more important? Being treated well or my career aspirations? Was there a reason I couldn't have both? I seldom had either, so was "one out of two" not bad? Maybe life would have been better if I had remained. But maybe not. The indifference shown to me at the end suggested I had overstayed my welcome, and it strengthened my disappointment with the entire job.

Eighteen months after I quit, the owners sold Katan for forty-two million dollars. I would assume some staff were absorbed into the new parent company that acquired Katan Corp, while others were let go. A duplicate and unqualified CTO like Dean was no longer needed and he moved on, dropping down a peg or two to lesser management roles that were more in line with his experience.

CHAPTER FOURTEEN

Lunatics Run the Asylum

With all the problems I'd had with managers, DataSoft attracted my attention partly by having a flat organization structure. Two men in their sixties co-owned the company, which they had started by accident when working together and stumbling into a chance to design software for an agency that became their first client. Aside from this, they had a woman Director of Operations, a single HR rep, a network guy, and one sales guy who tried to drum up new business for them. Otherwise, everyone was a project manager or a programmer.

But the latter were not all equals. Four of them, who I privately referred to as the Four Horsemen, had the title Senior Developer, but probably should have been called architects. At this point in my career, I was a senior developer regardless of what title I had. I didn't much care about titles except that it didn't look as good on my resume if my employer only considered me a Developer and not a Senior Developer. This was better than the non-industry standard titles at Katan Corp, which had already caused recruiters and interviewers to ask me what they meant.

The Four Horsemen designed virtually all the systems and decided how all programming was done, from the big picture down to the little. The latter mostly meant all pro-grammers had to use a custom library of controls that one of them was largely responsible for creating. This meant that, instead of using the built-in button control in ASP .NET, for example, I had to use the button control they had created. They based it on the built-in one but added additional properties and methods (aka actions) to it. I learned of this the hard way, when someone assigned me my first project to work on alone and no one told me this until weeks into working on it. They forced me to redo much of my work. Never a fan of bad processes, I couldn't help wondering why they didn't tell me their requirements beforehand. Was it an early sign of bad things to come?

They were in Herndon, Virginia, the farthest west I had traveled into NoVA for a job, but I took the twisting back roads through Great Falls, where the rich people had their mansions along the Potomac River. This helped me evade most of the NoVA traffic, and I often took the back roads in Maryland, too, but there's no escaping the dreaded American Legion Bridge over the river. I typically made it to work in 45 minutes with my now customary schedule of working 7 AM to 3 PM. My motorcycle helped, either from sheer acceleration or allowing me to more easily change lanes when problems arose. They also let me work from home on Tuesday and Thursday once I settled in.

And that became one of two reasons I hardly knew anyone. The other was my assigned cube on the ground floor of a long, two-story building. Only six others sat down in this overflow space. My cube was next to the window, and with unreserved parking, it took fifteen steps to reach my car instead of the fifteen minutes it took at the Pentagon years before. I was among the first two or three people at work and was sometimes the one to unlock the front door, no one else arriving for two hours.

Upstairs, the owners sat at the front end of the building, the HR rep and director just outside. There was a small meeting room and printers and cabinets, and then the long row of remaining staff, a single hallway separating sets of cubes to right and left. Most of the way down was the big meeting room, and then an area we were discouraged from entering because of the Four Horsemen and network guy being back there, plus the spare equipment room. The network admin sat guard, politely accosting anyone who stepped over the threshold. In fairness, it was probably to stop people from helping themselves to computer equipment, but it was still a bit off-putting.

My early sense that the staff were not friendly, inclusive, or even considerate crystalized within a month, during a luncheon the owners did in the large meeting room. There weren't enough seats for the 40+ staff to sit. I was one of those forced to eat while standing, and when those at the table finished eating, they didn't let someone who was still standing and juggling a plate, napkin, fork, and drink take their place. No one spoke to or even looked at me so that it seemed like a series of cliques. Having had speech problems for twenty years, starting as a child, had left me somewhat loathe to just barge into conversations with people who seemed oblivious to my existence. I stayed for what I considered to be a polite amount of time, looking for a conversation opportunity that never arose before leaving.

My first project was for the LSN, doing a prototype, which can be done in different ways. A poor way is to use an image program like Photoshop to do mockups of how the screens will look. It's a poor choice for at least two reasons. First, any work done just has to be duplicated in the program used to actually create the real app (in this case, ASP .NET). Second, a client can get used to how things look in that mockup, and they are bound to look different in the actual app, causing frustration. This is a notorious situation among coders. Fortunately, my employer agreed with my approach—create the screens for real in ASP .NET. It's just that if you clicked on a button that said "Save," nothing was saved to the database, which didn't exist. But the button navigated to another screen afterward if that was supposed to happen. In fact, that was the only thing that *did* work, allowing users to navigate the app and see how everything would function.

Since I didn't deal directly with the client, I only heard from the PM that they could be obnoxious, and the biggest sign of this was that they wanted to cancel a meeting and halt work until I did something they had asked for. There is known as a data grid. It is rows and columns of data, like a spreadsheet, embedded in a web page. This grid can be sorted and searched, and there are usually buttons or links on each row that say "Edit" or "Delete" and take the user to another screen to perform that task. The data comes from the underlying database, of course. But since this was a prototype, the data wasn't real. I had typed dummy data into an HTML table to simulate what the data grid would look like. But I only typed five rows. The client wanted ten in the final app and had asked for it among more substantial changes. I hadn't gotten around to the trivial task, partly because this was just a prototype, and was astonished to learn that they were so furious that they were demanding no more work be done until I did it. I knew then that they were impetuous and petty.

One day, the HR rep/recruiter, Katarina, stopped by my desk. She was black, mid-thirties, average height and build, laid back, easily excited, always pleasant, and easily relatable, like she could strike up a conversation with anyone. I had liked her immediately, and now that I had been there a month, I knew she stood out in stark contrast to our standoffish coworkers.

"Rands!" she said. "How's it going?"

"Good." I smiled, but stifled a smirk. I often asked people to call me Rand instead of Randy, and it was how I signed emails, but she got it wrong and appeared incapable of correcting herself no matter how many times I told her it was Rand and not Rands.

"I keep hearing great things about you," she said.

Now I smirked. "Naturally."

She laughed. "Anna says you're a huge help on the project." Anna was the young, blonde project manager on the prototype and the only person I worked with so far.

"I get the impression she doesn't have much experience, which–"

"Yeah," she interrupted, "that's why they paired her with you, because you have so much. They're looking for you to guide her. We didn't even tell you that and you're already knocking it out of the park! You're one of the most senior people here. It's why they were excited to have you onboard."

I had known none of that. "That's good to know."

"Yeah, they always want a senior person on everything, even a prototype like this. Sorry they have you working on one. Everyone hates that."

"What? A prototype?"

"Yeah. Everyone wants to be coding."

So did I, but being the one to lie out the entire app gave me prominence on it and it was part of coding, anyway. Unlike some people, I had an eye for screen flow and layout, which was one area where I had repeatedly nudged Anna. She, or the client, sometimes had bad ideas, and I had to explain to her so she could explain to the client, whom I wasn't allowed to talk to directly, a fact I found odd, especially now that I knew how little experience Anna had.

"I've been wondering," I said, "they don't let me talk to the client–"

Katarina shook her head, interrupting as she often did. "Yeah, they never let the programmers talk to clients. Just causes trouble."

I frowned. "Why?"

"Programmers aren't good with people. You guys should sit in a corner and code all day."

I laughed, not offended by the stereotype. "Some of us are better with clients than others."

"Yeah, I can tell you'd be good at it. You're personable, unlike most here." She leaned over and whispered, "It's not my decision, but I wouldn't let most of them talk to a client either, and I've talked to all of them."

I knew she was alluding to the owners having decided about this. But there was something else I had wanted to know. "Anna also doesn't let me see the requirements document. I find that–"

"No one ever does. Not the programmers. Even the four senior guys don't get to see them. Well, not usually."

"You're kidding."

"Nope."

"Why? I mean, that's the most important thing, like the Bible on a project." I wasn't sure how much she knew about software development and didn't want to insult her intelligence, but the requirements document is critical and I excelled at creating them. A detailed process took place to accomplish this and involved repeated interviews with the client/stakeholders to make sure every requirement was captured and documented accurately. All design, coding, and testing work followed and was done to that doc. The entire project schedule also resulted from this, and if it was inaccurate, not only would deadlines be missed, but the app would fail UAT (user acceptance testing), leading to rework at company expense. The requirements document was a contractual obligation to create but also to adhere to with the software. I didn't care that someone else had created it, but I needed to see it to do my job.

Katarina said, "They don't want coders seeing the document."

I opened my mouth, then shut it again, trying not to express my disbelief because I knew it would come across as disapproval and I wasn't in the position to do that. "Okay, but what's happening is that Anna is trying to interpret the requirements doc to create designs, and that's the programmer's job."

"Not here it isn't."

I stifled a shake of my head. This was insane. Project managers don't do app design. Software developers do. That Anna had almost no experience had repeatedly been obvious.

"The designs she comes up with are really just not workable most of the time."

"That's why we have her paired with you."

"Right, but she's showing them to the client, who likes them, and then she shows them to me and I have to point out what's wrong with them. She sees my point, which is great, but then she has to go back and show the client the changes and explain it. I know she has said they're frustrated."

"Okay, I see your point, and you're not wrong. I can talk to them and see if she can at least show you the designs before the client."

"That would be great."

"Sure, Rands."

I grinned to show no hard feelings. "You mean Rand?"

She smiled, then laughed. "I don't know why I keep doing that."

"No worries." Something was on my mind, and I added, "I know you might not be the one to ask something, except you seem to know everything."

"That's because I talk to everyone! And you're the only fun one to talk to, I'm telling you."

I hadn't complained about how anti-social everyone was, but you'd almost think I had. "We're almost done with the prototype. Any idea what's next for me?"

"No, but Rands, everyone is fighting over who gets you on their project next."

"Really?" I wasn't sure if I should believe her. She seemed prone to exaggeration, more from her demeanor than words. I seldom saw her talking to others, so I wasn't sure how much of the enthusiasm was normal or directed at me.

"Yeah. You know we have this project manager meeting every week and Anna is always saying she'd be lost without you."

Now I suspected hyperbole because people seldom say such things about themselves. But I didn't need everyone fighting over me. That appreciation existed, even if less than what Katarina claimed, was good enough for me.

With the prototype done and awaiting customer approval, they assigned me a second prototype for a pharmaceutical company. Coworkers had expressed sympathy when I had the first prototype, but that rose considerably with a second in a row, something they said never happened. I wasn't happy either because I hadn't been allowed to do much .NET coding at Katan Corp and now it was continuing. I also learned that I would not necessarily get to work on either project once the client approved them for coding. And sure enough, I would not work on them. The work was almost all HTML and something any junior developer could do. If I would not code the actual app, then this wasn't a good use of my skills.

I worked with another project manager, who was less experienced than Anna. She was so green that one owner stepped in as the real PM. I initially thought this was a chance to make a good impression on him, but he was extremely demanding, wanting an update at noon and by COB every day so that I was working my ass off. Along the way, I convinced him to buy a menu control we could use throughout the company and which added improvements to anything we were already using. He also asked me to do a presentation on it for the other coders, so I did and felt appreciated, which tempered my desire to look for another job.

My willingness to tolerate a lack of meaningful work was dropping. In my career, employers consistently denied me the one thing that mattered most—coding. By May I had been there four months and done none (HTML is not programming, but formatting). I had made my discontent with this known to Katarina, who talked with management several times, saying they understood how I felt. And so it came as a relief when one of the PMs, Derek, successfully fought to get me assigned to an IRS project because of all he'd heard from other PMs about how great I supposedly was.

The project's size meant there were two junior PMs aside from Derek, who was considered among the most senior and therefore trusted to get it done on schedule. He was my height, broad shouldered, lean but well-built, and balding with short brown hair. He seemed intelligent, astute, and aggressive in demeanor with how he moved, stood, and looked at those around him, as if he thought he had accurately sized up everyone's personality with a glance and knew how to get what he wanted from them. While I didn't find him intimidating, I could tell others might, especially women. I disliked him from the start.

The IRS app had two pieces: a website and an old-school desktop app. I had started my career doing the latter but had transitioned to the former at the Pentagon and then USAIS with Jack. Two of the Four Horsemen led the project, setting up the architecture. This means elements like the database design, and on a website, things like the menus, headers, footers, and overall look and feel. It also meant creating common functions. Let's say the hypotenuse of a rectangle needs to be calculated based on values given to a formula. And three screens need to calculate this. We can create a function to do this. If we add the function to all three screens, this duplicates it. If the function changes, we have to change it in three places. It's better to create a "common function" that is located in one place and "called" from the three screens with a line like "Hypotenuse = CalculateHypotenuse (value1, value2)."

When I joined the project, I was the first programmer who was not one of the Four Horsemen. One of them was largely responsible for the custom code base everyone at DataSoft had to use, and he fit the anti-social programmer stereotype perfectly. I seldom saw him and he looked visibly awkward, like he just wanted to be left alone. He was also a snob about programming and a real geek who loved tinkering with how everything worked, finding fault with it, and deciding he could do better. I found him unrelatable and increasingly gave into saying hello and then largely ignoring him unless he contacted me, which was rare, almost exclusively via email, and usually a somewhat commanding "do it this way" message.

Then there was Rod, the other horseman on the effort. He was either the technical lead or just seemed like it because he would actually interact with people. The first half dozen times I saw him, he was already sitting behind a table so that it came as a surprise the first time he stood up. His body was shaped like a pear so that he seemed to have a normal build from mid-stomach upward. But his waist ballooned out to twice his body width, his butt and legs enormous so that it looked like two halves of two different people had been stapled together. In retrospect, I can't help thinking he had been bullied as a kid from it (assuming he had always been like that), and that this helped Derek, a natural-born bully if ever I saw one, dominate him. I found Rod to be soft spoken, reasonable, and likeable, if not particularly friendly. And I mostly dealt with him.

It didn't take long to have my first run-in with Derek. One day, I was supposed to be at the IRS HQ in D.C. at 10 AM to get fingerprinted for yet another clearance, the appointment all of ten minutes with a single person. I decided to take the metro and give myself plenty of extra time for the hour-long trip to get there. I arrived at the metro parking lot at 8:30 AM only to find it packed. Me and twenty other cars circled the multiple lots and parking garages like vultures, to no avail. The Shady Grove metro was like an island in the middle of nowhere, and any side streets had copious signs warning of towing. And there were no spots, anyway. The radio indicated multiple accidents on the highways, too, so driving to D.C. was out because I'd never make it. Frustrated, I finally went home and called Katarina to see about rescheduling. She wasn't happy but agreed.

And then I got the super snotty email from Derek, saying Katarina was furious. I knew right then that he was lying because I'd already talked to her and "fury" simply wasn't her style. But Derek's? Definitely. The coward couldn't admit to his feelings and projected them onto someone else—a woman, no less. He snidely said she was nice enough to get me another appointment, that I had made the company look bad, that I was hurting our chances of ever getting business with the client again, and that I had no excuse for my unprofessionalism; I wondered what excuse he gave himself for his. He was laying it on awfully thick over so little.

I replied and CCd Katarina. Far from apologizing to the jerk, I told him his statements were out-of-line, that he was making a mountain out of a molehill, and that he owed me an apology. Within minutes, the phone rang.

"Hey Rands," began Katarina, sounding exasperated.

"Hey. I assume you're calling about our mutual friend."

"Yeah. Don't mind him. I'm not mad at you at all, but him for this. He has no business talking to people like that."

"Couldn't agree more."

"He thinks he runs the whole company."

"The only thing he runs is his mouth."

She cackled. "Rands! Spot on! Have to remember that one."

"What's his problem, anyway?"

"He turns on people like that all the time, eventually. I thought he wouldn't mess with you because you're as big as him and one of the most experienced people here."

"Don't think he cares."

"Yeah. I'm sorry about this. I will try to get you removed from the project if I can. Once he pulls this on someone, he rarely quits."

"Great."

But I heard nothing more about me being pulled off in the wake of Derek's tantrum. I wondered if my experience had put a target on my back for Derek. Did he consider me a threat because my experience and physical size suggested I couldn't be bullied? If so, I had just proven it with my response. In high school, I had once stood up to a dozen black guys who tried to jump me, so it was going to take more than a whiny email from an assclown to intimidate me.

I had immediately updated my resume in the incident's wake, but didn't activate on the job boards. I was now sensitive to the speed with which a job could go bad and didn't want to be caught flatfooted if the likely badmouthing behind my back started. Maybe I should have been impressed that he accosted me directly, but that just told me how aggressive he was.

By the time I joined the IRS project, none of the screens had been created, so I worked with mostly Rod to get one done according to how he envisioned the app to work. Then I was on my own, doing a combination of creating the interface and developing more common functions other screens would need. Since none of the programmers were allowed to see the requirements documents, I would only learn that two or more screens needed a function I'd written into one of them when sent a second design document for another screen that needed it. This caused me to move the function to a common location and adjust the previous screen to call it. It was a stupid way of doing things, because as other programmers joined the project, they might get a screen to work on and not realize there was already a common function they could use. This was solved, in part, by my frequent reminders to everyone to check the common function library every day, and to email the team when they altered or added anything; naturally, some of them didn't. I also brought it up at our weekly meetings as the team expanded to over a dozen programmers.

This included Julie, a tall, leggy woman with shoulder-length, straight blonde hair. She was a few years older than me and had worked there a couple of years. Julie was the first to join the team after me, Rod having relinquished the job of teaching others how to do the work to me. She and I worked well together and became work friends, the only one I would have there aside from Katarina. We sometimes thought of improvements to each other's work, peer-reviewing the code, a process that expanded to others as they joined us, either me or her bringing them up to speed.

A frequent problem was the design specs. Since the owners bizarrely prevented the programmers from seeing the requirements documents, we could not create the design docs that were usually our job as well. The PMs were doing it. And screwing them up. They went so far as to tell us which database tables we needed to use, and how to relate the tables to each other with a query, in order to grab the data required for a screen. And they were often wrong, partly because this is the sophisticated work of coders. Non-technical staff had no business doing technical work.

We would learn of the screwups after programming a screen and encountering errors or other problems. It caused repeated back and forth with the PMs, who seemed irritated to learn of their mistakes. This could cause hours and sometimes days of ripping out code and replacing it. And yet they were constantly on our asses about deadlines.

The PMs were sloppy and we all knew it. The evidence was in writing. I frequently worked with Henry, who often sent me a design doc riddled with typos and other signs of indifference to accuracy. He once sent three of them in a row for nearly identical screens, and the exact same typos were in them. He had duplicated the documents and changed the relevant parts. Shortly after sending me such a document early one Monday, he dropped by my desk.

"Hey Randy," began Henry. He was average height, small glasses making him seem beady-eyed as they sat on his head of short, curly brown hair. "When do you think this screen will be done?"

Not turning away from my computer as I typed, I said, "By the end of Wednesday, like I said in my email." I knew he'd seen it because he had responded to let me know he was coming to discuss it.

"It's really important that we meet our deadline."

I looked sideways at him, not liking his insinuation that I didn't meet deadlines. "Okay."

"I need you to take that seriously."

I stopped what I was doing and turned all the way around to him, leaning back in my chair. "Are you accusing me of something?"

"I just need you to get it done."

My hard gaze belied my feigned, polite tone. "I'm glad to see that this matters so much to you. I assume there are no errors in the document that will slow me down this time and that you've faithfully done your part to ensure we, as a team, meet our deadlines."

He looked unsure how to respond and walked away.

At lunch time, Derek stopped by. "So how's the screen Henry gave you looking?"

I arched an eyebrow at him, knowing Henry had said something. "Like a screen with four hours of work on it instead of twenty-four. Why do you ask?"

"I just want to make sure we're on schedule."

"We are."

"It's really important that we get this done."

I stifled annoyance. "Is it more important than it was four hours ago? Or about the same?"

"You don't seem to be taking this seriously."

I turned toward him, aware that he and Henry were badmouthing me to each other. Who else were they telling I didn't take the project seriously?

"You have no business saying something like that to me," I said, "or about me to anyone else. If you don't like my estimate, I'll discuss it with Rod and you can argue with him about it if you like. In fact, I'll forward Henry's document to him and CC both of you so you can see his opinion." I turned my back to him and started that email while he was watching. I sent it and Rod soon responded that he agreed with my estimate. But that didn't stop Henry from dropping by at the end of Monday to see if the screen was done.

"I assume you're kidding." I replied, rising to leave for the day.

"Why would I be kidding?" he asked.

"You don't seem to be taking my estimate seriously," I said, amused at turning the idea back on him.

"We're behind schedule and–"

"We probably wouldn't be if we didn't have to keep redoing screens when the design docs have errors in them. A better use of your time would be double-checking your work instead of looking over my shoulder at mine."

I walked away without waiting for a response. The next morning, I received an email from Henry asking if I did yet it. CCing Derek and Rod, I replied, and wrote something like:

I realize that technically it's the next day, but in work time, about two hours have passed since you last asked me that. I have said multiple times that it will be done COB Wednesday. That's 24 hours of work. You have asked if it was done at 4 hours, then 8, and now 10, which is less than 50% of the estimated time that Rod and I have agreed on. Please stop.

To my surprise, I heard nothing more. I finished the screen around lunch time on Wednesday but didn't turn in the code until shortly before I left for the day. I had been talking with Julie about this, as she was getting a similar treatment. We sometimes went to lunch together, talking about our mutual dislike of Derek and Henry. We discussed their behavior every week at our programming meeting, with Rod saying he would talk to them at our next discussion with the entire IRS team, where we all watched him back down, Derek bullying him. The subject had been the error-filled design documents, the unrealistic expectations, and the constant hounding of programmers to work faster. None of us wanted to work with them.

After a few weeks of work on the desktop portion of the app, they pulled me off it to work on the website version. Once again, I was the first person doing the screens, only Rod and the other Four Horsemen guy having touched it to set up the architecture. I took it as a sign of faith in my work, with me once again bringing other team members up to speed as some transitioned to the web app, too. The IRS was supposed to create the web app themselves but dropped the ball. We were just helping and there was no deadline because it wasn't even part of the contract. This meant I was now spared the hounding by Derek and Henry. And after nearly two years of not doing .NET website coding, I was finally doing it again... for all of a month.

They pulled me off the IRS project to send me to the headquarters of a major insurance company because I had experience with SQL Reporting Services. Not for the first time in my career, my employer took away me from a project doing the technology I specialized in to do some side thing I either had very little experience with, or quite a bit in the past, where I wanted to leave it. I was beyond sick of it and protested the change, to no avail.

And then it got worse when we learned more details. The client was trying to migrate from Microsoft Project Server 2003 to 2007. I had zero experience with either. Project Server was installed into a SQL Server database. My impression was that this meant that if you logged into Project Server and pulled up a screen, that screen grabbed data out of the database to construct itself. The database was not only what users had typed in, but stuff to make the app function. In other words, there was "user data" and "system data." The app broke without the latter, resulting in a potentially corrupted Project Server and total data/system loss—unless you figured out what had gone wrong in the database, among the "system tables" that Microsoft designed (good luck with that).

The client had written a bunch of custom reports using SQL Reporting Services, which they tied to that database to see their "user data" in ways not supplied by the built-in or customizable reports that came with Project Server. Well, in the new version of Project Server, Microsoft renamed all the tables. This meant the custom reports the client relied on would not function. Not even slightly.

To make matters worse, instead of renaming something like tblProjects (that's "table projects") to something intelligible, the new table name was something like tblASDOIHSAHLKN. Or maybe tblOIUDHFKSYTNA. Microsoft had randomized the table names to be indecipherable, probably on purpose. The reason was that if I went into tblProjects and deleted or renamed a field, like changing "ProjectID" to "MyProjectID," the entire Project Server might crash because all sorts of functionality was looking for a field called ProjectID and it was now "gone." Technically, it would still be there, but the app wouldn't know that. Likely to inhibit tampering with the database, Microsoft obfuscated every table and field name to be gobbledygook. And it was now my job to figure out which of the hundreds of tables was tblProject, and which field was which. And I needed to do it on dozens of tables.

To do this data mapping, I opened every table one by one so I could see the data in it. Based on the content, I surmised the table's purpose, noted it, and moved on to the next one. Partly by process of elimination, I whittled the possibilities down to the tables I needed to find. To verify I was correct, I needed to "join" tables in query; this basically means:

Give me these fields from tblASDOIHSAHLKN and these other fields from tblOIUDHFKSYTNA where field AISDSUDF from tblASDOIHSAHLKN matches LKHDFIND from tblOIUDHFKSYTNA.

If this makes little sense, that's kind of the point. Normally it would have read like this:

Give me these fields from tblProject and these other fields from tblProjectDetails where field ProjectID from tblProject matches ProjectID from tblProjectDetails.

If my query produced an error, then I was wrong about something. If it produced data, I still had to look at it carefully to see if it produced the right information. Slowly but surely, I got the job done, being given only four weeks to do it, with a week-long vacation in the middle of it and no computer to use at the client for the first week. On my return to DataSoft, they gave me a bonus.

While I succeeded, the project made me realize I wanted to end my career.

/

CHAPTER FIFTEEN

Malfeasance

I still loved creating an application. They were challenging, technical, and creative, a balance of considerations that, when done well, produced an app people enjoyed using and which made their lives easier. Meanwhile, behind the scenes, I had juggled all the concerns, both technical and business-wise. I prided myself on doing everything well, a kind of jack-of-all-trades.

I could interview stakeholders and answer their questions, teaching them the process of having an app designed to their requirements, which I excelled at gathering from them and documenting. Creating project schedules and meeting the deadlines came naturally. I could create prototypes and screen designs that had them excited about what we were building. I could write all the code to make the app function, and I produced few errors because I was Mr. Fix-It, not Mr. Introduce-Bugs (there was no secret to this—I just tested my code). Creating intelligent database designs and writing the complex queries to produce the needed reports was fun to me. I could write user manuals and other documents, and teach people how it all worked, either another programmer or an end-user.

The problem was that, while creating an app was still fun, I seldom did that. Instead, I was almost always fixing someone else's mess, learning their code, database designs, and way of thinking. Or dealing with an asshole manager. Or working on technologies I wanted no part of. Or being forced to do exclusively documentation when it was supposed to just be part of the job. Or having my location changed over and over, whether just my cube at my employer or being sent to one client after another and getting an awful commute that made me miserable. It was like every employer saw my versatility and decided I was their technical Swiss Army Knife.

They didn't care what I wanted to do, or about my career. Rather than providing me the promised opportunities that would grow my skill set, they shoved me down a path destined to ruin my career. I could not be a senior ASP .NET and SQL Server developer if I was constantly being given something else to do because that was what my employer needed, rather than what *I* needed. It was one thing for these asides to be part of my career goals, but they always replaced and thwarted them.

The whole reason I took the job with DataSoft was that they specialized in these two technologies, just like I now did. Or wanted to. And they only did software development, not "business process re-engineering" (or some other thing) like Katan Corp had. And yet they kept denying me it. If even this company kept sticking me with everything but what I wanted, with every *exception* to what they did as a firm, then no one could give me what I wanted: predominantly .NET coding work. With my resume repeatedly coming back to haunt me, because it revealed my versatility, I began removing or downplaying the evidence of those abilities.

But I didn't start looking for a job yet. Instead, I found myself looking for a project, because when I returned to

HQ, they did not give one to me for weeks. I could no longer ask Katarina what was going on. Though she was a recruiter and the HR rep, she seemed to know everything happening. But that summer, Katarina quit with little explanation to me. She was very upbeat about it, as if blatantly trying to sound like she loved it there, but just had to take another opportunity. I would eventually learn the truth and didn't push her at the time because she seemed determined to leave on good terms. Letting on that I hated my job when I did was an unwise weakness of mine. But I couldn't help it. I am honest to a fault. It is the bane of my existence. Whoever said "honesty is the best policy" was a liar.

As if to crystallize my hatred of projects not aligned with my career, another one arose. Our sales guy had found an opportunity with a federal agency in D.C. and the potential client wanted to interview someone, namely me. If successful, we would win the contract, and I already knew this meant being assigned to it, meaning I had incentive. Or not. My experience was once against poised to be used against me. At United Systems, I had supposedly done Microsoft Visual Basic (VB) programming for four years, but of course Hank kept preventing me from doing any coding. Now, the potential new project was VB 6, the last version before Microsoft retired it for ASP .NET. Going back was just that, going backwards. There was also a technology I had never done, tons of documentation, and the location was awful. It represented everything I hated in my career. So bombing the interview was the obvious move.

Except that one of the company owners was sitting beside me the entire time, the sales guy behind me, listening to every word. As if that wasn't bad enough, the interviewer was horrendous. Instead of just asking me a question, he would be purposely vague so that I had to first figure out what he was asking. I don't remember the technical questions, but an approximation of how the interview went would be like this:

"So let's say you had two piles of items, each with two things in them," he would ask.

"Okay."

"And you wanted to combine them. What would you do?"

I hesitated, as the answer seemed obvious, and he'd given it to me in the question. "Combine them."

"Right. But how?"

"You put them together?"

"Yes, but how?"

"By moving one pile to the other or moving both to the same spot."

"Okay. But what is that called?"

I hesitated, stifling irritation. "I'm sorry, I don't know what you're asking."

"Is there a word for that?"

A couple of words came to mind, but they wouldn't answer the question. "For what, exactly? Putting things together?"

"Yes."

I struggled to figure out what the hell he wanted me to say. "Are you talking about addition?"

"Yes! That's exactly right. So what happens when we put them together?"

Somebody kill me now, I thought. "They merge?"

"Yes. What is the result?"

Since I had already answered this, I admitted, "I'm sorry, I don't know what you're asking me."

"What happened to the piles now that we combined them?"

"They're one bigger pile," I said. He frowned, and I added again, "I'm sorry, I don't know what you're asking me."

He sighed in disappointment and finally gave me a clue what he was talking about. "If you had two items in the first pile and two in the second, what is the result?"

I suddenly realized what this entire chain of questions was about. I looked at him incredulously. "Are you asking me if two plus two equals four?"

"Yes!"

After forty-five minutes of this torture, I had to excuse myself to move my car from the 1-hour-only spot it was in because the guy was extending the interview. And then I couldn't find another place. The sales guy came out and yelled at me as I circled the building again. I gave in to responding that if it mattered so much to him, he could park it for me. Did he really think shouting at me was going to help a candidate during a job interview? When the ordeal was over, the co-owner said I had done a good job, but we didn't win the contract. I was heartbroken.

After this, I scheduled a talk with Mary, the Director of Operations, since she was one of the people likely deciding what I worked on. I politely admitted I was unhappy with the work I'd been doing since being hired because most of the company's projects were .NET and most of mine were not. She promised to resolve this and after weeks of no work to do, they assigned me back to the LSN project that had been my first prototype. She was overseeing the two PMs on it.

Steve, one of the Four Horsemen, and the one who interviewed me, was the technical lead on the app and had taken it over from me when I was put on the IRS project, which happened because I could get a clearance (that suggested Steve was not). But I wasn't doing the app itself, to my disappointment. Instead, I would be the architect of the reports using SQL Reporting Services, a component of SQL Server, the database I specialized in, so at least this was in my wheelhouse.

The reports were so challenging that even Steve didn't want to do them or figure out how. Our client interviewed survivors of landmines around the world and recorded the responses on paper, but the system was replacing this. The questions and answers could be in a half-dozen languages, and the app was designed in English. But screens existed to enter translations. Questionnaire #1 might have ten questions, but a staff member might have only entered translations for half of them. This meant that the reports needed to return a translation if it existed or the English if not. This wasn't actually that hard.

	Age	Range
Gender	20-30	31-40
Male	1	2
Female	0	0
Total	1	2

Example 1

Something was worse. The report needed to calculate totals into a chart like the first example here, where there is no data for the "Female" row showing zeros. The problem is that the report could only show data, not nonexistent data. Instead of looking like Example 1, the report would look like Example 2, where the Female row is missing altogether. But the client wanted it to look like Example 1. How could I make the chart show a row for data that didn't exist? Let's just say I added fake data for the missing row so that it would be sent to the chart, with all 0s as 1s. Then I used the charting software to make every 1 be a 0. The problem was that a legitimate 1 would *also* be made a 0, so I had to add a kind of tag to the fake column data so this subtraction would only happen where I told it to. Multiple problems like this existed in the reporting so that the coding became complex. But I found it fascinating, creative, and fun. For the first time in months, I didn't hate my job.

	Age	Range
Gender	20-30	31-40
Male	1	2
Total	1	2

Example 2

While this was happening, Mary made me supervise an offshore junior programmer in the Philippines, the first time the company had one, as an experiment. He was doing the easier reports at my direction. The 12-hour time difference complicated matters and meant almost exclusively email interaction. The guy reminded me of Dexter from Katan Corp in that he repeatedly bucked my directions. I had to look at his work every morning, tell him what he'd done wrong, and make him redo parts of it. In many cases, he repeatedly invented a function that I had already written when he should have known it existed. It wasn't like I hadn't told him or he couldn't look for one himself before inventing one.

By November, the project was largely done. And I had nothing to do for most of the month. I enjoyed the downtime while also wondering from experience if I was going to be let go. Other projects had finished at the company, including the IRS one and the second prototype I had done. Several programmers had been hired during the year to meet this demand, and a few more had quit, but now we had too many coders and not enough work. This was a problem I hadn't considered before, that my employer would win too many contracts, hire people, finish work, then let people go. When Mary called me into a meeting in her office, I feared the worst, but relaxed on not seeing the new HR woman. Mary asked me to close the door.

She was about my age, average height, a little pudgy, and Asian, with straight black hair halfway down her back. I had seldom seen her before the recent project, as if she hid in the shadows. She was sort of like the top PM and worked mostly with them. I found her distant, not personable, and unrelatable. She seemed phony. My wife eventually met her and thought Mary acted superior. I didn't dislike Mary so much as I never felt a connection with her, but then that was true of everyone at this job except Katarina and Julie. It might have been the coldest place I had ever worked.

"So," she began, sitting behind her desk, "I wanted to let you know something that's been going on for a while, since the IRS project."

I hadn't worked on the IRS thing since early June. "Okay."

"There's not an easy way to say this, so I'll just say it. We learned that no one here wants to work with you because of your behavior."

Shock passed over me before I flushed, an ugly mix of reactions and realizations rushing through me. Badmouthing. Rejection. Ostracism. Recrimination. Humiliation. Pain. Disbelief. Victimization. Bewilderment. Anger.

Mary continued, "They said you're difficult to work with and we can't find a PM who wants you on their project, which is why we haven't assigned you one."

Insulted, I immediately thought of suspects responsible for this and that I was being fired after all. "Who is saying this?"

"I don't really want to get into it."

Stifling a snort, I said, "I think I have a right to know who is badmouthing me to the other PMs. I assume it is Rod and Henry."

She pursed her lips, and I knew I had guessed correctly. Those assholes. "Well, most of what they're talking about is your emails."

I flushed anew. This seemed to be a common theme for me since someone had invented email in my mid-twenties, in the 1990s. Not really wanting to hear the answer, I asked, "What is wrong with my emails?"

"They said that they feel like they're being attacked."

That startled me. Was she serious? "That's a pretty awful thing to say and I think I would know if I was attacking someone."

"Well, they mean stuff like you pointing out mistakes they've made."

I almost laughed. "Are you saying I'm not supposed to say anything? I mean, isn't the problem that they made the mistake, not that I said something about it? I do this so that they will learn from it and not repeat it, and honestly, I consider that a responsibility of anyone who cares about their job. That is without question the point of me saying it and I know they are smart enough to see that."

I was certain of it, and that they were just pissed off that I'd said it, the egomaniacs. I wanted to say that it wasn't my problem that they couldn't handle learning they had screwed up, but I knew it would sound callous.

Mary said, "It comes down to your tone, and when I first read the emails, I agreed and found them off-putting, but when I read them a second or third time, I couldn't see it anymore and thought they were fine."

I shook my head in disbelief. As sometimes happened in my life, someone at work or outside of it often took exception to something I'd written even though I wasn't the sort to call someone names or type in all caps, for example. I wasn't overtly doing anything off-putting and by saying it was tone, Mary was admitting this. Even when upset, I tried to be polite, and yet I was learning over and over that it just didn't matter. No amount of care seemed able to hide an emotion like frustration from someone.

And why should we have to? Is everyone so incredibly bothered to learn others are not happy with them? Was everyone a snowflake? I felt like I had to bend over backwards to feign being happy with someone—because they were so sensitive—while they were going out of their way to take minor word choice issues in the worst possible way, then go after me over it. It was touchy and vindictive. I had seen it before and I was sick of being made to feel like I was some sort of email ogre, terrorizing villages of innocent victims that were forming a mob to hunt me down and destroy me.

And did my opinion of Derek and Henry really matter so much to them? They didn't act like it. Because if it did, maybe they should've stopped being obnoxious. Did they expect to be incompetent and overbearing, and have me like and respect them? Men like to pretend nothing hurts our feelings because it not happening supposedly means we're more manly, so for them to complain was especially odd, and even worse when you consider Mary's last statement that she couldn't see anything wrong with the emails on reading them again.

I said, "Doesn't that suggest there's no real problem with them?"

"Yeah, and that's part of why we don't think it's an issue."

That was something, at least. "You know what's a real issue? Two PMs badmouthing me to everyone so that none of them want to work with me. What have you done about this?"

She looked startled, and I knew the answer was "nothing." She said, "Well, we were looking into your behavior to see what the problem was."

"I think you need to look into *theirs*."

Mary frowned as if I was being ridiculous. "People are going to talk. It's normal."

"There's nothing *normal* about making a bunch of people at work not want to work with me. And you're right, people talk. The programmers don't enjoy working with either of them, especially Derek, and he causes serious morale problems while also doing sloppy work or overseeing other PMs who do. And that wastes time while he's pushing everyone to speed it up."

"He's one of our best PMs."

"Based on what criteria?" I rhetorically asked.

Dodging that, Mary admitted, "I did want to say we talked to everyone you've worked with."

Not for the first time, I felt like I had been put on trial behind my back, investigated for some crime, everyone who had a gripe against me given the opportunity to air it while I had no idea and didn't get to say my side of it until the verdict was handed down. This was fucked up.

"Everyone said that you're fine in person. Your emails can just be a little strong."

I almost laughed. After twenty years of speech problems starting when I was eight, my in-person style was actually the thing that was fine and my written words were the problem instead. "Fair enough. I think decisively. What can I say? Maybe I can hedge in my emails."

She perked up. "Yeah, that would be good. I mean, I appreciate that you have confidence, but it can bother some people. I know you had an incident with Derek early on and another with Henry always pushing things to be done way ahead of a reasonable schedule. I also noticed that neither of the PMs on the LSN project said anything, so it made me wonder if it was just the IRS project. Did you just not like that from the start?"

So it was only Derek and Henry. "It wasn't the project. It was the PMs and their behavior. Did the coders have a problem with me on that?"

Mary shook her head. "No, but Rod said your coding was sloppy and so we had to see what he meant."

That brought me up short and angered me. If there was one thing I wasn't, it was a sloppy coder. I may not have been a genius or one of those geeks who spent his free time programming, but if I had a reputation for anything in my career besides documentation skills, it was few bugs. Even when a screen I had done broke, it was usually because someone else changed a function that my screen was calling and didn't tell me or test every screen using it. This is such a known way to introduce bugs that preventing it has a name: regression testing. This type of breakage had happened repeatedly on the IRS project and been discussed in the developer meetings (I wasn't the only one affected by it).

Had Rod blamed me for someone else breaking my screens after I was done with them? That was taking a dim view of a bug on my screens being reported—sometimes a week or more after others had peer reviewed and *also* validated that it worked. Ironically, Rod was often the culprit of bugs because he had repeatedly changed the architecture of the apps, and this had always broken things en masse. Even before we had so many people coding on it, as the first programmer to work on the apps besides him, I had updated or fixed his code more than once. The pot had called the kettle black.

I asked, "What do you mean, you had to see what Rod meant? Are you saying you've been investigating my coding? Since when?"

"Yeah, the reason you were working on the LSN project with me and Steve is that we were evaluating your conduct and coding to see if there is a problem."

I went cold. I had been on trial and not known it. So much going on behind my back, so little time. This sounded strangely familiar.

"And the verdict?" I asked.

"We concluded that there isn't a problem with either, so you're good. We were actually really impressed with your work on the reports, and even your handling of the problems that the Filipino guy was causing, and the emails you sent out about all of it. Steve reviewed everything, too, and had no issues. We really needed someone to handle this as a senior developer and you did exactly that. So there's no problem at all."

Like hell there isn't, I thought, a little relieved I wasn't being fired, as far as I could tell, but I thought, *A third of the company has been badmouthing me for half a year and you've known for months and did nothing about it. There's definitely a problem.*

"Then why are we talking about this?" I asked, not sure I wanted the answer.

"Well, we just wanted you to be aware of the tone thing with email so you can make any adjustments, for your sake and anyone else's. We've decided anything going on with that is unintentional."

The conversation concluded shortly after and I left. I logged into SourceSafe to investigate something. SourceSafe was a code repository, like a library that we can check code in and out of. This is how programmers work on the same project. We can create each screen in ASP .NET and then add it to the repository. If I checked it out, like a book, no one else could change it or see what I had done until I checked it back in. They could update the project so that everyone's latest changes were downloaded into ASP .NET. Running the program would then have the latest code. This way of working is standard. A feature of repositories is that they let you see who checked things in and out and when, and even what they changed in case the alterations needed to be undone or rolled back.

I examined all of my work on the IRS project. After my final check-in of anything, between one and three other programmers had altered it to make what looked like minor changes to the approaches we were using. Each of those modifications had taken place after I left the project. But what I was looking for was Rod, and I found that he had altered several screens I had worked on. Without exception, his changes came after those of others and were of the same nature, updating methodology. There was nowhere that a change looked like fixing "sloppy" coding. Nothing had been rewritten, just a line or two altered to go with continuing changes.

The accusation made no sense anyway, for multiple reasons. I was the first programmer on the IRS screens for the desktop app, and literally everyone else that joined the project was basing their work on mine. Wouldn't my sloppiness have been noticed and commented on before? People would have suggested my screens be changed because they needed to be consistent so that there weren't ten coding styles from ten programmers. And then this was repeated when I was once again made the first programmer on the web app. Was the thought, "Well, Randy did such sloppy work on the desktop app that we should have him start off the web project that way, too." Wasn't I being chosen, at least the second time, proof that I had set a positive precedent they wanted to duplicate?

Then they sent me to that insurance company to fix a horrendously complicated problem on a technology I didn't even know. Who sends a sloppy programmer to do that? And then when investigating my sloppiness, they had me do something simple on the LSN project, right? Nope. They had me architect the reports, the most challenging data analytics the company had ever done, once again using tech I didn't know, because they needed a senior person (and the four "Senior Developers" were all busy). Then they had me mentoring the junior offshore talent.

It bears pointing out that the LSN client was high strung, demanding, and intolerant, and I not only got the reports done, but was asked to teach them how to use them. Did you have an asshole staff member like me, whom "no one" wants to work with, work directly with a touchy client? In fairness, by that point, they must have decided I wasn't a jerk after all. The whole thing boggled the mind, but I got clarity before long. I went to lunch with Julie, who told me that the co-owners sometimes blew offhand comments by one of the Four Horsemen out of proportion and that was all this likely was. Still, Rod had made me look bad.

At some point in all of this, I realized that, aside from the Four Horseman, I might have been the most senior programmer on staff, at least on paper, due to my certifications and ten years of experience, even if nearly half of that was shit work. This likely explained most of my assignments: create the architecture of two apps when prototyping; architect the screens on both the IRS desktop and web apps; fix Microsoft Project data mapping nightmare; and architect the LSN reports. I was also the one they sent on that awful interview to win a client (because you obviously send someone no one wants to work with to impress a client and then work with them).

That Sunday, the company had a Christmas brunch that I no longer wanted to attend, given that so many people who hated me would be there. My wife agreed, but we went anyway and didn't overstay our welcome. That night, I updated my resume on Monster.com and didn't block DataSoft from being able to see it. I had heard that employers fired staff for looking to leave, but I didn't really care. I didn't understand it either, as it seemed vindictive.

They had destroyed my job, anyway. Mary seemed to think they had set in motion fixing my email tone, as if I'd become a more pleasant coworker, but what she'd done was alerted me to copious bullshit that would make anyone want to leave. I knew they hadn't done a thing to quell the terrible reputation Derek and Henry had given me, and I knew from experience that I would never recover from it. Both of them had tried to bully me to my face and failed, and my pushback was the reason they went with Plan B— do it behind my back. They succeeded. If you can't beat 'em, destroy 'em.

My resume was more popular than ever, with scores of recruiters contacting me about jobs in one week. I didn't have to take this crap at work, but I soon learned I wasn't the only one to get such treatment.

Despite the conversation with Mary and her statement that everything was fine, signs grew that they weren't. I had noticed since August that when I saw either of the owners, they would not only not greet me at all, like they used to, but would immediately look away as if they had seen a stranger on the street. What this told me was *when* they heard I was a sloppy jerk no one wanted to work with—after I returned from the insurance company gig. And it continued.

In early December, my employer loudly announced that "everyone" was getting the annual holiday bonus, a $500 gift card. They did not hand these out all at once. At first, Julie and I were among those who didn't receive one, but then she got hers. I began asking the new HR woman, a girl in her early 20s who had almost no experience (it showed), and she finally told me they were "discretionary" and not everyone got one after all. I was not getting one. On hearing this, I flushed, feeling deeply disapproved and like they had lied me to that everything was supposedly fine. Was this a passive aggressive action? It seemed like it.

Suspicion loomed and I didn't like feeling like more nasty things were going on behind my back and I wasn't being told what they were. Julie had one PM friend she trusted and who told her they did this every year to at least one person. That they had singled me out over the badmouthing seemed obvious and I was angry.

The company also announced that everyone who didn't already have a 17" monitor was being given one by New Year's Day. I saw them appearing on everyone's desks, and on my first working day in January, I arrived first and unlocked the front door. Seeing I still had a smaller monitor, I went upstairs and confirmed every last person had a bigger screen now except me. I didn't care about the monitor so much as what seemed like another silent swipe at me, and my suspicions that this was personal grew. They had also said everyone was getting a "phone switch" by then, and I was also skipped for this.

My annual review two weeks later had been on my mind, a black cloud of passive aggressive nastiness over my head. Not for the first time, I wanted to be a contractor for the rest of my career because, as an employee, I was consistently treated like shit or given bad assignments. Since the meeting with Mary in November, I still hadn't been assigned a project by mid-January.

I wasn't the only one being screwed with. I was now regularly talking with Julie, who told me the company had given her a lot of crap her first year, PMs having also said she was hard to work with. Nothing could have been farther from the truth, in my experience with her. Their reason had been a stunner—she asked too many questions. It still makes me laugh. The PMs produced horrible documentation that caused confusion, but programmers can't code vagueness. We need accuracy. That PMs thought her desire for clarity made her hard to work with is some next level stupid. Julie was now informed that she had a meeting with Mary that week to prepare for her own annual review to ensure it went well, because if that review happened now, "it wouldn't go in your favor." We were both shocked by that. She also told me some stories I don't remember, of others being given similar crap and lectured in meetings like the one I'd had with Mary.

The lunatics were running the asylum, despite virtually all the PMs having less than two years' experience. DataSoft was a software development company that seemingly hated software developers. Not for the first time, on my way out the door, I was learning things I wish I had known before.

Around this time, the company fired a programmer named Zain. His offense had been doing his job, making updates to a prototype website on a development machine. The problem was that one update broke the site. At that moment, one of the co-owners was trying to demo the site to the customer and couldn't. Rather than warning Zain to ensure it was running and push no updates until after the meeting, they told him nothing, so that it was at least partially their fault. They made the network admin disable all of Zain's access to his computer, etc., so that when he tried to log in the next day, he couldn't and didn't understand why. For help, he went to the network admin, who found himself in the uncomfortable position of knowing Zain had been fired and not been told yet.

I was starting to think I had been treated fairly.

In discussing my situation with Julie and my wife, both thought it unlikely they would fire me because I had done nothing wrong. I wasn't so sure. Two weeks into the new year, I finally couldn't take it anymore, this feeling of impending termination. I emailed Mary to get an update on what my project would be. Instead of a response from her, I got one from the HR girl asking me to come in on a Monday for a 3 PM meeting when I was normally working from home. That day at noon, one co-owner arrived, and they asked me to do the meeting now. When he walked in to join us, I knew what was happening.

CHAPTER SIXTEEN

The Value of a Good Pitch

Wade said, "It's not working out, so we're gonna let you go."

Irritated by the confirmation of my suspicions, I frowned at the co-owner Wade, who had once sat beside me while I went on that awful interview months earlier. He was more personable compared to the other owner, who seemed farther into his 60s and gave the impression of being the gruff, technical one. I had liked Wade prior to the cold shoulder he started giving me in August. Now I scrutinized his balding head with its patchy, salt-and-pepper stubble beard, seeing a carefully neutral expression mixed with a matter-of-fact demeanor. I sensed he just wanted to get this over with and wasn't interested in talking to me, but I wanted information. He seemed uncomfortable, even intimidated.

I asked, "What is not working out?"

He hesitated and vaguely said, "I understand some conversations have happened."

I interrupted. "Only one with Mary."

"One is enough. Things haven't changed, and it's not working out."

"I have had no contact with PMs since that conversation and no actual work to do, so how could I have upset a PM or write supposedly sloppy code? Mary claimed there was no issue anyway, so what changed?"

"No one wants to work with you and it makes it difficult to find projects for you."

I frowned at him, offended by this sentiment. "You know that's an insulting thing to say to someone, right?"

A brief scowl appeared. Then Wade said as if having caught me and not to bluff him, "We know you posted your resume on Monster."

Did that explain everything since the meeting with Mary? "So that's what this is about?"

"We're not happy. You're not happy, so we're letting you go."

Only a dick repeats it. "I heard you the first time. Did you expect me to be happy after what Mary told me?"

"Like I said, you're not happy, and we're not happy. We're giving you two weeks' severance. She can give you details on your termination." He indicated the HR girl, who silently sat there looking uncomfortable. Severance meant this was a layoff, not firing, and the vague "letting you go" was a way to indicate my termination was not for misconduct. Here, it was just personal animosity toward me. I had thought that was true of just Derek and Henry, but the way he and the other owner had been acting made me feel like they thought I had created a hostile work environment and ruined the job for everyone else. The irony.

I said, "You know, termination is an ugly word you don't say to people."

Ignoring that, he replied, "We want you to get your things and leave immediately. If you need a reference, I'd be happy to be one."

My eyes likely widened in disbelief. Was he kidding? If he was serious, this seemed to say he knew that this was injustice. Or was this and the severance an attempt to buy my silence? Because I was angry and my indignation was not for sale.

Snidely, I said, "Thanks, but I'll pass."

Since I kept a light desk, I was gone in five minutes, turning over my key to the building. I had no chance to say goodbye to anyone, and though I haven't mentioned them, I had gotten along fine with all the developers, including the Four Horsemen.

In the aftermath, when I told Julie, she was mad and ready to quit. She called all the PMs she had worked with in the last year and asked if any of them had a problem with her. Several hesitated before denying they did, and she knew they were lying. We didn't think she was getting fired because they gave her the bonus and other things denied me, but she was in peril. At her review, she was told that Derek and Henry liked her but that two other PMs on another project thought she needed too much hand-holding, a variant on "you ask too many questions." Julie also forwarded the email that HR sent out to everyone, making it sound like I voluntarily quit. They were liars. And petty.

I called Katarina and told her the whole story. She was both shocked and not shocked, admitting that this sort of thing was the reason she quit. She had to sit there while good people were treated like this. They had tried to force Julie out the previous year, so I told her they were after Julie again right now. She said the gift cards were not discretionary and that everyone got one unless the co-owners or Mary decided they didn't like someone, and they always did this shit of announcing everyone got one and then bypassing someone, a passive aggressive stunt.

Since she already knew my salary and worked as a recruiter, I asked her what I should be making, as I suspected I was too low (now that I had those certifications). I was intending to ask employers for another $10k. She told me I could make up to $25k more! After she had left the company, she asked me to be a reference and to pretend she was still the recruiter there, so I had done so. Now I asked her to return the favor—*she* would pretend she was still the HR rep there and be a reference. She agreed, of course. To this day, she's a Facebook friend, and probably still calls me "Rands!"

I filed for unemployment and indicated I had been laid off. To my surprise, the MD unemployment office called back and said DataSoft had indicated they had fired me for misconduct and a dispute was underway. If I lost, I would collect no benefits for five weeks. Upset, I called the HR girl, who said she had made a mistake, that the forms for this were confusing, and that she would correct it. And she did, but it was just another sign that, except for the programmers, virtually everyone in the company was incompetent. Less than a decade later, the owners sold DataSoft to another company, and it effectively ceased to exist. Wade retired and the other co-owner started another firm.

My resume continued to be hot, and I soon had three interviews in one day. I wasn't worried about finding a job and told those who asked that DataSoft had won an unusual number of contracts, hired people, delivered projects, and then didn't have enough work for people. I was among those laid off. This had an element of truth to it, and no one questioned it.

The only thing stopping me from getting some jobs was the technical interview, like usual.

One tech exam featured such poorly worded, written questions that I had to figure out what they meant. When the guy came back and said I'd gotten those two wrong, I explained my interpretation and why the wording suggested that. He was the one who had written the questions, and now he grudgingly admitted what I did was right based on my understanding, but then he told HR I failed the test and not to hire me. What that told me was that the guy was full of shit and I didn't want to work with him, anyway.

Another guy asked me to say the worst thing that happened with developing. Then he told the recruiters I was too negative. He also said I would be overwhelmed by leading a project from start to finish simply because I hadn't on the same project before; I always got pulled off, but I had repeatedly done every phase of one: requirements gathering, design/architecture, coding, reporting, testing, deployment, and maintenance, not to mention user training and all documentation. He actually said I was perfect except for that and refused to hire me. Little did he know I had now released two albums of my music, with me as composer, performer, recording engineer, producer, record label, promoter, band manager/leader, and sometimes graphic designer—after building the guitars I used on them and even assembling the computer used to record them in my home studio. Oh, and never mind gaining four years of classical guitar skill in only two years to earn my Bachelor of Music, Magna cum Laude, all while dealing with horrible personal troubles. Overwhelmed my ass.

Each time someone asked me to recite the definition of something I barely remembered or never heard of, I looked it up later and added it to my list of terms to re-memorize. Sometimes a concept had been invented or popularized after I started my career, and since I didn't spend my free time perusing programming websites, I hadn't heard it. Other terms were new but referred to something I had been doing for years before someone named it, so I already implemented it but didn't know it now had a name, so it looked like I didn't do the practice in my work, and I shouldn't be hired. I found much of this aggravating.

So often while I was job searching, companies would insist that if I didn't have the exact experience in every last piece of technology they used, I would be unable to learn it and do the job. And yet once they hired me, employers consistently refused to let me do the technologies I *did* have experience in, while sending me on projects to do new ones I had never used.

For a year, recruiters had been calling me about Microsoft SharePoint, something I had only recently heard of and had no experience with. It wasn't on my resume. I didn't understand why people were pitching me jobs that were exclusively that or SharePoint *and* ASP .NET. Then a recruiter explained it to me—SharePoint was an OOTB (out-of-the-box) intranet that someone could install into a SQL Server database, kind of like Microsoft Project, which I had briefly worked with at the insurance company client of my last employer. Using the resulting website screens SharePoint auto-generated, users could auto-generate more screens/sites and change them with button clicks or by dragging "web parts" around on screen to rearrange them. But if someone wanted to programmatically alter the way SharePoint worked, they had to write ASP .NET code. As someone who specialized (or tried to!) in the Microsoft "stack" (i.e., their tech), I knew this fell into my wheelhouse and I should probably learn it.

One interview produced my next job, the first doing SharePoint, but I ran into one problem that I didn't mind and another that I did. The first was that the person expected to do the technical part of the interview became unavailable and I could skip it altogether! The other arose as I was getting in the elevator to leave after the non-technical interview. The recruiter jogged up and stopped the door from closing.

/

"Hey," he said, "there's a problem with your clear-ance."

"What?"

"I couldn't find it in JPAS."

"What's JPAS?"

"It's the DOD security clearances app that allows peo-ple to verify clearances. Yours isn't showing up."

I frowned. "What does that mean?"

"I'm not sure, but I would check with your recent em-ployers to see if they transferred it to them. If it's gone inactive, we would still move forward with hiring you but have to reduce the salary."

That was just what I needed. "Okay, I'll check and let you know."

I left, not worried about this. An employer has to "hold" a clearance by transferring it to them, possibly through that JPAS app, and if no one "holds" it for two years, the clearance goes inactive. I had been at DataSoft twelve months and Katan Corp before that for fourteen months, so if my clearance had gone inactive, then USAIS was the last one to hold it. It would also mean that neither employer since then had transferred it despite telling me they had. What were the odds?

But that's exactly what had happened. I first confirmed that DataSoft never transferred it, and then that Katan Corp hadn't either. I was furious. There was nothing I could do and no way to prevent that from happening in the future because all an employer had to do was lie to me that they'd done it and I had no way to verify it, as only a com-pany's security officer had access to JPAS. When I told the new company, they said they would sponsor me for a new one and lower my salary offer.

To quote my diary:

I got lucky with the tech interview for these guys. It was supposed to be in person last Thursday, then on the phone with the CTO on Friday. He cancelled and on Monday, I learned the recruiter was trying to line up someone else. I grew worried, thinking a CTO was less in the weeds and might ask fewer technical questions or less troublesome ones. With no warning, the phone rang for the interview. It was a programmer who admitted they had given him 2 minutes warning that he was doing a tech interview, and he wasn't prepared. I smiled. He asked all of 5 questions that were super easy, though we spent 25 minutes on the phone just talking about being programmers. He wanted me to ask questions! I was pacing around, smiling and laughing, knowing I had the job now.

Within 5 minutes, Julie sent an instant message saying the recruiter had just called her. Checking references is the last step, usually. He spoke to Katarina, and Dean from Katan Corp. I hadn't talked to Dean since I left, and it surprised me at how happy he seemed to hear from me. It was more like when we first worked together. After he became CTO, he was all business, or hanging out with his Marine buddy. He agreed to be a reference and within minutes, the deal was done and the recruiter was moving forward with paperwork. That's when he told me the salary reduction amount. I am trying hard to tell myself I'm going up by $13k and should be thrilled, especially after being laid off, but I would make $20k more if I hadn't just been screwed again. They dropped the offer by $7k.

Because of this salary cut, I was already a bit sour on MicroSys, my new employer. I tried to shake it off and hope for the best despite my history, but the salary drop proved an omen. The problems started on day one and were initially trivial. I had no computer because someone thought I was starting a week later. When they finally gave it to me, they had spelled my last name wrong in the system; changing it was labor intensive and caused minor problems with things like email for weeks.

They had an upper floor of a glass and steel high-rise in Tyson's Corner, VA, so that I saw the USAIS building on my left as I exited the beltway into the city streets to my right. The parking garage was a plus, but my lack of an assigned workspace was the worst desk situation I had faced.

Every day, I sat in a large conference room with a table in the center. Along the walls were alcoves, not cubes. Each was just deep enough to fit a keyboard, mouse, and monitor on. They weren't much wider. The walls were no deeper. Alcoves lined three of the room's walls so that I was practically shoulder-to-shoulder with peers, each of us able to see those beside us from the corner of our eyes.

I needed to choose a spot each morning and hunt for a chair in other offices or conference rooms, sometimes being accosted by someone telling me I could not have that one. My bad neck from a 1997 car accident and my body adjusting to a new chair every day sometimes meant neck stiffness, pain, and a headache. I couldn't leave any personal office supplies at work because someone else could take my seat and my stuff the next day. Renovations were taking place in part of the office and more permanent seating was in the works.

The people I shared the room with were not friendly. They considered the location transient; no one was supposed to be here for long and yet I would spend two months there, seldom seeing the same people so that I hardly knew anyone. Those present were often there for a day and not seen again. They knew no one in the room, too, and they already knew they might never see us again once they deployed us to a client site. Maybe they saw no reason to speak to anyone, but I felt like I didn't belong there and already didn't like my job.

And I had no work for weeks. This was surprisingly common in my career when starting a job (or even after being there for months). I was bored, but there are worse problems to have at work and I had probably had most of them. I didn't feel needed or particularly wanted and was already questioning why they hired me. And part of me just didn't care anymore.

My ambition was slipping. There seemed no point in working hard when it wouldn't be appreciated, or I'd be shown the door over something trivial. At least I had more sense now that it wasn't just me, as I had seen others treated badly. There's an old idea that people will work just hard enough to not get fired. If I was going to get fired anyway, maybe I shouldn't be working hard to begin with? I was starting to just want a paycheck. At United Systems with Hank, I had felt like I'd lost my soul, meaning my work ethic. I found it happening again, but not from a specific employer or manager. Maybe all of them. My career was destroying my desire to continue it, but I had tripled my salary and risen to six figures. Trying to switch careers would mean a significant pay cut. I wasn't serious about walking away, but something needed to change, and in the short term, that thing was my attitude. I was finding harder to give a shit anymore.

And my first project made this worse. They assigned me to help with a SharePoint task for the U.S. Navy, which had me visiting both the Navy Yard and Bolling Air Force Base across the river, south of D.C. Entering such places was one perk of my career, though most of these locations were unexciting, old, and a little run down. Some, like the Navy Yard, built in 1799, even predated cars. While I have some interest in historical places, working in such a place doesn't allow one to enjoy that aspect. There's no tour guide to make it interesting and any significance to the things I saw was lost on me. Those who take a tour may envy those who work in these locations, but it can be the other way around, where the staff may not understand the uniqueness of the location because doing a job is the focus, not appreciating the place's significance. Still, I always perked up on learning I got to enter one.

The problem was the project itself. The work was non technical, like writing a user manual or training Navy personnel in a classroom setting on how to use the site my new coworkers had designed. I wanted no part of this and knew I would get questions I could not answer. This was unacceptable. Then someone said I would morph into a customer service representative and I flat out said no, not caring if my refusal got me fired. I was drawing a line in the sand and thou shalt not cross it. My manager said being flexible is part of being a good contractor, to which I privately thought that they were the contractor and I was a software developer who didn't care about being *that* flexible. My flexibility had caused nothing but problems. I was already eliminating or downplaying documentation experience on my resume so no one would realize how good at it I was, and stick me with that instead of coding.

Someone told the client I was doing SharePoint taxonomy (a hierarchical classification of items), which I had never heard of, and the client cornered me, wanting me to break the task down into smaller ones with due dates I would be accountable for. This was an awful position to be put in and a sign of things to come. My manager was doing all of this so that I was "billable" and earning them money, rather than me being on company "overhead" and costing them it. He and the team were very nice, at least, one guy even reading a fantasy book I had recently finished writing. But this wasn't what I was looking for, my eyes already on the door.

During my interview, MicroSys had told me that a shortage of SharePoint developers had them hiring .NET programmers that they would train in SharePoint development. This sounded like a great way to learn a tech I hadn't used, so I took the job. They also had straight-up .NET projects, and while they weren't a software development company, providing technical staff of various kinds to federal clients was their business. This included SharePoint and network admins, or whatever else came up.

As it turned out, I was the first of these .NET guys to be trained in SharePoint, and therein lay the problem. They didn't have any idea how to go about training me. There was no one to do it. They had plenty of qualified developers, but they were all offsite on projects. There was no plan. They didn't even have a SharePoint development environment for me to use. As the Navy project continued, my manager finally said he wanted me to train myself. I wasn't sure where to begin other than researching on the internet, and when he said I should get certified, I almost laughed. There was no way I was going from total ignorance to certified by myself, especially when I checked for brain dumps, and none existed.

And then someone promoted my manager, and a new hire took his place. Dick was a few years older than me, with receding brown hair and a gut. He exclusively wore a suit and tie without the jacket. I eventually learned he was a Mormon with at least six children, living in a big house out in Leesburg, VA, a rural community that had recently exploded in population, becoming a kind of suburb of itself. Dick reminded me of the stereotype of a used car salesman—a guy who would say anything to gain someone's confidence. He never stopped smiling, but there was something obscene about it. He could tell someone they would die a horribly painful death and still have the creepy-ass grin on his face.

I first met Dick in June in a conference room he had to use for meetings because he didn't have somewhere to sit every day, either. I had asked to talk to him about my projects and his intentions for me.

"I agree we aren't using you effectively as a resource," he admitted. "What they have you doing is for very junior people."

Referring to me as a resource to my face always bugged me. I was a person, not a thing. "Couldn't agree more," I said, relieved.

"I see you more as a team lead than a developer."

I arched an eyebrow. Having some authority sounded like a good idea. Maybe it would minimize someone screwing with me, but I wasn't sure I wanted to be a manager after what many of mine had done to me. "So how do we go about getting me on something different?"

"I'm pulling you off that Navy project. I want you to resume this SharePoint training work. I'd like you to learn how to create a SharePoint development environment and document it so others can create one for themselves. You would be the lead on this, and you'll be able to delegate some things to others. After that, we'll have you as the technical architect on projects. That would be your title, probably within six months."

"That would be great." Training myself still wasn't what I wanted or had been told, but being the guy who created something everyone else needed could give me some esteem if done well. The rest sounded like I would finally move in the right direction and I came away from the meeting relieved and even a bit excited. Finally, I had a manager who agreed to give me the assignments I should've been doing. I just had to get past this training thing, but with a brighter prospect on the other side of it, I dove in.

It wasn't just my work that I found new enthusiasm for, but the social aspects there. After being ostracized out of my last job, I felt determined to at least get along with everyone, even if I thought they were an ass. This was not my strong suit because I don't suffer fools gladly, and my honest opinion emerges, no matter how subtly I make it, via a knowing look I seem unable to eliminate. My wife had once told me she married me because she knew she could trust me, precisely because I don't hide what I think very well. There's a good reason I never play poker.

I had so far been a bit stifled in any attempt to be social there because I didn't know anyone except the Navy project people, who never came to HQ. The company did many happy hours in a large game room they had for entertaining clients. It had a pool table, bar, dart board, shuffleboard, and a big screen TV with Wii and at least Guitar Hero set up. I initially ignored these because I left at 3 PM and they didn't start hanging out until 5 PM, often with no announcement happening so that I did not know I was missing them.

But then MicroSys finished renovations and I finally got a cube, something that is often despised compared to an office, but I now knew there was something worse. This helped me get to know those who sat near, though none were coders. And they told me about the happy hours. Being a little quiet in large gatherings, I didn't fare very well at them at first because people naturally talk to those they have a rapport with first, but I slowly knew people more. But I was still on the outside looking in when the company also took us on two party buses to the Washington Nationals baseball game. I spent much of it alone because no one I had a rapport with was there, or they excused themselves (I wasn't being invited to go with them) to go talk to someone else and never came back. It was a little pathetic and turned embarrassing after the game, when some drunk coworkers were grinding against each other on the party bus back to HQ. Was that what I was missing? Was it the fast track to being social? My wife would've killed me.

The recruiter who found me, and told me about the problem with my clearance, helped my social life at work without meaning to. My first week, he took me to lunch as part of the corporate hiring routine, and he asked several people from the office to come so it wouldn't just be us, but a more social experience. Well, now he routinely asked me to join these on another person's first week, especially if they were technical like me; I was often the only tech person at HQ. The result was that, as they continued hiring people frequently, I was getting a free lunch almost once a week and knowing yet another person who associated me with this welcoming experience. I liked the recruiter and we were work friends of a sort. Little did I know he would betray me.

Up to then, the only team I had been on was for the Navy project, but I basically saw none of them again except the PM, a beautiful Latina woman who I got along with very well. To my surprise, she invited me to her wedding that summer and I brought my wife, who agreed that I must have turned a corner on social elements at work to secure this invitation. We clicked with the couple and talked of outings together, but it never happened. I always remember the PM because she agreed with me that, at many jobs, once you leave, almost everyone there acts like you died, not answering emails or returning calls. We both thought it was silly, so it surprised me when she did that very thing to me when I left.

It wasn't until I joined the newly formed company softball team that they finally socially accepted me at work, one reason being that I had something to do with other people instead of being isolated. I had never played softball, just baseball as a kid. And I sucked. I was a poor batter but a decent outfielder able to catch fly balls with ease but discombobulated by grounders, mostly because on the uneven outfield, balls took surprising bounces and ended up going by me.

But even the softball team offered politics. I wasn't sure I wanted to do it and had to miss the first two games due to band practice. By now I had disbanded my instrumental band because too few places would let us perform and it wasn't worth it. But I still wanted to do concerts, so I had recently joined an Iron Maiden tribute band that was gearing up. When I arrived to watch the third pair of games (they were always doubleheaders), I would not play, but they were short-staffed and someone had a spare glove. I ended up playing and had a lot of fun. We went out for drinks after, and it was the first time I felt like I belonged there. And so I meant to play every week.

But I was out of shape. On the drive home, my ankles started to hurt, and by the time I parked in my garage, they hurt so badly from the running that I was not accustomed to that I could not put weight on either foot. I literally crawled across the garage floor, into the house, and up the stairs, my wife getting ice for me. I couldn't walk for two days and had to work from home. It still makes me laugh and was the first time my body told me I wasn't in my teens or early twenties anymore, but in my mid-thirties. Being older than many at work was the other reason I didn't fit in before.

Within days of this, they included me in a silly email game with a dozen people from the office. They called it "Story Time" and everyone replied to the same message, adding a few more words to the sentence being written. There was no way that would've happened without the softball games because I hardly knew anyone doing it were it not for that. Happy hours were infinitely more pleasant, too. I had turned a corner and was happy with my social life at work, more so than ever before.

Despite my ankle injury, I bought a glove and came to the next doubleheader, but the two guys running the team refused to put me in at all and ducked questions about why. In the following weeks, I fared only slightly better and even the team members started giving them shit about it, recognizing the unfairness. They came to my aid partly because I was the only one taking photos, with a 35 mm camera (the smartphone revolution had only just started), and uploading them to the company network, a fact they appreciated. That I was doing something positive for everyone instead of sitting there resentfully might have helped.

One co-captain, Jason, was the team's primary pitcher, but he was increasingly unpopular. He yelled at everyone who made a mistake. He often tried to play someone else's position for them, such as him having the ball and instead of throwing it to first base, running over and tagging it himself. His arm tired easily so that he seldom finished a game when pitching. To our growing relief, he rarely showed up, but that left us with the other co-captain as pitcher, and he sucked, once walking a dozen batters in a single inning; we lost games from that alone.

I'd always had good aim and had dabbled in baseball pitching in little league, so I tried pitching during warmups one night. Teammates slowly noticed my aim as I calibrated it. During the first game, the opposing team scored twenty runs in a single inning and Jason quit and put me in. I did better than him and pitched both games. The following week, he was absent, and I exclusively pitched, hearing a lot of "great pitching" and "It looks like we found our pitcher." We had much more fun without Jason, a fact people loudly commented on before someone told the other team captain to "fire your boyfriend." I tried not to laugh. I had taken the place of the jerk who wouldn't let me play at all and saw it as sweet revenge. The pitcher is the most important person on a team. And suddenly it was me. I loved it. And this was what finally had me fully accepted, not only on the team, but around the office.

I had come to like my job and my peers.

But nothing lasts forever.

CHAPTER SEVENTEEN

The Bait and Switch

While I continued making strides on the softball team and on a social level at work, I was also teaching myself SharePoint. The problem was that I needed a development environment before I could code in one, and it had become my job to create one. While I knew Microsoft Windows well, I had seldom touched Windows Server, a more sophisticated version. How to install and configure it for SharePoint preceded doing the same with SQL Server and finally SharePoint itself. This was a tall order, but I had fulfilled those before and did it again, documenting how I had done so.

With that settled, I started on the software development piece but only got as far as the "Hello World!" app known to all programmers. It's a simple first program that makes the platform, in this case SharePoint, respond to a button click by putting those words on screen. There was a reason I got no farther, and my boss was it.

They had wanted to hire .NET developers like me and train us in SharePoint until hiring me and deciding to make me train myself. After months of not hiring anyone else like me, they finally had me be the person doing the technical interview of other guys, with Dick handling the rest of the interview. We hired another guy, who I subsequently trained. Then he, instead of me, was deployed on a project while they left me behind at HQ. Then all of this happened with another person. Then a woman. Each time, I protested to Dick, as I once again did in his office.

I asked, "Why do they get to be sent out as SharePoint developers and I'm still here training people?"

"Because you're our trainer."

I frowned. "That's not why I'm here. Instead of training me, you made me train myself, but now you're making me train everyone else, and they get the kind of work that I came here to do while I don't."

His grin increased. "But you're so good at it."

"Flattery will get you nowhere. I want a programming assignment. I wrote all this documentation about this so that no one needs me for this, and they don't."

"Forward that to me. I want to see it."

"Sure."

"We'll see about getting you other work."

"That would be great."

I left and reviewed my *SharePoint Installation and Configuration Guide*, the product of months of work, one last time before sending it to him for review. I wrote it in Microsoft Word, which has a feature called "Track Changes." This means that when he edited it, I could see everything he had changed and accept or reject the alterations. He sent the document back a couple of days later, asking me to review his modifications. To my disbelief, one change he made was to remove my name from the "Author" line on the title page and replace it with his! This was the most blatant attempt at taking credit for my work that I had seen.

I replaced his name with mine amid other changes and sent it right back to him. He returned it hours later with only one change—his name in place of mine. I changed it back to mine again and returned it. I didn't see the document again. With the possible exception of his superiors, everyone knew I was working on this, so if he tried to pass that document off as his, everyone would know what he had done. Was he really that stupid? I had no doubt that he forwarded it to the Vice President and CTO with his name on it.

Shortly after, he unveiled another unpleasant surprise for me in his office. "I want you to go to a university in Lexington with the CTO and Conner," Dick said. We were now in his room, with its frosted glass windows to either side of the door. Aside from that touch, it was as boring as any other I had seen.

I had lived near D.C. since the early 1980s and was unaware of where he meant. "Where is Lexington?"

"An hour south of Charlottesville," he said, meaning Virginia. My sister lived in Charlottesville, and I knew it was a 2.5 hour drive. No wonder I had never heard of it.

"Why am I going there?"

Referring to our CTO, he said, "Martin will install and configure SharePoint for a University there and we want you to shadow him."

I scowled. "What for? I'm a developer, not a SharePoint admin."

"Martin is a CTO and has better things to do than this sort of work, but he's the only one at MicroSys who knows how to do this, except you."

I shook my head, not flattered. "I've only done it in development, not production. That's a very different setup." A dev box could have SQL Server and SharePoint on the same computer, but a production environment had these installed on separate ones, and it was more convoluted.

Dick's smile grew, as if I had set myself up. "That's why you're going to learn it from him. You'll be the new person who sets up SharePoint for our clients."

I again shook my head. "No, I'm a developer. This is not what I do for a living."

"Sometimes we have to do what we have to do," he said, as if sagely.

Yeah, like find another job.

Despite my objections, he sent me and Conner, a .NET developer I had helped interview and recommended for hire, to Lexington. We stayed for two nights in a motel apart from Martin, who had nicer digs. We watched him struggle to implement SharePoint on the university's network as he ran into multiple problems and the client watched and peppered him with questions, to which I did not know the answers. I watched in utter boredom, resolved to quit before this became my job. Martin had played a few games of the softball team and been surprised by my pitching, but we otherwise had nothing in common and he chatted it up with Conner while I got slightly drunk each night at dinner. Martin was paying for everything, generous with the bar tab, and openly encouraging us to order another round. One thing about the company is that they were big on socializing and drinking, and I sometimes felt like that was my job rather than doing any actual work. It was working, at least. That summer, a VP threw a pool party at her house and invited me, so I went on my motorcycle without my wife but didn't stay overlong.

We hired several more people with me interviewing many more. I trained each new person, and they were still deployed while I was not. I was increasingly certain Dick was reneging on the promise to let me do SharePoint development. While this was happening, he sometimes conducted a meeting with me and the others at HQ, airing the attitudes that he wanted us to adopt. He repeatedly stated that one should never show weakness to the customer. If you didn't know the answer to something, you lied, looked it up later on your own time, and smooth-talked the client into accepting any changes to what you had previously said. If this was an estimate and you screwed up with an unrealistic one, then you worked unpaid overtime to meet the date you had given rather than admitting it.

I shook my head as I sat among those I had helped hire and train, already sensing they found his take on this odd. "I don't agree with any of that. It's lying to the client."

Dick said, "This is how consulting works."

I laughed a bit, seeing coworkers scowling. I had the room's support but would've said what I had to say even without it. "No, it's not. I've been doing this for ten years and no one has ever told me to lie to a client."

"Then they aren't doing a good job."

I knew better but asked, "Isn't honesty the best policy?"

"It's not dishonest to give an answer and then update it later."

"When you know you're full of shit, it is." Those in the room laughed. For once, Dick seemed genuinely amused, and I added, "You're never going to convince me of this."

He let it go, but me and the others talked about it more than once and thought Dick was giving awful advice none of us intended to follow. Since I had interviewed all of them, recommended they be hired, gone to the welcome lunch with them and the recruiter, and then trained them, I had a kind of unofficial authority among them. Dick had official authority, but not their respect, and maybe this contrast played a role in my fate.

By now, they all knew (because I had told them) that he had taken credit for the very documentation they had used to get up to speed and begin having a successful career that I was still being denied, to their consternation; they understood that this was not cool. I thought if telling people he had stolen credit cost me my job, then so be it. I could not sit silently by and let it happen. This likely also played a role in what was to come, but I'm at peace with it. Someone could make the case that I should've let Dick steal credit for my work without comment, because thwarting your boss leads to nothing good. But I can also make the case that I had done the right thing in putting my name back where it belonged. I would rather die on my feet than live on my knees. Am I a fool? Maybe. But I also sleep well.

One day, my manager called me into his office and said, "There's a project I think you're a good fit for."

I can't say I really believed him as I asked, "Let's hear it."

"There's an eight-year-old project that has been badly managed, so much so that the government agency took it away from the previous contractor and we won it. It's a mess, but we get to fix it and save the day."

I stifled a sigh. "What's wrong with it?"

"You're going to find that out. It's an Oracle database, by the way."

I tried not to scowl. "I don't know Oracle at all." It was one of the other industry leading databases besides SQL Server, so it wasn't a bad skill to gain. Still, I felt a little ambivalent because, for the umpteenth time, they would prevent me from working with my chosen technologies.

"I'm sure you'll have no trouble. Be prepared to work fifty-to-sixty-hour weeks."

My eyes widened before I laughed a little. "Sorry, but no. I don't do that."

I would say he smiled, but he never stopped. It was just the degree of smile that changed. His increased. "You do if I say you do."

I held his gaze, wiped the smile from my face, and slowly shook my head.

"Well," he said, "we'll see."

No, we won't. No job was worth that. And I had a life outside of work. I wasn't giving it up for a company that had already stiffed me on salary, was still dragging their feet on starting a new clearance for me, and was giving me shit assignments. This was the kind of bullshit they could do to a salaried employee but not an hourly contractor—unless they paid me to do it. I had an ego now, I admit. My phone lit up when I posted my resume and I did *not* have to do work that was off target from what I wanted.

Frustrated with the lack of a SharePoint development project, I found an opportunity for one, to gain some practical experience. People were talking about keeping track of the softball team's metrics, including things like strikeouts and RBIs, so I created a SharePoint site to track all of it, our schedule, and anything else related to the team. This included pages designed to inspire more of the company to either join the team or come to games. When I was done, I forwarded it to Dick and Martin but heard no response, so I shrugged it off and moved on.

But as the summer's end neared, the county posted a deadline for signing up for the fall league and I was the one who asked people, including the CTO, if they wanted to continue. They did and at the last minute, Martin signed us up. While I wasn't the reason, the team had done a first season, I was the reason we had a second, though I was destined to not play a single game.

In August, Dick called me into his office and told me I was finally being deployed to do SharePoint development work at the National Institute of Health (NIH) in Bethesda. I could hardly believe it. But then I learned he had told them I was a "Senior SharePoint Developer." I balked.

"Dick," I began, "I may be senior in .NET, or in general, but I'm hardly a senior SharePoint developer. I've barely done anything beyond the Hello World app."

"I understand," he said, sounding like he meant it. "We have a SharePoint Architect who is part of the project."

I breathed a sigh of relief. An architect was a notch above senior developer. This was the guy who would field all the tough questions from the client, being the lead. And he would help me understand what I needed to do, and how. With that in mind, I relaxed and looked forward to the assignment. After nearly six months, they were finally deploying me! At this time, Dick also gave me access to the online app to do a security clearance request and paperwork. They had stalled a long time on this, another source of frustration fading. Everything looked to be going well.

But then I started the project and learned that the architect was disappearing on vacation for two weeks the day after we met the client. I was on my own during this. And every day, the client peppered me with questions. He was a SharePoint guru wannabe, eager to know every last thing. He knew more than me, and he would ask me which of two approaches I would use in SharePoint to solve a problem and why. Most of the time, I didn't know either element he was asking about, not to mention be able to compare them. This happened several times a day and was horribly uncomfortable. I kept having to say I would have to look into it and get back to him because I couldn't even bullshit him, as Dick had so often suggested I do.

Within days, the client called for a meeting with me, to create a list of features he wanted, with an estimate for how long each would take to implement. I was in no position to even guess at this. I typed up his list with the caveat that the architect and I would discuss this when he returned, but he made me add a column to the list called "guestimates." And when we were done, he insisted I send it to Dick, who was not pleased, and called me to HQ.

Smiling while his eyes glared, Dick said, "I can't believe you wrote guestimates on that document."

I flushed, suddenly realizing how it had looked. I hadn't given it any thought before because it wasn't my idea. "He was the one who added that column name."

"You should have overruled him," Dick said. "And the whole idea of giving estimates you can't back up is problematic."

I snorted. I hardly needed that one explained to me. "You know, I told you I wasn't comfortable with this, and you said the architect would be there and he's not. This is not a problem I created."

"You should give the client an answer and worry about how honest it is later."

I shook my head. "And how does that make me or the company look if I'm off by a mile?"

"You're giving comfort to our competitors."

I scowled. That reminded me of the war in Iraq in the early 2000s, when some said you were either with the President of the U.S. or against him, and if you questioned what was happening, you were giving "comfort to the enemy." Dick's version was no less obnoxious.

"It's not okay to say that to me."

"What's not okay is you making the company look bad."

Offended, I remained silent because saying what I was thinking would get me fired on the spot. I left shortly thereafter.

On Friday, while home, I tried to email Dick, saying I was working from home unless he wanted me to come in. This was how we always handled this. But while logged into work, I couldn't get an email to send from Outlook. I didn't know why. I finally went into my personal email account and sent the note from there, then worked the rest of the day, noticing as I did so that I was not receiving any work emails. This was not uncommon because I didn't really work with anyone. Around the time I was going to log off, Outlook suddenly started working and a deluge of emails came in. And I grew worried.

One email was from the network admin, informing everyone that the company network had suffered a massive outage the night before and email was not working properly. Anyone onsite at HQ could send and receive emails, but no one else could. This meant that Dick had not received my email. And then I learned Dick had taken the day off without warning, and told no one who worked for him. The result was that no one knew where I was all day.

Normally, no one was looking for me, but in a coincidence that reminded me of my old nickname, The Black Hole of All Luck, upper management had suddenly become desperate to have my security clearance paperwork submitted by COB. I never learned why this was unexpectedly so urgent, given that they'd had six months to get me started on this and hadn't granted me access to the clearance questionnaire system before that week.

The company executives had been looking for me all day, repeatedly emailing me via the company email that wasn't working. The #2 guy in the company finally emailed asking if I was on PTO, a kind of stupid question if the answer was yes because I wasn't going to see his email. Apparently, every last one of them had forgotten how to use a phone. As if that wasn't dumb enough, they knew they had an email outage at work and yet were exclusively trying to contact me that way. To make matters worse, I had already submitted the clearance paperwork, and all they had to do was ask their security officer this, but this apparently never occurred to them. I knew this was bad. Perception is reality, and in their eyes, I had taken the day off without warning, even though I had emailed Dick and worked the whole day. I immediately responded to the #2 guy and explained some of this. He responded that he was okay with all of it and I relaxed.

But on Monday, I went to HQ and soon received a snotty email from Dick, lecturing me that "resources" like me were required to be at MicroSys when not at a client and that "core hours" were 9 AM to 3 PM. The cold, disciplinary tone had me fearing for my job and I posted my resume on Monster.com. But then I talked to my wife and my first manager there, and both said I had done nothing wrong and shouldn't have to worry, so I took the resume down. I suspected that Dick had gotten shit for his own disappearing act on Friday and passed the buck.

We soon met to discuss the client's wish list and a schedule I had tried to create for it, even though either Dick or the vacationing architect should have done that. He said everything looked fine, while wearing that obscene grin of his, like usual. I went home for the day and checked my email from there, seeing a request from him to meet in the office of his manager, Bob. And I knew. I was so certain I was being fired that I wrote and signed a resignation letter and dated it the next day so that it would look like I quit instead of being fired. When I arrived at work the next morning, I spent my time cleaning out my desk and putting everything into my backpack or my car. My desk was virtually empty by the time Dick moved up the meeting to immediately, and I followed his grinning ass to Bob's office, a notebook in my hand and the resignation letter inside it. I had been working there for six months and knew it was ending.

After we both entered, Dick said over his shoulder, "Shut the door." And I was even more certain as he joined Bob at a round table. At least there was no folded letter on it with my termination inside, but I knew what was happening anyway. I took a chair and didn't bother hiding the frown on my face. An atmosphere of doing something bad to someone hung in the air, more from Bob than my jerk manager. Dick wasted no time, still wearing the grin he always wore.

"I don't enjoy doing things like this," he began.

Then why are you smiling while doing it? I thought.

He continued. "You're being let go."

I wasn't in the mood for ambiguity. "Am I being fired?"

"If you don't quit, yes. We know you're looking for a job, so we're dismissing you for disloyalty."

I did a double-take and scowled. Well, at least they were admitting to not having a good reason. "What makes you think I'm looking for a job?"

Dick smirked obscenely. "You posted your resume on Monster yesterday."

I met his gaze and saw that he thought he had out-smarted me, had caught me. It was true and I didn't under-stand how, which added to my irritation. "I blocked MicroSys from seeing it."

This time Bob spoke up, amusement in his eyes. "One of the company owners owns another, smaller firm that our recruiters do recruiting for, under their own account. The side effect is that when they're logged in for the other company, they can see if anyone from this company has posted a resume even if we've been blocked from seeing it."

I went cold and stifled a curse, feeling caught by some awful loophole. I had once heard a rumor about this other company and the recruiter thing, but it had never occurred to me to block them. Part of me felt stupid, but I didn't. Not really. It was too far removed from every day con-cerns. It's not so much that I was stupid to not recall it and take precautions so much as it would have been impressive if I had. But then maybe I just had too much faith that peo-ple were not raging assholes. I certainly saw little sign that anyone had any integrity or decency at all. I had taken a precaution and still gotten nailed. What was the point of anything in this damn career of mine? The recruiter I had become friends with at work was the only one who looked for prospects with my skill set. The son of a bitch had just gotten me fired.

Dick leered at me. "This sends a loud and clear message to us that you would be happier somewhere else."

I glared at him. "When I want to send you a message, I'll do it to your face. It was up for less than a day before I took it down, and you're the reason it was up. That snotty email you sent me yesterday had me concerned I needed to be looking for another job."

"You're disloyal," he said, like this was some awful rebuke.

I frowned. "It's not the 1960s anymore. No one is loyal, and given that you're firing me for considering leaving, which is not exactly you showing me loyalty, you're just sounding like a hypocrite right now."

"There are other issues with you," began Dick, and I braced myself for unfair insults. "You aren't making an effort to learn SharePoint."

I snorted. "Oh that's rich. First of all, you're the one responsible for all of my assignments, so if I haven't learned it yet, then it's your fault. More to the point, we've hired a half-dozen people that I subsequently trained."

As if this proved his point, he said, "And they all know more than you now."

I bristled. "That's because you sent them on projects while refusing to do so with me until a week ago. You've got me on a hamster wheel running in place while they get more experience that you deny me."

Bob added, "All you seem to care about is the softball team."

I looked at him in surprise. "Seriously?"

"You spent unauthorized time setting up that Share-Point site."

I let fly with my contempt. "Okay, so first you say I'm making no effort to learn SharePoint and need to be fired for it, and now you're saying that me trying to use what I've learned on a project is also a problem and I need to be fired for *that*. You know, if it weren't for me, Martin would have missed the deadline to apply for another season, and people voted almost unanimously to do it again. How about a big thanks for causing something that makes dozens of staff happy?"

To think my last job had ostracized me, only for me to become popular at this one partly over softball, and now *that* was being used as an excuse to get rid of me. There was no winning.

"You also lack confidence," Dick said.

That was a new one. My last job told me my confidence made people feel attacked. "What are you talking about?"

"You wrote 'guestimates' on that list of things the client wanted."

I glared at him. "I already told you he was the one dictating everything on that list, and I was just typing it up for him. Jesus, it's like every time I do something positive for someone, you find a way to make it sound bad." I was a glass-half-full guy living in a glass-half-empty world.

"You should have been able to answer those questions."

"No, I shouldn't have, because I don't have the experience. Gaining it was the whole reason I came to this company, and you have consistently denied me the chance. You are at fault for putting me in that position with the client and setting me up to fail. You are the one making the company look bad."

Bob had been wiggling his hand as if to wave me off because he didn't care about that accusation anymore. He apparently had another line of bullshit he was impatient to say. "You also waited six months to start your clearance investigation."

I looked at him in surprise. "So let me ask you something. Do I have to wait for the security officer in this company to give me access to the app to do the paperwork?"

Bob nodded.

"When my manager tells him to, right?"

"Sure."

He looked about to say more, but I cut him off. "Well, Dick here only told him to give access to me a week ago, and I had it done within a few days, not six months."

Genuinely and visibly surprised, Bob turned to Dick. "Is that true?"

Dick looked startled, the truth on his face. I didn't expect him to admit it. "Yes."

Caught you lying in front of your boss, asshole.

"Well," Bob started, "that doesn't change anything."

I gave Bob a withering look of anger and he fell silent. One thing they were not getting out of me was any impression that I was cowed, because I was not. They were railroading me with bullshit and I wasn't letting them think I wasn't aware of it. They were beneath me, not the other way around. They could sit there trying to disapprove of me with lies all they wanted, but that was only earning my contempt. It was they who were not measuring up to professional standards, and that was the reason we were having this conversation, not their attempts to find fault with me. Bob might have wilted a little, but Dick hadn't.

Smugly, he said, "Don't waste your time trying to contest any of this. I made sure the owners are aware of everything we're saying here today and that you are not a fit for this company."

I shook my head in disbelief. "So you're actually proud of throwing me under the bus to management behind my back with bullshit. That's what you're saying."

"You're disloyal and giving comfort to our competitors."

"Hypocrite! It's hardly scathing coming from you. You can stop saying that now, or are you still trying to convince yourself?"

Still wearing that shit-eating grin, he said, "If you don't quit, we'll make it look like we fired you for poor performance."

My eyes widened in shock that he was actually admitting they were going to lie about me to the unemployment office. They likely didn't know I had seen this trick before and beaten it. The threat was arrogant and a way to tell me off. Why the personal animosity?

"So first I catch you lying in front of Bob, who made it clear he doesn't care about that, and now you're admitting you're going to lie again. You know, Bob, I knew Dick was an asshole, but I thought better of you before today. You're just as bad. Most of the bullshit is coming out of his mouth, but you condone it."

Bob pursed his lips in such a way that I knew I had nailed him. I put a big dent in any attempt to disapprove of me like they had apparently thought they were going to do. A small victory, but turning the tables in a moment like this is a worthwhile consolation. So is standing up for yourself and succinctly calling out the fucked up stuff people are doing. Given that I couldn't change the outcome, I was quite pleased with the way the conversation was going. I had one more way to prove that they weren't as slick as they thought—the letter, the existence of which said, "As much as you did shit behind my back, I still saw this coming, assholes."

Dick repeated, "As long as you're on staff, we're going to lose business to companies that we compete with for work."

I was sick of hearing this stupid, insulting line, and I snapped, "Fine, then I'll go work for one of your competitors. I quit." Pulling the resignation letter from my notebook, I threw it on the table. I rose without looking at them and left what struck me as a sudden, startled silence behind me. Did they think this would be amicable? You have to be honest to get that. Bullshit gets you a "fuck off" vibe.

I strode straight to my cube, which wasn't far away. All the apps like Outlook on my work computer were already closed and I just instigated a laptop shutdown that I wasn't staying to watch. I thrust my notebook into the backpack, which was technically their property, but I decided I was taking it. I heard them hesitantly come up behind me as I was slinging the bag over one shoulder. Something about their uncertainty makes me wonder in retrospect if they had intended for me to do two more weeks, or turn over work to someone else, or anything but quit and stride out the door, but I was fucking out of there. I had already thrown my badge on the desk and was about to leave when Dick spoke, his tone helpful and smug.

"Is there anything I can—"

Outrage tore through me. How dare he now try to act like he was going to do me some sort of favor? I loudly snapped over one shoulder, "No, there isn't."

A straight line ran from Bob's office to my cube and the exit so that I never looked at them or even had to pass by as I strode away, silence reigning behind me. At the elevators, I passed a work friend and told him they had fired me, so he asked me to email him. When I got home, I tried logging into work email over the internet and got in because they were too stupid to immediately lock me out. I emailed a dozen co-workers, telling them what had happened, why, and how, and that if anyone had any jobs they could refer me to, to please contact me at the personal account I provided. Almost all of them replied in shock. I had interviewed and trained several them. Most gave me contact info for various agencies and past employers or suggested being a reference. I also emailed my first manager, who responded that he had no idea any of this was going down and that he would've prevented it if he'd known. He offered to be a reference. It seemed that the only person at the company who had an issue with me was Dick, and that was all that mattered.

Over the next few days, the fallout continued, the biggest revelation being that Dick emailed everyone that they had laid me off for posting my resume and that he considered me to not be a long term person as a result. This was stupid for two reasons. First was that I had already told them what he'd actually done, and I had far more credibility because Dick was sleazy. But second, he had just put everyone on notice that they would be fired if they looked for a job. I had now warned my former peers to block that other company, not just MicroSys, from seeing their resume online. Several said they did so at once and thanked me. At least I had done some small good in the world. And sometimes that is all you can hope for.

I activated my resume and had recruiters once again blow up my phone and email with twenty potential jobs within days, an experience to which I was now accustomed. It felt like the equivalent of "go to hell" money; I had plenty of options and wasn't worried. I had a job within days, but I was now seriously contemplating my future as a software developer. Almost without exception, my employers had treated me like shit, usually sooner rather than later. MicroSys had been screwing with me from the moment they dropped their salary offer, and it continued even after I was told to quit or be fired. I didn't know I would have a job so soon, so I filed for unemployment. And then a woman from the state office called me.

"When you filed for benefits, you indicated that you voluntarily quit," she said.

"No, the woman I spoke with when filing the claim said there was no option for involuntarily quit, so that's what she put down."

"So what actually happened?"

"They found out I was looking for a job and told me I could quit or be fired."

Sounding exasperated with MicroSys, she said, "Why would they do that? That's messed up."

I laughed. She must have been new to this. "A lot of companies do."

"Well, I spoke with them to get their side, and they said they fired you for not doing your job."

Maybe I should've been shocked that they carried through with the threat if I didn't quit, even though I had. Why were they doing this? What had I done to this fucking company? Anger boiled. "That's a lie. I have a bunch of people who would be happy to set the record straight. Is there any sort of documentation I can submit? I gave them a resignation letter, too, so there is written, signed proof I resigned."

She laughed. "No, it won't matter. I'm siding with you anyway."

Sudden relief washed over me. Someone besides me was sane and not a total asshole? I let out a breath. "Okay."

"They admitted they didn't warn you so that you could improve."

I snorted. "That's because there was nothing for them to warn me about."

"Right. We always want to see documentation of it, too, like a review. We want to see that people are given another chance, not just shown the door. Since they didn't do those things, then the responsibility for you being unemployed is theirs and you are entitled to full benefits."

Wow. They were smart. And fair. It was a miracle. And now Maryland was basically saying MicroSys was wrong to do this. "Well, thank you. I really appreciate this. I mean, I found a job anyway and am here now, so it hardly matters, but thank you."

"That's great. I'll update your file. They can appeal the decision, but they probably won't, especially with you already employed again."

I nodded. The amount of money MicroSys would have to pay a state unemployment office would be negligible because I wasn't being paid by the state now that I had a job, so it wasn't worth their time. And I had thought of a way to never be on the receiving end of this again.

CHAPTER EIGHTEEN

Consulting Calls

In the wake of leaving MicroSys, I decided to never spend so much time socializing at work. I don't mean doing that instead of working, but attending events outside of work hours. After being ostracized out of DataSoft, I had given up considerable personal time to form a connection at MicroSys. It had worked and paid dividends, but I lost my job anyway. With no warning, and not a single conversation with me to understand my side of things, senior management turned on me with a few manipulations from Dick. It was a slap in the face. I had come away from MicroSys with nothing to show for my social efforts...

Except for a new hobby of playing softball, which I continued to do. In fact, in less than a week, I had a superior job and a better softball team with me as the main pitcher. I stood on the pitching mound the first night, musing about how fast my life can change. Knock me down and I just get back up again with a speed that can make your head spin around. Far from discouraged, I vowed to do something about my career, taking more control. And that meant not working for anyone else anymore after the current gig, which was contract-to-hire, ended in six months. I had thought about it for years, and my resolve had strengthened.

I could never be part of a company. I had always been a loner in my life, and the corporate version of that was being a consultant. I was a tramp, a wanderer, and I needed to be free, and the idea of being on my own made me feel invigorated. If someone pulled a bait and switch on me again, I would just smile politely while getting another client and then moving on. No more getting entrenched anywhere again, like United Systems, where I became complacent about leaving. I would have one foot out the door at all times and companies would know better than to screw with me because I was that good at finding another job. I didn't have to take any bullshit.

I also knew now that I could not be a manager. With almost ten years' experience, I likely should have been one by now, but then I also should not have had the experiences I was repeatedly having. It was obvious that being a manager meant fucking people over and first lying behind their back about it and then to their face while firing them. I couldn't do it to people. I wouldn't have been able to before I started my career, just out of conscience, but now that it had been done to me so many times, I wouldn't have been able to live with myself. "Never become the enemy" was one of my personal slogans, meaning don't become the type of person you hate. I wasn't cut out to be a manager. And they had to work over 40 a week quite a bit; my personal time was already too cramped. This meant remaining a software developer.

I was senior now, having become that way without help from anyone at my jobs except for Jack back at USAIS. I was always on my own, even when MicroSys was supposed to train me. This mattered because I was now thinking I didn't need these people. Far from helping me, they stood in my way, with job assignments that deprived me of the experience I wanted. I should have been better than I was, but it's hard when you seldom get to do your actual profession.

Every recruiter approached me for jobs with "Senior Developer" in the title. And this wasn't just tenure, but capabilities. My resume showed a great variety of abilities, some of which had come back to haunt me. The only way to control all of this was being a consultant, choosing my projects myself every time. This happened when an employer tried to entice me to come aboard, but once I was did, I handed this ability to choose my projects over to them, and they abused it almost every time. Only SysCorp, United Systems, and USAIS, less than half of my employers, had me coding from day one. And United Systems largely stopped me for the next three years. No one pays a consultant who specializes in something(s), to do the wrong job.

I had made mistakes in my career, but learning from them doesn't help me when the next company finds a different way to stick it to me. And none of the errors had warranted the over-the-top responses. Employers always sat there firing me and acting like they were so much better, disapproving of me for something while what they were doing was worse—blown out of proportion, planned in advance, coordinated, executed behind my back, with multiple justifications (each one outrageous), and vindictive. Those retaliating seemed to feel justified in going for my throat, smug in their unwarranted feelings of superiority that they were putting me in my place and showing me how powerful they were.

But this did not cow me for one simple reason—you can't act morally superior during this if you're the one acting horribly and I, at worst, made an innocent mistake. If you want the moral high ground, you have to actually stand on it, not wallow in your own filth and try to build yourself up at someone else's expense. It doesn't work that way. When evil people condemn a decent person using such tactics, that condemnation rings hollow for all its empty pretenses. Visiting injustice on the innocent doesn't convey power over them, but that you are powerless in the face of their decency and your own vileness.

I don't know what happened to MicroSys, but as of this writing in 2021, the company no longer exists. They may have been sold to another firm. Most of the ones I worked for from 1999 to 2008 are gone. Only United Systems and the Pentagon employer, RCS, still exist. I would like to think that the aftermath of my employment had something do with these places going under, for revenge's sake, but it's just an idea they put into my head; a surprising number of companies had claimed I was going to destroy them in some way if I remained employed there, a laughable, heavy-handed exaggeration to justify my termination. RCS said the Army would learn they could get damaging info on the company from me; it turned out they were right when I threw them under the bus on my way out the door. USAIS said I had threatened the security of the company network. DataSoft said the project managers felt like they were being attacked. MicroSys said I gave comfort to their competitors and would cost the company business

I was Randy Zinn, Destroyer of Companies, Scourge of Businesses, Annihilator of Firms. Bunch of freakin' drama queens. Maybe I should have put those titles on my resume instead of Senior Developer. They admittedly have a nice ring to them. Most of those companies got rid of me and disappeared anyway. Maybe I wasn't the problem?

It was time to form Zinn Consulting and be an independent consultant, working for me. Little did I know that by doing so, I would indeed solve certain recurring problems in my career, but that I would just exchange one set of issues for another.

To be continued in *Consulting Hell: A Memoir...*

— ●·●—

If you enjoyed this book, more Randy Zinn memoirs are available at https://amzn.to/2XZWwFw or use the QR code below:

About the Author

Randy Zinn is a proud father to a son (b. 2012) and daughter (b. 2016) and loves spending time with them when not writing memoirs, making music, playing golf, or lap swimming. Under another name, he's published non-fiction and fantasy stories with a literary bent, and released several albums of his music (hard rock and acoustic guitar). He holds a Bachelor of Music in classical guitar, Magna cum Laude, and has worked as a software developer/architect in the Washington D.C. area for over 20 years as an employee, contractor, or consultant through his own company.

He's also faced a variety of personal issues, including Attention Deficit Disorder, speech problems, sexual assaults, depression, suicide, bullying, being Learning Disabled, and a devastating injury, all of which he overcame. The tales in his memoirs cover them all and his dramatic, life-changing transformation.

Connect with me online

http://www.Randy-Zinn.com
https://www.facebook.com/pg/randyzinnauthor
http://bit.ly/ZinnAmazon

If you like this book, please help others enjoy it.

Lend it. Please share this book with others.

Recommend it. Please recommend it to friends, family, reader groups, and discussion boards
Review it. Please review the book at Goodreads and the vendor where you bought it.

JOIN THE RANDY ZINN NEWSLETTER!

Subscribers receive the latest updates, the chance to join the ARC Team, and bonus content like deleted scenes, short stories, private/color photos, and priority access to learn more from Rand about what interest you.

http://www.randy-zinn.com/newsletter

Randy Zinn Books

Memoirs

A Storm of Lies
Corporate Hell: A Memoir
Consulting Hell: A Memoir

A Silence Not So Golden Trilogy
Book 1: *Refusal to Engage: My Voice is Become Death*
Book 2: *A Blast of Light: My Rebirth Through Music*
Book 3: *The Wine-Dark Sea: My New Life Awaits*

The Memoir Shorts
Book 1: *Adventures in Opposite Land*
Book 2: *Am I Evil?*

Other Non-Fiction

The Corporate Life Survival Guide
Tips on Surviving Corporate Hell

View all books at Amazon:

Made in the USA
Coppell, TX
29 September 2022

83812493R00203